Complete Malay

Christopher Byrnes and
Tam Lye Suan with Eva Nyimas

First published in Great Britain in 2006 as Teach Yourself Malay by Hodder Education, part of Hachette UK.

This edition published in 2016 by John Murray Learning.

Copyright © Christopher Byrnes and Tam Lye Suan 2006, 2010, 2016

The right of Christopher Byrnes and Tam Lye Suan to be identified as the Authors of the Work has been asserted by them in accordance with the Copyright, Designs and Patents Act 1988.

Database right Hodder & Stoughton (makers)

The *Teach Yourself* name is a registered trademark of Hachette UK.

British Library Cataloguing in Publication Data: a catalogue record for this title is available from the British Library.

Library of Congress Catalog Card Number: on file.

ISBN: 9781444102000

10

The publisher has used its best endeavours to ensure that any website addresses referred to in this book are correct and active at the time of going to press. However, the publisher and the author have no responsibility for the websites and can make no guarantee that a site will remain live or that the content will remain relevant, decent or appropriate.

The publisher has made every effort to mark as such all words which it believes to be trademarks. The publisher should also like to make it clear that the presence of a word in the book, whether marked or unmarked, in no way affects its legal status as a trademark.

Every reasonable effort has been made by the publisher to trace the copyright holders of material in this book. Any errors or omissions should be notified in writing to the publisher, who will endeavour to rectify the situation for any reprints and future editions.

Cover image © Anchalee/Alamy

Typeset by Cenveo® Publisher Services.

Printed and bound in Great Britain by CPI Group (UK) Ltd., Croydon, CR0 4YY.

John Murray Learning policy is to use papers that are natural, renewable and recyclable products and made from wood grown in sustainable forests. The logging and manufacturing processes are expected to conform to the environmental regulations of the country of origin.

Carmelite House
50 Victoria Embankment
London EC4Y 0DZ
www.hodder.co.uk

Contents

Acknowledgements

We are grateful to the staff at Teach Yourself books for their diligence and patience.

In particular I would like to thank:

Tam Lye Suan, for her expertise and input, and without whom this work would not have been possible.

Eva Nyimas, for her assistance and encouragement throughout.

Ginny Catmur, for her assistance and immeasurable patience during this project.

John Pride, and **Julia Spencer**, for their work on the new volume.

Christopher Byrnes

Credits

Front cover: © Anchalee/Alamy

Back cover: © Jakub Semeniuk/iStockphoto.com, © Royalty-Free/Corbis, © agencyby/iStockphoto.com, © Andy Cook/iStockphoto.com, © Christopher Ewing/iStockphoto.com, © zebicho – Fotolia.com, © Geoffrey Holman/iStockphoto.com, © Photodisc/Getty Images, © James C. Pruitt/iStockphoto.com, © Mohamed Saber – Fotolia.com

Meet the authors

I am a language teacher and an avid language learner. I have studied over a dozen languages and continue to study new ones, while adding to my knowledge of those already learned. I hold a modern language honours degree and teaching qualifications in MFL (Modern Foreign Languages) and TESOL. I also wrote **Complete Indonesian** (also part of the 'Teach Yourself' series), published by Hodder & Stoughton, and other works on learning and teaching languages.

Having spent over 25 years learning languages, both formally and through self-study, and over 12 years teaching them at every level from infants to adults, I have packed all my experience and love of languages into this course.

Christopher Byrnes

I am a Straits-born Malay speaker with over 20 years' writing, editing and translating experience. For this project I have teamed up with Christopher Byrnes to bring you a complete course in spoken and written Malay.

Tam Lye Suan

I am a native of Sumatera, and was formerly a teacher of languages and tourism at the LIBMI school in Jakarta. I speak Indonesian and Malay, and am conversant in several local Indonesian languages including Javanese and Sundanese. I have taught languages to children and adults alike.

Eva Nyimas

Only got a minute?

Malay has been officially known as Bahasa Malaysia, which means *Language of Malaysia*, since 1971, although it is also the language of the Malays of Singapore and the Sultanate of Brunei Darussalam.

In fact Malay exists in two forms: Bahasa Indonesia, the official language of the Republic of Indonesia, is also a form of Malay, although it has been significantly influenced by the indigenous languages of Indonesia and the colonial Dutch. On the other hand, the Malaysian form of Malay has been influenced by British rule, and has adopted a significant number of English borrowings.

This makes Malay, in both its forms, the most important language in South East Asia by number of speakers. It is a language well worth learning for anyone with an interest in South East Asia, not just for business, but also for tourism.

Malay spelling is easy to master because it is quick to learn and very regular, so you will find the language easy to pronounce.

In contrast with English and other European languages, words in Malay are often left out of sentences when the context is understood. Also, Malay shares the concept of counting with many East Asian languages, using words which convey an object's inherent characteristics. You will also find Malay has an extensive system of building vocabulary by adding prefixes and/or suffixes to a word, so your ability to identify word roots, and understand how particular affixes alter and extend their meaning, will give you a short-cut to deciphering the language.

Finally, if you've ever struggled with the complicated verb endings and tense forms of a language like French, or the formidable noun cases of German, then you're going to find Malay to be a pleasant surprise!

Only got ten minutes?

Malay, or **Bahasa Melayu** (*Language of the Malays*), has been officially known as **Bahasa Malaysia**, which means *Language of Malaysia*, since 1971, although it is also the language of the Malays of Singapore and the Sultanate of Brunei Darussalam.

In fact, however, Malay exists in two differing forms: Bahasa Indonesia, the official language of the Republic of Indonesia, is also a form of Malay, although it has been significantly influenced by the indigenous languages of Indonesia, especially Javanese, and later by the colonial Dutch. On the other hand, the Malaysian form of Malay has been influenced by British rule, and has adopted a significant number of English borrowings accordingly.

This makes Malay, in both its forms, the most important language in South East Asia by sheer force of numbers of speakers. It is a language well worth learning for anyone with an interest in South East Asia, not just for business, but also for tourism.

Malay spelling is easy to master because it is very regular. Once you learn how the sounds relate to the written word, which is a quick task in itself, you will be able to pronounce Malay easily. There is only one sound that poses any significant challenge to English speakers, and then, only when it appears in certain positions in a word. This is represented by **ng**. This sound is the 'twangy' sound found in **orang**, where it poses little difficulty for English speakers. However, it also occurs initially in some words, and in the middle of others, where it must still retain its sound, in the word **jangan**, for example.

The rest of the pronunciation is straightforward, as is the spelling system, which is almost completely regular. Some Malay speakers trill their **r** sounds; others do not, as you will hear on the recordings accompanying this course. If you cannot trill yours, you will not sound any less Malay.

In contrast with English and other European languages, much of the way Malay is understood relies on context rather than the actual words used. Redundant words are often left out of sentences when the context is understood. For example, a typical Malay greeting, **Mahu ke mana?**, which means *Where are you going?* contains neither the word for *you* nor the word for *going*, whose omission is unthinkable in English. However, in Malay this is commonplace, especially when the verb *to go* is implicit.

If you've ever struggled with the complicated verb endings and tense forms of a language like French, or the formidable noun cases of German, then you're going to find Malay to be a pleasant surprise…

There are no tenses in Malay. That is to say, there are no lexically expressed tenses, nor do Malay verbs change to express person. This means that a verb, such as **pergi** *to go*, does not change its form to express *I go*, *he goes*, *we went*, *they will go* etc. The pronouns alone tell you who is doing the action expressed by the verb.

Of course language needs to express present, past and future events, because these concepts exist as very real parts of our life experience. So how does Malay do this?

Points in time are simply expressed by stating when an action is supposed to take place. For example, **Saya makan nasi lemak setiap hari** means *I eat nasi lemak every day*. **Saya** means *I*, **makan** means *eat* and **setiap hari** means *every day*. There, the present tense is conveyed by the context. If I say, **Saya makan nasi lemak semalam**, where **semalam** means *yesterday*, the verb automatically conveys the past. So the meaning automatically translates as *I ate nasi lemak yesterday*.

Where a time expression is not appropriate, Malay uses what we call tense markers. These are words that, when used before the verb, convey the idea of tense. **Sedang** means *now* in Malay, but placing it before a verb conveys the idea of what we call a continuous tense in English. For example, **Saya sedang makan murtabak** *I am eating murtabak*. Replace **sedang** with **sudah**, which literally means *already*, and you've got *I ate* **murtabak**. **Akan** expresses the future tense, so **Saya akan makan murtabak** means *I will eat murtabak*.

Malay shares the concept of counting with many East Asian languages. Objects are counted according to the category they fall into; according to their inherent characteristcs, rather than just by number. Chinese does this; Japanese does this and Malay does this too!

For example, people are counted as **orang**. So *two teachers* (*teacher* – **guru**) is expressed as **dua orang guru**.

Animals are counted in *tails* (**ekor**) whether they have one or not: **dua ekor kucing** *two cats* (*two tails of cat*, if you will. We count cattle in heads, after all, which is a hint at a concept that is commonplace in Malay).

Flat objects, such as *paper* (**kertas**), are counted using **helai**: **lima (5) helai kertas** *5 sheets of paper*. And so on...

There is a range of these counting words, depending on the characteristics of the object concerned. However, they can be omitted without rendering what you are saying inaccurate.

Malay vocabulary is built extensively around root words or word bases. These root words, once they have affixes applied to them, form new words. Affixes are 'bits' that are appended to words to create new words, much as we use *re-* in English. In application, when you apply *re-* to build, you get *rebuild*, which means *to build again*. When you encounter *re-* again, in such words as *redraw*, you know instinctively that the *re-*, in this instance, means *again*. So it is with Malay words, only more so! The way in which Malay vocabulary is built up is far more predictable than it is in English, if you were learning it as a foreign language. This makes Malay particularly transparent, when you know how to look at it in a certain way.

While you could learn vocabulary words as you come across them, without paying any particular attention to the root, or base word, if you do incorporate them into your study, they will help you to gain a deeper and more rapid mastery of the language than you might otherwise have had.

While new words cannot be formed arbitrarily simply by attaching affixes, knowing the function of such affixes can greatly accelerate your ability to assimilate the language. Let's take a look at some affixes, and how they affect vocabulary, just to get a feel for what this is all about...

Pe- added to the beginning of a verb (a prefix), creates a noun that means the 'doer' of the action: **main** means *to play*, **pemain** means *player*.

Using **main** again, the addition of **-an** creates a noun from the verb, so we get **mainan**, which means *toy*.

Ber- added to nouns creates related verbs with a range of meanings. It can simply make a verb of what the noun is expressing: **gerak** *movement*, **bergerak** *to move*. **Ber-** with clothes words means *to wear* (whatever the item is). **Topi** is a *hat*, **bertopi** *to wear a hat*.

Vocabulary words may also consist of a combination of affixes. For example, **sihat** means *healthy* in Malay. To create the noun *health*, Malay surrounds this adjective with **ke-** and **-an**, giving us **kesihatan**. Many adjectives are changed into nouns in this way.

Ke- -an applied to a noun can create an extended meaning of that noun. For instance, **bangsa** means *nation*; **kebangsaan** means *nationality*.

Similarly, **per- -an** is applied to certain nouns to extend their meaning. For example, **rumah** means *house*; **perumahan** means *accommodation*.

While Malay vocabulary can be learned word by word, and effectively so, the ability to identify word roots, and understand how particular affixes alter and extend their meaning, offers you a short-cut to deciphering the language.

In *Complete Malay* we will introduce the most common affixes, step-by-step, in word-building sections, alongside your learning of conversational Malay.

Introduction

Welcome to this brand new edition of *Complete Malay*. This fresh approach to learning the language is based on the standard, colloquial Malay spoken in Kuala Lumpur, Singapore and Brunei Darussalam. Malay is also spoken in parts of Thailand, the Cocos Islands and in other areas of Indonesia that are close to Malaysia, namely the Riau Archipelago and parts of Sumatera and Kalimantan. In fact, Malay and Indonesian are both forms of the same language, Bahasa Melayu, which means that, once you've learned Malay, you get Indonesian almost for free, allowing for differences in pronunciation, idiom and a significant number of borrowings into Indonesian from Dutch owing to 350 years of contact through trade and Dutch colonization.

We developed this course with three considerations in mind. Our main goal was to produce a course that would give you, the reader, an introduction to real, everyday Malay, as it is used in the Malay-speaking world. We began with the premise that you want to learn to speak and understand the language as it is really used, rather than present the textbook-only style of language that you might find elsewhere. Secondly, we have endeavoured to make the language as easy to learn as possible by focusing on the vocabulary and structures that you will really need. Specific terminology has been included only where absolutely necessary so that you can become functional in the language in the shortest time possible, without the burden of learning unnecessary features of the language. Malay is rare amongst languages in that it is a lot less complicated than others you might have learned, so we have built upon this advantage. Thirdly, we have chosen to concentrate on language that is functional and, above all, useful. To achieve the goal of presenting authentic situational language we have built the course around a series of dialogues that reflect the way in which Malay speakers use language naturally.

By the end of the course you will be able to function with confidence in Malay on a variety of topics and situations, and, most of all, you will understand and be understood.

Although the scope of a course such as this is necessarily limited, it does provide a good grounding in the language that you can use as a base for more advanced study. Later in this Introduction several suggestions are given to help you locate resources for further study.

The structure of the course

Each unit (apart from Unit 1) contains two dialogues based around situations in which you will most probably find yourself in the Malay-speaking world. The first dialogue in each unit deals with the language you will require for handling certain situations such as booking a hotel room, or talking about your family. The dialogues in **Part One** are centred around Stan Davies, a businessman from the USA with a Singaporean-Chinese wife and a son and daughter who arrive later. The dialogues in **Part Two** reinforce the theme of the unit, consolidating what you already know and extending the knowledge and skills gained in **Part One**, often taking similar situations and adding the sorts of complications you are more likely to have to handle in everyday interactions. In **Part Two** we meet Tom Black, a student from Sheffield in England who has flown to Malaysia to meet his e-pal Serena for the first time.

The two sets of characters carry out a further function in the course: the language in **Part One** tends to be rather formal: the sort of language you will be using if you are on business or if you want to carry out tasks such as booking hotel rooms and asking for tourist information. The interactions between the characters in **Part Two** have been orchestrated so that we can introduce you to the more informal, chatty language you are likely to want to use amongst friends. It is important to know and be able to use both varieties of Malay.

Each unit is split into two parts and begins with a **Dialogue** followed by **Words and phrases** and a natural **Translation** of the dialogue. Note that the translations are not necessarily word for word and are intended only as a guide in case you find difficulty in understanding the dialogue from the accompanying vocabulary. Brackets have been used in the translation to indicate words that have been omitted in the Malay that are needed in English. Following the translation, there is a section of language notes called **How the language works**. This section introduces you to various important features of language structure and usage. For many of these sections, a short and simple exercise **Check you can form** exercise is included to practise the specific point that section of the language notes refers to. **Part One** ends with an exercise section called **Understanding Malay**. This section focuses on the receptive skills of reading and listening, and includes exercises that ask you to put to the test what you have learnt in **Part One**.

Part Two follows the same format as **Part One – Dialogue**, **Words and phrases**, **Translation**, **How the language works**. However, the final exercise section **Using Malay** concentrates on the so-called *production* skills, that is, writing and speaking, and features mainly communicative exercises that are designed to develop your functional ability in the topic area of each unit. This section requires you to look at both **Part One** and **Part Two** of the unit to complete the exercises. The final exercise in this section, **Over to you!**, simulates a situational conversation that you will be able to take part in if you have the recording or another speaker to practise with. In this exercise, you should complete the part indicated in English and then check your answer in the **Key** before using the tapes for fluency practice. There may be more than one way of conveying the information in each of the utterances, but we have chosen just one version that either uses language structures and vocabulary you have encountered in the unit, or indicates in full a new form to be used.

Complete Malay is not an instant solution to your immediate communication needs, in the way that a phrase book is. Nor was it ever intended to be. The goal of *Complete Malay* is to make you an autonomous and accurate speaker of the language in the most rapid and efficient way possible. This is best achieved by focusing on presenting the structure of the language in a logical sequence, with each unit building upon the last. For this reason, and to preserve the natural quality of the dialogues, the order in which vocabulary is presented has been deemed secondary to the all-important structure. It is on completing the course that you will find yourself armed with all the tools you need to function accurately and independently in Malay.

How to use the course

Start with the **Pronunciation guide** and work through it until you are sure that you are familiar with it. Some letters represent different values in Malay from what you might expect in English, so you need to be sure that you are not embarking on the course with bad habits that may go unchecked and that will be very difficult to eradicate later. If, however, you have the recording, you can move onto the language units after only a brief run through the **Pronunciation guide** as you will be hearing correct pronunciation of the dialogues from the outset.

1 As not all people like to learn in the same way, we can suggest two equally effective methods of approaching a part of a study unit:

Listen to (or read) the **Dialogue** first without concerning yourself with the meaning. This is likely to be the first time that you are being exposed to the language taught in a particular unit, so you should concentrate on the sounds of the words and intonation rather than meaning at this early stage.

Alternatively, if you are the type of person who prefers to know what the dialogue means as you listen to it, you could go straight to the **Words and phrases** sections before you even look at the dialogue and learn the words and phrases first. Then you can see how the words and phrases fit into the dialogue to create interaction and meaning.

2 Listen to the **Dialogue** again several times so that you understand what is going on. You should be starting to get a feel for the language with this repeated listening. You can't overdo listening!

3 Move onto the **How the language works** section and study the language notes one by one. If there is a **Check you can form** exercise, complete it and check your understanding by referring to the **Key** before moving on.

4 It is a good idea to listen to the dialogue again several times, now that you know how the language points covered in **How the language works** relate to the meaning in the text. It is recommended that you start to use the recording to repeat the **Dialogue** at this stage, in order to build speaking skills. When you have finished the unit, you should go over it again, and practise speaking the parts in the **Dialogues** as much as possible. For best results make sure you have fully understood and mastered all the points in the language sections, and that you can speak all the parts of the **Dialogues** as fast as the native speakers on the recording, if not faster!

Throughout each unit, we have added more vocabulary for you to acquire in the various exercises and activities. In addition, in some units we have also varied the range of language expressions on a certain topic to help you broaden your language ability. For example, in the **Over to you!** exercise, you are expected to use what you have learnt in the unit to construct a conversation that might be on the same theme as the unit topic, but might require you to adapt the language to a different context. On occasion we have introduced another way of expressing something that is different from a phrase or word used earlier. These alternatives are all, of course, in current use. You can get a lot from this exercise if you are using the audio component of the course because it features extensive guided fluency drills designed to help develop oral skills.

The first six units give you the basic sentence patterns and lay the foundation for the language so it is recommended that you master these fully before moving on in the course. If you can, work through these units again to reinforce your learning.

Learning tips

DO'S

1 Give yourself time for what you have studied to become part of your repertoire. A language is not a series of facts; it is a skill and a habit that needs to be learnt. Practice makes it a habit.

2 Play your language recordings as much as possible. This could be while you are exercising, doing the washing up, driving to work and even at a low volume while you sleep! Do not make the mistake of thinking that passive listening alone will do the work for you. It will not. It will, however, create an environment which will allow your mind to become fully attuned to your new target language, in the same way as it would if you were living in the country.

3 When you listen to the **Dialogues** after you understand the meaning, listen again several times with your eyes closed and try to imagine the 'action' that might accompany the conversation as you listen.

4 Learn the **Dialogues** by heart to the extent that you know exactly what is coming next, and so that you can respond in place of either speaker when you play the **Dialogue**.

5 Master one unit in its entirety before moving on, and still keep revising it to keep the language fresh in your mind. For each new unit you progress onto, it is a good idea to go back two or three units and revise them fully too.

6 If something does not make immediate sense come back to it a day later. Remember that, when you are learning a language, you are exposing your mind to a new way to relate to concepts and ideas. It can take a little time for your brain to begin to accept this, but you can be sure that it will if you persevere.

7 Study or practise the language every day. If you cannot find time for active learning of new language try to spend time playing the recordings or going over language that you have already studied.

8 Go over what you have learnt during the day just before sleeping.

9 Get as interested in the country and culture of Malaysian-speaking peoples as you possibly can. Find as many reasons as possible why learning Malay is important and enjoyable to you!

DON'TS

1 Do not try to learn too much at once, especially in the early stages. Language learning, and learning in general, becomes a habit that you can develop. The more you learn, the more you are capable of learning, so allow yourself to develop the art of acquiring a language over time.

2 Do not underestimate the value of revision. Learning a language is a cumulative task. You will find that, at a later stage, when you return to a unit that you completed earlier, you will have a deeper sense of knowing and understanding as more parts of the language already learned fall into place.

3 Do not be disheartened if results do not appear straight away. When you have finished a unit, do not be irritated if you do not have that information at your fingertips straight away. You will find that as you progress through the language, things that you have learned before start to become available to you and make more sense! Allow time for the new information to 'gel' in your mind and become part of your linguistic repertoire.

4 Do not feel that you have to start speaking the language straight away, if you do not want to. Some language courses emphasize speaking and using the language from the very outset. It is up to you, of course, whether you do this. An effective strategy is to spend time learning to understand the language in the unit without speaking, and go over the unit, or even a few units afterwards. If you have the time to do this, you may find it beneficial, as you are mimicking what you did when you learnt your first language. You spent months listening to the language around you before you ever started to speak it! The process of understanding and then using is built into the course to a certain extent.

5 Above all, do not cram learn! Cram learning the night before an exam in which you have to produce factual information may result in you being able to retain facts in your short-term memory long enough to pass, but if you have tried it, you will know that in a matter of days most of the information is lost. Languages are skills that need to be developed over time. Do not try to rush through the course, for the same reason.

Learning Malay as an English speaker

Most languages belong to a language group. For example, Spanish and Italian belong to the same group, the Romance family, which means that if you learn one, the other is far easier than it would have been to start it from scratch because you have already put the time and effort in to understand the new and 'foreign' concepts, and a lot of the vocabulary is easy to understand because both languages developed from Latin. The foreign languages you choose to learn will have features that are easier because your native language is English, or harder because they are so unlike English. If you know the nature of the language you are going to learn, it can really help to have a strategy to put into play against the aspects that could, potentially, cause you difficulties. In the following section we are going to look at the areas that might cause difficulty for English speakers learning Malay, so that we can suggest some tactics for dealing with them, head-on, and make learning as smooth as possible. The good news is, that compared to other languages you might have learned, the basic grammar of Malay is very user-friendly. Malay is logical, economical and elegant. Naturally, if you want to progress to advanced levels, then you will find that there are nuances of meaning that need careful study, but to gain a mastery of the basic language you have an advantage in that much of the mechanics of the language will seem simplistic.

POSSIBLE PITFALLS

This may sound obvious, but in learning a new language you have to learn to think differently. Languages, especially unrelated ones, express concepts in very different ways. You can rarely just translate exactly what you would say in English and hope that it comes out as authentic Malay, and vice versa. Malay has its conventions, as does English.

For example, Malay has a variety of ways of saying *You* depending on the level of politeness required in a given situation. In English, when we want to refer to *You* we just think, and say, *You*, but for the native speaker of Malay who wants to express *You* the choice will need to be made from a range of options, and, what is more, s/he will make that choice in a split second. When you learn to think differently, you will be able to do that too.

The best strategy is first to be actively on the look-out for the differences. Then, learn what they are as you go along and start to apply them deliberately as you use the language. The correct choice will probably rely on a slower, conscious process at first but with exposure and practice, the convention will soon become an automatic response.

Pronunciation: follow the guide in the book carefully and do pay special attention to the *ng* sound, which can be awkward for English speakers especially when it occurs at the start or in the middle of a word. Apart from that, if you can roll your *r's* there is very little you will need to practise extensively where pronunciation is concerned.

The other area that might slow you down is that of learning vocabulary. Many European languages share *cognates* with English, that is, words that share similar origins with English words. You can immediately see the common ground in Swedish *hus* and English *house*. Sometimes the link is not immediately apparent, but it is there if you look at the word from a different perspective. For example, in French *sheep* is *mouton*. Although this bears no relation to the Anglo-Saxon word *sheep*, it is the form that gave us *mutton*. Similarly from German *Hund – dog*, we get *hound* in English and so on …

Few languages exist without influence from other ones. Malay is no exception! Over the centuries trade to the Malay Peninsula brought loan words from Sanskrit, Persian, Portuguese, Hindi, Hokkien (a form of Chinese) and, of course, Arabic. While many scientific words in English are borrowed from Greek, and although many of these have now become adopted into Malay, the ones that are not from Greek (introduced by Europeans) tend to be borrowed from Arabic, the language of Islam, and therefore also of important religious significance, as Malaysia is officially a Muslim state. Of course, if you happen to know any of these languages you have an immediate advantage in that some more of the Malay vocabulary will already seem familiar to you.

Unfortunately, Malay offers very few usable cognates to most English-speaking students, although there are many borrowings in Malay owing to over 200 years of British rule in Malaysia. In spite of the differences in spelling, words like **fesyen**, **basikal**, **filem** and **televisyen** probably need no further clarification, once you understand the highly regular Malay spelling rules. But what about the thousands of words you need to learn that do not resemble English ones? If you have a so-called 'good' memory, you might find it easy to learn and recall words, but if you do not have a 'good' memory, or rather a *trained* memory, rest assured that your memory for languages will improve with practice. Alternatively, you could employ a memory trick known as *mnemonics* to create what I call *false cognates*, that is, words for which you invent a link, however obscure, with English – or any other language you already know, for that matter. Here is how it works: take the Malay word or phrase and see which elements remind you of something else you can use as a 'hook' to link it to something you already know. These hooks can be direct, or they can be as obscure as you like. The secret here lies in what *you* did to create the mnemonic; in what the images and links *you* create mean to *you*.

Let's look at an example. Take the word **suntik** in Malay, which means *to inject*. If you break that word down you have two English words you know already, *sun* and *tick*. Now you have two words you recognize, but what on earth do they have to do with injections? This is where creativity comes in, and the more creative you are, the better this technique will work. Add imagination, colour, excitement, smells, feelings and action, and you have all the ingredients to create a memory: imagine a yellow cartoon sun round and grinning in a blue sky. All of a sudden, out of nowhere, a huge tick appears and plunges into the sun, 'injecting it'. Hear the sun yelp and observe the pained look on his face. What kind of noise does the tick make as it flies through the air? etc. This is the most elegant use of mnemonics because not only can you find almost exact equivalent sounds for the English, you can also work them into an imaginary scenario that you can make highly memorable by use of action, movement and amusement. This example is very direct, because the sounds you are playing with already have meanings in English that you can weave into a memorable scene.

Here, we created a mnenonic that didn't just contain the sounds of the word to be memorized, we also created a mental skit that had the meaning of the word embedded in it too.

Another example we could take is **mandi**, which means *to bathe*. There are no immediate connections, but if you imagine 'Mandy bathing', you have an immediate link, right to the word, and not just to the word but also the meaning. If you know a Mandy, this is even easier.

Mnemonics for words like **suntik** are offered to us on a silver platter. For many words, though, you will have to be far more imaginative in order to create a usable mnemonic, and very often all you will be able to come up with is an approximation of the English sounds.

Take **bungkusan**, for example, meaning a *package*. Allowing for differences in pronunciation you could take **bung** as *bun*, as in a roll of bread, and **kusan** to mean *cousin*. Now you have the sounds of the word broken down into something familiar, how are you going to weave them into a meaningful memory story? Maybe your *cousin* comes home one day with a huge, brightly-coloured box, wrapped up like a Christmas present. Can you see it? How big is it? Ridiculously big – larger than life is better! Watch her as she struggles to get her huge *package* through the narrow front door. Watch her force, it, straining and heaving until it bursts open sending you and her flying to the ground. And what should the parcel be stuffed with but hundreds – yes, hundreds – of buns! And they aren't just ordinary *buns*, they are sticky, sweet and messy. Can you smell the buns? Feel the stickiness against your skin and see the mess the icing leaves on your clothes? Can you taste the sweet icing all over your fingers? From this moment on, your cousin is known as the *bun-cousin* who brought a huge *package* for you, stuffed with *buns*.

I know this might seem ridiculous, because, of course, it is!

Another way to learn vocabulary is via the flashcard method. Copy the vocabulary and phrases from the units onto flashcards and carry a handful of them with you wherever you go; that way you can look at them when you are commuting or waiting in a queue. Put the foreign word or phrase on one side and the English translation on the back, and just cycle through them whenever you get the chance. Test yourself both ways, first of all aiming to recognize the meaning of the Malay words and phrases, and, when those are well established, to produce the Malay using the English as a prompt. The regular exposure will do the job of learning for you! An extra benefit can be gained if you keep all your cards so that you can recycle through sets of words and phrases for review.

We hope that you will enjoy working through this course and enjoying the interaction with Malay speakers that learning this wonderful language will give you. **Selamat belajar!**

The authors' companion website to this course is at http://www.bahasamalaysia.co.uk

Pronunciation guide

You will be happy to know that Malay pronunciation is very regular. With one or two exceptions what you see is what you say.

The guide we give here will help you to pronounce Malay in an acceptable way. It must be stressed, however, that all a written explanation of these sounds can provide is an approximation of the real sounds. There is simply no substitute for hearing foreign sounds produced by native speakers so if you do not have access to a native Malay speaker, then you would benefit greatly from hearing the real Malay sounds on the recording that accompanies this book.

Modern Malay spelling is much more regular than English spelling. With very few exceptions, separate letters or certain combinations always have the same pronunciation. As far as possible, we have deliberately chosen useful, high frequency words to illustrate the pronunciation of the sound within the word for this pronunciation guide.

Vowel sounds

 00.01

All vowel sounds are short:

a is pronounced like **a** in f**a**r

l**a**gu   *song*   t**a**m**a**n   *garden*

unless it occurs at the end of a word when it is greatly reduced to the sound of **a** as in **a***gain*:

tig**a**   *three*   nam**a**   *name*

e has two distinct sounds, one is pronounced like the **a** sound in **a***gain*. This is, by far, the most common **e** sound in Malay.

e   **e**mpat – *four*   t**e**rus – *immediately*

The other sound is pronounced like the **e** in **e***gg*. In texts produced for native speakers this **e** is not distinguished from the other **e** sound. This can make it difficult for a beginner to know where these **e** sounds are. It is surprising that most text books and dictionaries, even those intended for foreign learners of the language, do not point this out, especially as it occurs in some very common words!

é   mer**é**ka – *they*   **é**nak – *delicious*

Throughout this course an acute accent has been used to indicate this second sound. Note, however, that it is only used as a guide for learners of Malay as a foreign language so you should never use it in your own writing. Note further that this accent does *not* mark stress in a word, as it does in some languages.

i li*ma five*   like the *i* in Capr*i*

o to**lo**ng *please*   like *o* in *ho*t but with lips more rounded

u sat**u** *one*   like the *oo* sound in *coo*l but short

aa s**aa**t *moment*   pronounced as two separate *a* sounds rather like the two *a* sounds in the phrase *sa(t) at* with the *t* missing! If you are British, imagine how a Cockney might say this.

ai samp**ai** *until*   like *ie* in *tie*

au h**au**s *thirsty*   like the *ou* in *hou*se

Consonant sounds

 00.02

The following consonants are pronounced as in English:

b	**b**as	*bus*
d	**d**ua	*two*
f	**f**oto	*photo*
g	**g**i**g**i	*teeth* always as a hard *g* as in *g*ot
h	**h**ari	*day*
j	ra**j**in	*diligent*
k	**k**eras*	*hard*
l	**l**apan	*eight*
m	se**m**bilan	*nine*
n	e**n**am	*six*
p	se**p**uluh	*ten*
s	**s**ayur	*vegetables*
t	**t**empa**t***	*place*
v	**v**egetaris	*vegetarian*
w	**w**arna	*colour*
ya	**y**es	
z	**z**ebra	*zebra*

*When **t** or **k** occur at the end of the word they are pronounced so lightly as to seem not pronounced at all.

bara**t**   *west*   tida**k**   *no*

These consonants are pronounced differently from English:

c cari *look for*	like **ch** in **ch**op
h sekola**h** *school*	at the end of a word it is pronounced as a puff of air
tuju**h** *seven*	
k tida**k** *no*	at the end of a word it is not pronounced
r tidu**r** *to sleep*	**r** can be pronounced rolled as in Spanish or soft as in English
kh khusus *special*	like the **ch** in the Scottish word *lo**ch***
ng ora**ng** *person*	like the **ng** in *lo**ng*** but not pronounced as far as the final **g** sound. It can occur at the beginning of words and is still required to be pronounced as indicated above.
ba**ng**un *to wake up*	
ny ba**ny**ak *a lot of*	like the **ne** sound in the word **ne**w
ngg me**ngg**osok *to brush*	like the **ng** in *lo**ng*** but this time as the full sound
sy i**sy**arat *sign*	like the **sh** in **sh**in
syarikat *company*	

STRESS

 00.03

Although stress may differ depending on where you are in Malaysia, as an English speaker you will probably find it more natural to follow the pattern of stressing words on the penultimate syllable.

se**ko**lah	*school*
members**ih**kan	*to clean*

Later on in Unit 3 you will have the option of listening to a Malay speaker recite the whole alphabet. You may well be surprised to hear that the letters are pronounced just as they are in English!

Exercise 1

Although you will meet all these words in the study units of the course, any words that you can learn now will give you a head start! Look at the clues and fill in the crossword, saying each word out loud as you write it in.

Across

2 four
4 delicious
5 they
7 please
8 fantastic
10 food
12 one
14 like
16 two
17 three
19 five
20 room
21 colour
22 first

Down

1 school
3 place
6 six
7 new
11 name
13 no
15 shop
18 special

1 Welcome to Singapore

In this unit you will learn how to:
▶ *greet people*
▶ *introduce yourself and others*
▶ *say where you come from*

PART ONE

Dialogue

 01.01

Selamat tengah hari!
Nama saya Stan Davies.
Saya berasal dari Amérika.

Selamat tengah hari!
Nama saya Sue-Ann.
Saya berasal dari Singapura.

Hélo!
Saya Tom.
Saya dari England.

Hélo!
Saya Serena.
Saya dari Malaysia.

Quick vocab

selamat tengah hari	*good day, good afternoon*
nama	*name*
nama saya	*my name is*
berasal	*to be from*
saya berasal dari	*I am from*
Amérika	*America*
Singapura	*Singapore*
hélo	*hello*
saya	*I am*
dari	*from*
saya dari	*I am from*

How the language works 1

1 Hélo is a multipurpose greeting just like *Hello* in English. In addition, Malay has four greetings for the specific time of day: **Selamat pagi** in the morning, **selamat tengah hari** which would correspond to *good day* in older style English**, selamat petang** which is used between 2 and 6 p.m. and **selamat malam** which is used throughout the evening and night. So we could say that the Malay greetings roughly correspond to the English in the following way:

selamat pagi	*good morning*
selamat tengah hari	*good afternoon*
selamat petang	*good evening*
selamat malam	*good evening, good night*

2 You do not need to use words for *am*, *are*, *is* in Malay. So **saya** can mean both *I* and *I am*. Compare the following sentences in English and Malay:

I am Tom.   *I am from England.*

Saya Tom.   **Saya dari England.**

Exercise 1

See if you can make these sentences. The names of the countries can be left as they are.

  a I am John. I am from England.
  b I am Kylie. I am from Australia.
  c I am Fatimah. I am from Malaysia.

3 To give your name or introduce yourself in Malay you can use **nama saya** + your name or you can just use **saya ...** *I am ...* **Saya** is far more natural and consequently, more frequently used, especially in the spoken language, than **nama saya**. We do the same in English. Consider how much more likely you are to say *I am John*, for example, rather than *My name is John*.

Understanding Malay

 01.02

Exercise 2

First familiarize yourself with the new vocabulary.

 Quick vocab

usahawan	*businessman*
mahasiswa	*student (at college or university)*
pelancong	*tourist*
penari	*dancer*
joget	*a traditional dance*

> ● **INSIGHT**
>
> You'll also hear the word **seorang** in the listening exercise, which means *a*. It is a feature of Malay we will be dealing with later in the course.

If you are not using the recording turn to the transcript at the back of the book and treat this as a reading exercise. You will hear these people introduce themselves in the order indicated by the number below the picture. Listen to what each person says and link the person's name, the country he/she is from and the other piece of information about that person.

(1) Kamal

(2) Huzaini

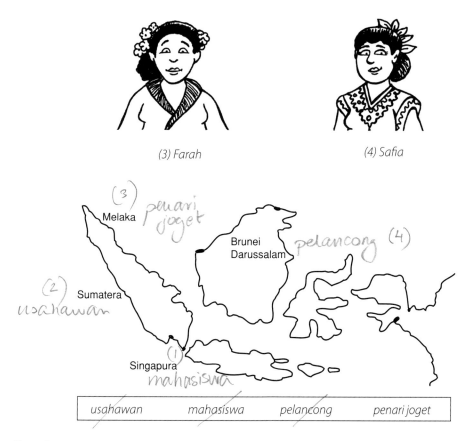

(3) Farah

(4) Safia

| usahawan | mahasiswa | pelancong | penari joget |

Exercise 3

True or false?

When you have completed the listening exercise above try the following true/false test.

    a Kamal is a student from Singapore.

    b Huzaini is a tourist from Sumatera.

    c Farah is a dancer from Melaka (Malacca).

    d Safia is a tourist from Brunei Darussalam.

PART TWO

Dialogue

Mr Davies, a businessman from the USA, has arrived at Singapore Airport. He has come to Singapore for several months on business. His Singaporean wife, Sue-Ann, and the rest of his family will be joining him later. Two men from the Maju Jaya company have come to meet him.

01.03

Encik Zamani	Maaf! Adakah saudara ini Encik Davies?
Encik Davies	Ya, saya.
Encik Zamani	Selamat datang ke Singapura. Kami dari Syarikat Maju Jaya. Saya Zamani dan perkenalkan, ini Encik Baharom.
(They shake hands.)	
Encik Baharom	Gembira dapat bertemu dengan Encik Davies.
Encik Davies	Saya juga, begitu.

 Quick vocab

maaf!	*excuse me, I am sorry*
adakah saudara ini …?	*are you …?*
Encik	*Mr*
ya	*Yes*
selamat datang	*welcome*
ke	*to*
kami	*we*
dari	*from*
syarikat	*company*
dan	*and*
ini	*this/this is*
perkenalkan, ini	*let me introduce*
gembira	*happy*
dapat	*to be able*
bertemu	*to meet*
dengan	*with*
gembira dapat bertemu dengan	*pleased to meet (you)*
juga	*too, as well*
begitu	*so*
saya juga begitu	*I am (pleased to meet you) too*

> **●INSIGHT**
>
> In the early stages of learning Malay, try not to worry about words like **begitu** and **dengan** in the vocabulary above: just concentrate on learning the phrases for now.

6

Translation

Mr Zamani	Excuse me! Are you Mr Davies?
Mr Davies	Yes, I am.
Mr Zamani	Welcome to Singapore. We are from the Maju Jaya company. Pleased to meet you. I'm Zamani and this is Mr Baharom.
Mr Baharom	Pleased to meet you.
Mr Davies	Pleased to meet you, too.

How the language works 2

1 In this unit you have come across words like **saya** *I* and **saudara** *you*. Words such as these that can be used instead of repeating a person's name are known as personal pronouns. Here are the formal personal pronouns in Malay:

saya	*I*
saudara	*you*
saudari	*you*
anda	*you*
dia	*he/she*
kami	*we*
kita	*we*
meréka	*they*

They are called formal personal pronouns because you should use them in a situation where you are not familiar with the speaker or where you would be expected to maintain a respectful tone to whomever you are addressing.

As you will have noticed there is more than one word for *you* and *we* in Malay. **Saudara** can only be used when addressing a male and its counterpart **saudari** can only be used when addressing a female.

> ● **INSIGHT**
>
> These **-a** for males and **-i** for female endings exist elsewhere in Malay too. **Mahasiswa**, that you met in Part One, has another form, **mahasiswi**, which refers to a female student.

Anda, on the other hand, can be used to address both male and female speakers. In addition, in Malay, a person's name, with or without the title, is often used in place of a personal pronoun out of deference. In the dialogue for this section you will notice that Mr Zamani uses Mr Davies' name and title when addressing him directly: **Gembira dapat bertemu dengan Encik Davies**. This may seem awkward at first to an English speaker, as we only use names in this way to refer to a third party and never to address someone directly, but it is a very common feature of Malay and one that would be very advantageous to you to be sensitive to, especially in highly formal situations where it is more or less expected.

The words for *we*, on the other hand, have specific meanings and usage depending on the situation. **Kita** is used when you are including the person or people you are speaking to in what you say. **Kami** is used when you mean *us* but not *you*. For instance, imagine you are at a party with your spouse. When the time comes for you and your spouse to go you announce your departure by saying **We** *must be leaving now*. You would use **kami** in Malay. If you used **kita** it would mean that you expect all the others to go with you! Obviously it would not be taken literally. It is just an illustration, but it is worth bearing in mind the distinction when you are speaking Malay as you may unintentionally find yourself altering the meaning of what you want to say otherwise.

2 To introduce yourself to someone in Malay simply use: **nama saya** + your name

To introduce someone else use the phrase **Perkenalkan, ini** + someone's name. Notice the slight pause marked by the comma.

Perkenalkan, ini Peter Robinson.   *This is Peter Robinson.*

Note the set phrases:

Selamat berkenalan.   *Pleased to meet you.*
Gembira dapat bertemu dengan anda. *Pleased to meet you.*
Gembira dapat bertemu dengan   *Pleased to meet you too.*
   anda juga.

> ● **INSIGHT**
>
> Remember that you could use the other person's name to mean *you* instead of **anda** or **saudara/saudari** as appropriate. Refer to point 1.

Or, in response to the first utterance, you could use **Saya juga begitu** or **Begitu juga dengan saya** as alternatives to vary your Malay.

3 In Part One you saw that you do not need to use words for *am/are/is* in Malay. You may have also noticed that you do not need to use a word for *a (an)* or *the* either. You just say *I from ABC Exports* or *I businessman*, etc. Compare the following English and Malay sentences:

I am a businessman.
Saya usahawan.

This is a book.
Ini buku.

In a sentence such as *That is timber.* where there would be no *a* in English anyway, the pattern is the same:

That is timber.
Itu kayu balak.

 Quick vocab

buku	*book*
kayu balak	*timber*

Exercise 4

Put these sentences into Malay.

   a This is a dictionary.
   b He is a businessman.
   c That is coffee.
   d This is a shop.
   e She is a teacher.
   f This is water.

kamus	*dictionary*
kopi	*coffee*
kedai	*shop*
guru	*teacher*
air	*water*
nasi	*rice*

4 In any language there are two types of question – one that requires an explanation (indirect) and one that simply requires the answer *yes* or *no* (direct). One way to form a yes/no question in Malay is by using **adakah**. In English we change the word order, for example to turn the statement *This is a book* into a question we say *Is this a book?* To form the question in Malay simply take the statement and add **adakah** to the beginning:

Ini buku.	*This is a book.*
Adakah **ini buku?**	*Is this a book?*

Similarly:

Anda usahawan.	*You are a businessman.*
Adakah **anda usahawan?**	*Are you a businessman?*
Itu nasi.	*That is rice.*
Adakah **itu nasi?**	*Is that rice?*

> ● **INSIGHT**
>
> Note that in the dialogue, the phrase **Adakah saudara ini …?** is a very polite idiomatic expression for *Are you …?* and is best learnt as a set expression.

Notice that the punctuation rules – capital letter at the beginning of the sentence and question mark at the end – apply in Malay too. Also, as in English, you should use a rising intonation at the end of the question.

Exercise 5

See if you can form **adakah**-type questions using the statements in Malay you made in Exercise 4. For example:

a *(This is a dictionary.)* **Ini kamus. Adakah ini kamus?**

Using Malay

Exercise 6

Look at the following dialogue between two people. Can you unscramble it so that it makes sense? Then translate it.

01.04

Ya, betul.
Saya gembira dapat berkenalan dengan anda juga.
Selamat datang ke England. Nama saya Robert Davies.
Maaf ... Adakah saudara ini Encik Salleh dari Malaysia?
Ya saya. Selamat berkenalan.
Adakah anda dari syarikat perniagaan Singapore Seas Imports?

 Quick vocab

perniagaan	*business*
syarikat perniagaan	*trading company*
betul	*correct*
Ya, betul.	*Yes, that's correct.*

Exercise 7

Over to you!

Imagine that you (**A**) are from a company called ABC Exports. As the only Malay speaker at your firm you have been sent to the airport to meet a Malaysian lady (**B**) called Mrs Fauziah (Puan Fauziah). You see a lady waiting who might just be Mrs Fauziah. Write out the dialogue replacing the English with suitable Malay phrases you have learnt in this unit.

When you check your answers in the **Key to the exercises** note that there could be several different ways of expressing the English in Malay, so if your answers are different it does not necessarily mean that they are wrong. We have just chosen one alternative as an example.

 01.05

A	*Excuse me. Are you Mrs Fauziah?*
B	Ya betul.
A	*I am from the ABC Exports Business Company. Welcome to England. My name is (your name).*
B	Gembira dapat bertemu dengan anda.
A	*Me too.*

It's normal if you found the **Over to you!** exercise hard-going to begin with! It is expected that you will have to listen, and interact with it several times to be able to do it perfectly. Trust us on this one. The **Over to you!** exercises are designed to stretch you linguistically, and the only way to do that is to push you slightly beyond your comfort zone, so do persevere with them!

Test yourself

1 How would you greet someone at 1 p.m.?

2 How would you greet someone at 9.30 a.m.?

3 How would you give your name in Malay?

4 How would you say *I'm from Singapore*?

5 How would you say *Welcome to England*?

6 What is the difference between **saudara** and **saudari**?

7 **Kami** or **kita**? Which one do you use to include everyone in what you say?

8 How would you introduce Mrs Walters to someone in Malay?

9 What word can you add to the beginning of a statement to form a question?

10 If someone said **Gembira dapat bertemu dengan anda** to you, how would you respond?

2 Arrivals

In this unit you will learn how to:
- ▶ *use less formal yes/no questions*
- ▶ *show possession*

PART ONE

Dialogue

Having met at the airport, Stan, Baharom and Zamani continue their conversation.

 02.01

Baharom	Keréta kami sudah menunggu di luar.
Zamani	Apakah ini bagasi anda? Biar saya bantu.
Baharom	Anda bercakap Bahasa Melayu dengan baik sekali.
Stan	Terima kasih. Saya cuba tetapi saya hanya tahu beberapa patah perkataan sahaja.
Baharom	Tidak mengapa. Sedikit-sedikit nanti lama-lama menjadi bukit.

 Quick vocab

keréta	*car*
sudah	*already*
menunggu	*waits, to wait*
di luar	*outside*
apakah	*an alternative to **adakah***
bagasi	*luggage*
biar	*let, allow*
bantu	*help, to help*
biar saya bantu	*let me help*
bercakap	*speak, to speak*
bahasa	*language*
Bahasa Melayu	*Malay (language)*
baik	*well, good*
sekali	*very*
dengan baik sekali	*very well*
terima kasih	*thank you*
cuba	*try, to try*

tetapi	*but*
hanya	*only*
tahu	*know, to know*
beberapa	*a few*
patah	*broken*
perkataan	*words*
sahaja	*just/only*
tidak mengapa	*that's all right/no problem*

Malay proverb: **Sedikit-sedikit nanti lama-lama jadi bukit.**

Take it one step at a time.

> ● **INSIGHT**
>
> **Bahasa Melayu** means *language of the Malays*. However, in Malaysia itself Malay is officially known as **Bahasa Malaysia**, and has been since 1971, so as to include all the ethnic groups in the country, not just the Malays. Be aware that the term **Bahasa Melayu** is politically incorrect in Malaysia.

Translation

Baharom	Our car is already waiting outside.
Zamani	Is this your luggage? Let me help you.
Baharom	You speak Malay very well.
Stan	Thank you. I try but I only speak a little.
Baharom	That's all right. Take it one step at a time.

How the language works 1

1 To express thanks in Malay use the phrase **terima kasih**. Adding **banyak**, which means *many* or *much* gives you **terima kasih banyak**, *thank you very much*.

To respond with *don't mention it*, use **terima kasih kembali** (often shortened to just **kembali**) or **sama-sama**.

2 Kereta kami *our car*, **bagasi anda** *your luggage*. The same words that are used for the personal pronouns are also used to show ownership or possession. Take careful note of the position. When they are used to show possession, they are placed after the noun they refer to. It is important to be aware that, as these words are the same, meaning depends exclusively on position. When they are placed before the noun they refer to, they have a different meaning, as discussed in Unit 1.

Study the following:

guru anda	*your teacher*
kawan saya	*my friend*
buku dia	*his book or her book*

Exercise 1

How would you say the following:

  a her photo
  b their present
  c my watch
  d our picture?

 Quick vocab

foto	*photo*
hadiah	*present*
jam tangan	*watch*
gambar	*picture*
kawan	*friend*

The **kita/kami** distinction applies here too. Baharom uses **kereta kami** in the dialogue because in Malay he is obliged to convey the idea that the car that is waiting is from the company Zamani and he work for and came in, and not the one Stan works for.

3 Biar means *let* or *allow*. It is used to form expressions like **biar saya bantu**, *let me help*, or, more commonly with **kita** in making an invitation **biar kita pergi**, *let's go!* (i.e. *let us go*.)

> ● INSIGHT
>
> **Saya** means *me* as well as *I* as in the expression above. We'll meet this formally later in the course.

Exercise 2

Can you make the following sentences?

  a Let me wait here.
  b Let me take that bag.
  c Let's speak Malay!
  d Let's go to Ipoh!

4 Verbs are often described as the action words of a language, such as *run*, *speak*, *take* and *try*, although they do not necessarily have to indicate action to be verbs. *Be* and *have* are also verbs.

In English, verbs change their form to indicate tense (i.e. whether they refer to the present, past or future), and sometimes to indicate the person who is performing the action. For example, we say *I speak* and *they speak* but *he speaks*, and *she speaks*. In Malay, the same form of the verb is used no matter which tense or person is being expressed. So, **bercakap** may mean *speak, speaks, spoke, speaking, to speak*, etc.

Note that in the vocabulary sections in the text and at the back of the book the *to* form (such as *to run*) is used to indicate a verb.

Understanding Malay

Exercise 3

True or false?

Read these statements in Malay based upon the dialogue in Part One, and say whether each is true or false.

- **a** Keréta Stan menunggu di luar.
- **b** Zamani membantu Stan.
- **c** Bagasi Stan di luar.
- **d** Stan bercakap Bahasa Melayu dengan baik sekali.

 Quick vocab

membantu   *to help/helps*

Exercise 4

Fill in the gaps in the following sentences with the verbs listed in the vocabulary section, concentrating on the meaning of the Malay only. Then match up the sentences in Malay with the correct English version.

Dia sudah _____ surat.	*She teaches Malay.*
Meréka sedang _____ akhbar.	*We are watching TV.*
Dia _____ bahasa Melayu.	*He has written a letter.*
Saya sedang _____ teh.	*They are reading a newspaper.*
Kami sedang _____ televisyen.	*I am drinking tea.*

 Quick vocab

membaca	*to read*
mengajar	*to teach*
menulis	*to write*
menonton	*to watch*
minum	*to drink*
surat	*letter*
akhbar	*newspaper*
televisyen	*television*

> **● INSIGHT**
>
> Words like **sudah** *already* and **sedang** *now* are how Malay conveys the idea of tense. They will be fully explained later, but if you need to know now, **sudah** makes a past tense and **sedang** a continuous one.

PART TWO

Dialogue

Tom Black, a student from the UK, arrives at Kuala Lumpur International Airport to meet his long-standing e-pal Serena for the first time. He passes through customs and baggage reclaim without a hitch but there is no sign of Serena! Looking like a lost tourist, Tom is approached by several private taxi drivers offering their services.

 02.02

Pemandu teksi 1	Teksi, Encik?
Tom	Tidak, terima kasih.
Pemandu teksi 2	Encik nak naik teksi?
Tom	Tidak, terima kasih.
Pemandu teksi 3	Encik, mahu ke mana?
Tom	Saya sedang menunggu seseorang.
Pemandu teksi 4	Saya boléh menghantar Encik ke hotél. Encik hendak pergi ke hotél mana?
(Presently, a young lady approaches Tom and starts speaking.)	
Serena	Maaf. Adakah saudara bernama Tom? Maaf, saya terléwat. Saya tersangkut dalam kesesakan lalu-lintas.
Tom	Ya. Anda Serena?
Serena	Betul. Gembira bertemu dengan saudara.
Tom	Saya juga begitu.
Serena	Adakah semua ini bagasi anda? Biar saya bantu.

 Quick vocab

teksi	*taxi*
pemandu	*guide, driver*
pemandu teksi	*taxi driver*
tidak, terima kasih	*no, thank you*
nak	(short for **hendak**, see below) *to want, to need*
naik	*to take some form of transport*
mahu	*to want*
mahu ke mana	*where to?*
sedang	*now*
menunggu	*to wait*
sedang menunggu	*am waiting (for)*
seseorang	*someone*
boléh	*can/to be able to*
menghantar	*to take (someone somewhere)*
hotél	*hotel*
hendak	*to want, to need*

mana	*which*
ke hotél mana?	*to which hotel?*
maaf	*excuse me, I'm sorry*
bernama	*to be called, to be named*
terléwat	*(to be) late*
tersangkut	*(to be) stuck*
dalam	*in*
lalu-lintas	*traffic*
kesesakan lalu-lintas	*traffic jam*
gembira bertemu dengan saudara	*glad to meet you*
semua (ini)	*all (this)*

● **INSIGHT**

This may interest you: often, verbs beginning with **ter-** such as **tersangkut** and **terléwat** refer to an undesired outcome of a result beyond the speaker's control.

Translation

Taxi driver 1	Taxi, Sir?
Tom	No, thank you.
Taxi driver 2	Does Sir need a taxi?
Tom	No, thank you.
Taxi driver 3	Where do you want (to go), Sir?
Tom	I am waiting for someone.
Taxi driver 4	Can I take you to a hotel (Sir). Where do you want to go?
Serena	Excuse me, are you Tom? I'm sorry I'm late. I was stuck in traffic.
Tom	Yes. Are you Serena?
Serena	That's correct. Pleased to meet you.
Tom	Me too.
Serena	Is this all your baggage? Let me help.

● **INSIGHT**

Malaysians affectionately refer to their capital as KL. KLIA stands for Kuala Lumpur International Airport. There is a rapid and efficient train system (KLIA Express) from the airport to the city centre that takes around 30 minutes and, in spite of what eager taxi drivers may tell you, works out as a cheaper and faster way to get to the city if you are travelling alone. If you are not travelling alone, some careful negotiation should land you a cheaper ride to your hotel by taxi.

How the language works 2

1 In the dialogue, **encik** is used to mean *you*. **Encik perlu teksi?** Used in this way, **encik** can be likened to the older style, hyper-polite English, *Does Sir require a taxi?*, although its usage is still common place in Malay-speaking countries. Any title or a name can be used to mean *you*. Therefore, if you say, for example, **Apakah Siti dari Kuala Lumpur?** this could mean *Is Siti from Kuala Lumpur?* but if you were addressing Siti directly, the meaning would be *Are you from Kuala Lumpur (Siti)?*

2 In Unit 1 we saw that **maaf** can mean *excuse me*. It can also be used to apologize for something in the following way:

Maaf, saya terléwat.   *I'm sorry I'm late.*

3 In Unit 1 you were introduced to **adakah** as a means of forming a yes/no question. As in the dialogue above, you can make the same type of question by using **apakah**. The meaning is the same and is subject only to the speaker's personal preference:

Adakah **dia sedang menunggu**   *Is she waiting for someone?*
  seseorang?
Apakah **dia sedang menunggu**
  seseorang?

Exercise 5

Use **apakah** to ask the following questions:

   a Is this all your (use **anda**) luggage?
   b Are they waiting outside?
   c Is he stuck in traffic?
   d Are we (use **kami**) late?

4 Did you notice that not all the questions in the dialogue are formed with **adakah** or **apakah**? In informal style, these may be omitted when forming a question, especially in the informal spoken language. Another way to form a yes/no question is simply to take the statement and add a rising intonation at the end; that alone forms the question.

 02.03

Look at the following examples and, ideally, follow along with the recording if you have it, as this type of question relies solely on the rising intonation you use.

Itu menarik.	*It's interesting.*
Itu menarik?	*Is it interesting?*
Dia penat.	*She's tired.*
Dia penat?	*Is she tired?*
Ini kucing anda.	*This is your cat.*
Ini kucing anda?	*Is this your cat?*

 **Quick vocab**

cantik	*beautiful*
menarik	*interesting*
penat	*tired*
kucing	*cat*

Using Malay

Exercise 6

Choose the correct response from the choice of three for each question or statement.

1 Maaf, apakah anda pemandu teksi?
  a Terima kasih.
  b Ya betul, Encik mahu ke mana?
  c Tidak mengapa.

2 Biar saya bantu.
  a Terima kasih, bagasi saya di luar.
  b Saya sedang menonton televisyen.
  c Saya bercakap Bahasa Melayu dengan baik.

3 Encik mahu ke mana?
  a Mahu ke Hotél Istana.
  b Selamat berkenalan.
  c Tidak, terima kasih.

4 Apakah anda sedang menunggu seseorang?
  a Ya, saya sedang menunggu pemandu teksi.
  b Tidak, dia pelancong.
  c Gembira dapat bertemu dengan anda juga.

Exercise 7

Over to you!

While you are working at your desk your Malaysian friend Mustafa (**A**) comes up to you to ask for help with something. Use the English in the prompts to answer Mustafa's questions in Malay. You are (**B**).

 02.04

A	Boléh anda membantu saya?
B	*I'm sorry. I'm busy now.*
A	Anda sedang belajar Bahasa Melayu?
B	*Yes.*
A	Boléh saya kembali nanti?
B	*OK.*
A	Selamat belajar!

Quick vocab

sibuk	*busy*
belajar	*to study*
sedang belajar	*to be studying*
kembali	*to come back*
nanti	*later*
Baiklah kalau begitu	*OK*
Selamat belajar!	*Happy studying!*

> ● **INSIGHT**
>
> Extending from the meaning given above, you can probably see why **Kembali** also means *Don't mention it*, in reply to **terima Kasih**.

When you have finished writing in the answers, check that you know what Mustafa is asking you, then use the recording to practise the dialogue.

Test yourself

1. How would you say *Thank you very much*?
2. What is the difference in meaning between **saya guru** and **guru saya**?
3. What is the difference between **bahasa kami** and **bahasa kita**?
4. Which word would you use to make an invitation?
5. Why are tenses so easy to express in Malay?
6. Which word would you use to begin an apology?
7. Give an alternative question marker to **adakah**.
8. How can you make a statement into a question without adding any words?
9. How do you say *Malay* as in *the Malay language*?
10. What does a verb beginning with **ter-** sometimes mean?

3 Tell me more about yourself

In this unit you will learn how to:
▸ *give information about yourself and ask about other people*
▸ *express nationalities and languages*
▸ *ask basic questions*

PART ONE

Dialogue

On the way to the hotel, Stan, Zamani and Baharom pass the time by getting to know each other a little more.

 03.01

Stan	Apa khabar Encik Zamani?
Zamani	Khabar baik dan anda pula bagaimana Encik Davies?
Stan	Saya juga baik, terima kasih.
Zamani	Bagaimanakah dengan penerbangan anda?
Stan	Sangat selésa, walaupun agak meletihkan.
Zamani	Anda mémang fasih bertutur dalam Bahasa Melayu.
Stan	Terima kasih. Saya belajar daripada isteri saya. Dia berasal dari Singapura. Apakah Encik sudah berkeluarga?
Zamani	Belum. Saya masih bujang.
Baharom	Saya sudah berkeluarga.
Stan	Maaf. Boléhkah anda bercakap dengan lebih perlahan?
Baharom	Baiklah. Maafkan saya.

 Quick vocab

apa khabar?	*how are you?*
khabar baik	*I'm fine*
dan anda pula bagaimana?	*and how about you?*
pula	*likewise*
Bagaimanakah dengan ...?	*How is ...? How was ...?*
penerbangan	*flight*
sangat	*very*

selésa	*comfortable*
walaupun	*although*
agak	*rather, somewhat*
meletihkan	*tiring*
mémang	*really*
fasih	*fluent*
bertutur	*to speak*
daripada	*from*
isteri	*wife*
berkeluarga	*married*
belum	*not yet*
masih	*still*
bujang	*single*
dengan lebih perlahan	*more slowly*
lebih	*more*
perlahan	*slow*
baiklah	*all right, OK*
maafkan	*to forgive*
maafkan saya	*I'm sorry, forgive me*

Translation

Stan	How are you, Mr Zamani?
Zamani	Fine, and you, Mr Davies?
Stan	I'm fine too, thank you.
Zamani	How was your flight?
Stan	Very comfortable, although somewhat tiring.
Zamani	You really are fluent in Malay.
Stan	Thank you. I learnt (it) from my wife. She is from Singapore. Are you married?
Zamani	Not yet. I am still single.
Baharom	I am married.
Stan	Sorry, could you speak more slowly?
Baharom	OK. I am sorry.

How the language works 1

1 *How are you?* in Malay is **Apa khabar?** The standard response is: **Khabar baik, terima kasih**, *I am fine, thank you*. You could use **Baik sekali**, *Very good, very well*, for short.

> ● INSIGHT
> **Khabar** on its own means *news*.

Other common answers are **sihat**, *I'm healthy* or **alhamdulillah**, **baik**, *I'm well, thanks be to Allah*. The last response is partly Arabic and widely used by Muslims.

> ● INSIGHT
> You should only use this expression if you, too, are Muslim.

2 Countries, nationalities and languages.

 Quick vocab

Belanda	*Holland*
Amérika	*America*
Kanada	*Canada*
China	*China*
Jepun	*Japan*
Jerman	*Germany*
Indonesia	*Indonesia*
Singapura	*Singapore*
Itali	*Italy*
Sepanyol	*Spain*
Perancis	*France*

> ● INSIGHT
> New Zealand, Australia, Ireland, Scotland, Wales and England retain the same spelling as in English and do not conform to the Malay pronunciation rules you have learnt in this book, so the pronunciation is the same as you would expect in English.

(i) To talk about nationality simply take **orang** which means *person* and add the name of the country to it:

orang Amérika	*an American (person)*
Saya orang Ireland.	*I am Irish. (I am an Irish person.)*

(ii) Talking about languages is just as simple. Take **bahasa** which means *language* and add the name of the country that corresponds to the language you want to express:

bahasa Itali	*Italian (language)*
Dia boléh bercakap bahasa Perancis.	*She can speak French.*

Note, however, that when talking about the English language, only the **Inggeris** form can be used. So English is always **bahasa Inggeris**.

> ● INSIGHT
> When Malays talk about their own language they often just refer to it as **bahasa**, taking it as read from the situation that it is **bahasa Melayu** they are referring to. As you know, the Malay language is also referred to as **bahasa Malaysia**.

As you know, Malay likes to use English words, so the word China (as in English) is common. However, you should still refer to a Chinese person as **orang Cina** and the language as **bahasa Cina** or **bahasa Mandarin**.

Exercise 1

How would you say:

a a Spaniard

b Chinese

c a Scot

d an Indonesian

e Dutch

f an American

g a New Zealander

h Malay

i a Singaporean

j Japanese?

2 Now that you can refer to any language you want, you need to know how to talk about speaking such and such a language. In Unit 2 you met **bercakap** + language:

**Anda bercakap bahasa Melayu
  dengan baik sekali.**

You speak Malay very well.

In this unit we introduce you to two more ways namely **bertutur dalam** and **berbual dalam**. With both of these verbs you need to use **dalam** whereas you do not need to with **bercakap**. **Bercakap** is probably the most common of these verbs, but you need to at least understand the others in case someone uses them while speaking to you, as your ability to speak Malay will no doubt set you apart from the usual tourists, and you will be commended on your efforts, if not the quality of your Malay.

**Meréka bertutur dalam bahasa Cina
  dengan fasih.**

They speak Chinese fluently.

**Boléhkah Devinder berbual dalam
  bahasa Melayu?**

Can Devinder speak Malay?

 Quick vocab

dengan fasih   *fluently*

3 Some question words.

So far we have seen two ways to make yes/no questions in Malay. The other types of question are those that require an answer and begin in English with question words such as *what? who? how?* and *when?*

In Malay these are:

i Apa or **Apakah?**   *What?*

Apa itu?   *What's that?*

ii Siapa or **siapakah?**   *Who?*

Siapa ini?   *Who is this?*

Siapakah orang itu?   *Who is that person?*

iii Bila or **Bilakah**?	*When?*
Bila penerbangan ke London?	*When is the flight to London?*
Bilakah mesyuarat?	*When is the meeting?*
iv Bagaimana or **bagaimanakah**?	*What kind of?/What's … like?/How's?/*
	How are?/How was?/How were?, etc.
Bagaimanakah filem itu?	*How was that film?*
Bagaimana emak anda?	*How's your mother?*

All the question words can occur with **-kah** attached to them without altering the meaning. As we shall see later on, **-kah** often features in question formation in Malay.

 Quick vocab

mesyuarat	*meeting*
filem	*film*

4 In English, nouns can be described by an adjective, for example: *a **big** car*, *a **happy** occasion*, or they can be described by another noun whereby the first noun gives more information about the second, for instance: **life**style, **book**shop and **fighte**rpilot. In English, the describing word occurs before the main noun.

In Malay, nouns can be modified by adjectives or by nouns and even verbs which also carry out the role of describing the noun. When any of these are used to describe a noun they are placed after the noun they refer to.

Study the following. The describing words are in italics in Malay and in bold in English:

▶ with adjectives

keréta *baru*	*a **new** car*
gambar *menarik*	*an **interesting** picture*

▶ with nouns

stésen *bas*	***bus** station*
orang *Wales*	*a **Welsh** person*

▶ with verbs

lapangan *terbang*	***air**port (or, originally **air**field)*
bilik *mandi*	***bath**room*

▶ When more than one describing word, including possessive pronouns (*my, your, our* etc.) and personal names, occurs in a phrase, the word order is the reverse of the English:

sekolah bahasa Inggeris   *English language school*
pasport teman saya   *my friend's passport*

 Quick vocab

baru	*new*
stésen	*station*
bas	*bus*
lapangan	*field*
pasport	*passport*
terbang	*to fly*
bilik	*room*
mandi	*to take a bath*
sekolah	*school*

Exercise 2

How would you say:

   a heavy luggage
   b sports clothes
   c bedroom (say: *room (of) sleep*)
   d My Malay language teacher's friend
   e My friend's Malay language teacher?

 Quick vocab

berat	*heavy*
sukan	*sport*
pakaian	*clothes*
tidur	*to sleep*

 03.02

When you are learning a language you may need to ask for clarification or repetition. You will find the following phrases very useful so you should learn them by heart:

Maaf, saya tidak faham.   *I'm sorry, I don't understand.*
Boléhkah anda ulangi sekali lagi?   *Could you repeat that please?*
Boléhkah anda tolong tuliskan?   *Could you write it down please?*
Boléhkah anda tolong éjakan?   *Could you spell it please?*

Boléhkah anda bercakap dengan lebih perlahan?   *Could you speak more slowly please?*

Boléhkah anda bercakap dengan lebih kuat?   *Could you speak more loudly please?*

 Quick vocab

faham	*to understand*
ulangi	*to repeat*
sekali	*once*
tuliskan	*to write down*
tolong	*please*
éjakan	*to spell*
kuat	*loud, strong*

You will notice that most of the expressions above use **boléhkah …?**, which corresponds to the English *could you …?* The **-kah** is actually optional and used colloqually in all the above, but Malays tend to use it wherever questions are being asked in the written form. **Boléh** means *can*, as in to have the ability to as well as meaning *to be permitted to*. More on **boléh** later!

Understanding Malay

Exercise 3

Say whether the following statements based on the dialogue are true or false.

    a   Penerbangan Encik Davies sangat meletihkan.
    b   Isteri Encik Davies berasal dari Singapura.
    c   Encik Davies belajar bahasa Malaysia daripada isterinya.
    d   Encik Zamani belum berkeluarga.

 Quick vocab

isterinya	*his wife*

Exercise 4

 03.03

First familiarize yourself with the vocabulary then listen to Rani interviewing a young lady and circle the correct answer to each question:

    a   What nationality is the interviewee?
       British – Indonesian – Chinese – Malaysian
    b   How well can she speak Malay (according to the interviewer)?
       like a native – fluently – only a little
    c   What other language can she speak?
       Chinese – Welsh – English – Japanese
    d   What problem does she have with the interviewer's Malay?
       It's too fast – It's too unclear – It's heavily accented

lancar	*fluent*
lembut	*gentle, (here) refined*
jelas	*clear*
tidak jelas	*unclear*

PART TWO

Dialogue

Tom is staying at Serena's house on an estate in the suburbs of Kuala Lumpur. Serena's neighbour is an elderly gentleman who tends to be a bit nosey! Tom and Serena are just leaving the house when they are caught by the inquisitive Encik Hanif who is sitting on his verandah …

 03.04

Encik Hanif	Saudari hendak ke mana? Siapakah lelaki itu?
Serena	Saya mahu pergi berjalan-jalan. Dia teman saya dari Sheffield.
Encik Hanif	Sheffield? Di mana tu? Di Amérika?
Serena	Tidak, di England.
Encik Hanif	Jadi dia orang Inggeris. Suatu masa dahulu saya pernah belajar bahasa Inggeris, tapi sekarang saya sudah lupa.
Tom	Jangan bimbang, saya boléh berbual dalam bahasa Melayu.
Encik Hanif	Di mana anda tinggal di Kuala Lumpur?
Serena	Dia tinggal di rumah saya.
Encik Hanif	Bila anda tiba di Kuala Lumpur?
Tom	Kelmarin bersama penerbangan Malaysia Airlines.
Encik Hanif	Berapa lama anda akan tinggal di sini?
Tom	Mungkin selama dua minggu saja.
Encik Hanif	Bagaimana pendapat anda tentang orang Malaysia? Anda rasa selésa?
Tom	Meréka semuanya peramah macam Encik. O, ya. Siapakah nama Encik?
Encik Hanif	Anda boléh panggil saya, Pak cik Hanif. Harap anda akan seronok tinggal di sini.
Tom	Terima kasih. Sehingga kita berjumpa lagi.

Siapakah?	*Who?*
lelaki	*man*
mahu	*to want, to desire to*
pergi	*to go*
berjalan-jalan	*to walk (for pleasure)*
pergi berjalan-jalan	*to go for a walk*
di mana	*where*
tu	*that (short for **itu** in speech)*
bukan	*no*
jadi	*so*
suatu	*a*
masa	*time, occasion*
dahulu	*before, in the past*
suatu masa dahulu	*a long time ago*
pernah	*(see language notes)*
sekarang	*now*
tapi	*but*
lupa	*forget*
sudah lupa	*already forgotten*
jangan	*don't*
bimbang	*worry*
tinggal	*to stay*
rumah	*house*
bila	*when*
tiba	*arrive*
kelmarin	*yesterday*
bersama	*with*
berapa lama	*how long*
akan	*will (verb)*
di sini	*here*
mungkin	*maybe*
selama	*for (with time)*
dua	*two*
minggu	*week*
saja	*only, just*
pendapat	*opinion*
tentang	*about*
Bagaimana pendapat anda tentang…?	*What's your opinion of…?*
rasa	*to feel*
semuanya	*all of them*
peramah	*friendly*
macam	*like*
O, ya	*By the way*

panggil	*to call*
panggil saya...	*call me...*
Pak cik	*Mr, form of address for older man*
harap	*hope*
seronok	*enjoy*
tinggal	*stay, live*
sehingga	*until*
Sehingga kita berjumpa lagi	*Until we meet again/See you again.*

> ● **INSIGHT**
>
> **Pak cik** means *uncle*, but it is also used as a polite form of address for older men. You can append this to the name, as in the dialogue, or you can use it without the name to mean *you* or to call out to someone older or elderly. The female equivalent is **Mak cik**. You should always make a point of using these with older people.

Translation

Mr Hanif	Where are you going? Who is that man?
Serena	I'm going for a walk. He is my friend from Sheffield.
Mr Hanif	Sheffield? Where is that? In America?
Serena	No, in England.
Mr Hanif	So he's an Englishman. I studied English a long time ago, but I've forgotten (it) now.
Tom	Don't worry, I can speak Malay.
Mr Hanif	Where are you staying in Kuala Lumpur?
Serena	He is staying at my house.
Mr Hanif	When (did you) arrive in Kuala Lumpur?
Tom	Yesterday afternoon with Malaysia Airlines.
Mr Hanif	How long will you stay here?
Tom	Maybe just for two weeks.
Mr Hanif	How do you find Malaysian people? Do you feel comfortable (with them)?
Tom	They are all friendly like you. By the way, what's your name?
Mr Hanif	Just call me Pak cik Hanif. (I) hope you enjoy your stay here.
Tom	Thank you. See you again.

How the language works 2

1 Negation. Malay makes sentences or phrases negative by using **tidak** or **bukan** depending on the situation. It is important that you understand the distinction between the usage of these two words.

▶ To make a verb negative in English, we use *don't* or *doesn't* before the verb. For example, we would say *He **doesn't** speak English* or *They **don't** eat beef.*

In Malay, insert **tidak** directly before a verb to make it negative.

dia minum	*he drinks*
dia *tidak* **minum**	*he doesn't drink*
saya tahu	*I know*
saya *tidak* **tahu**	*I don't know*

▶ In Malay, adjectives are also made negative by using **tidak**.

dia sihat	*he is healthy*
dia *tidak* **sihat**	*he isn't healthy*
meréka mabuk	*they are drunk*
meréka *tidak* **mabuk**	*they aren't drunk*

▶ When what you want to make negative is a noun (a thing) or a pronoun, **bukan** must be used. Again it is inserted directly before the noun (or pronoun) it refers to.

Saya orang Malaysia.	*I am a Malaysian.*
Saya *bukan* **orang Malaysia.**	*I am not a Malaysian.*
Ini kucing.	*This is a cat.*
Ini *bukan* **kucing.**	*This is not a cat.*
Dia presidén? Bukan dia.	*Is he the president? It's not him.*

Quick vocab

mabuk	*drunk*
presiden	*president*

Exercise 5

Complete the sentences with either **tidak** or **bukan**.

  a Dia _____ sopan.
  b Meréka _____ buta.
  c Kami _____ tinggal di Johor Bahru.
  d Itu _____ keréta saya.
  e Dia _____ gembira.

Quick vocab

sopan	*polite*
buta	*blind*

Finally, both **tidak** and **bukan** mean *no* as a one-word response to a yes/no question. You need to recognize what the focus word is in the question. Is it a noun, verb or adjective?

Apakah kawan anda *penari*? **Bukan.**	*Is your friend a **dancer**? No.*
Apakah dia *péndek*? **Tidak.**	*Is she **short**? No.*
Apakah dia *bekerja* **di Sabah? Tidak.**	*Does she **work** in Sabah? No.*

Exercise 6

Answer *no* to these questions:

    a Adakah itu pensél anda?
    b Adakah pensel anda patah?
    c Apakah ibu anda peramah?
    d Apakah meréka tahu?

 Quick vocab

péndek	*short*
pensél	*pencil*

2 In the dialogue did you notice that Encik Hanif asked Serena **Saudari hendak ke mana?** without including a pronoun? This is perfectly acceptable and widely used in conversational style. Native Malay speakers like to express themselves in the simplest and most economical way possible which leads to them omitting certain words from the sentence when the context is fully understood. In this case, it is obvious that Encik Hanif is addressing Serena and no-one else. It would be unthinkable to miss words out like this in correct English, even when the context is fully understood. The omission in the sentence above is optional. It is just as correct to say **Saudari hendak pergi ke mana?**

> ● **INSIGHT**
>
> As you work through this book, and especially if you have the opportunity to converse with Malay speakers, you will begin to get a natural feel for which words can be dropped when the context is understood.

3 To ask *where?*, *where to?* and *where from?* Malay uses:

di mana ...?	*where …?*
Di mana anda tinggal?	*Where do you live?*
ke mana ...?	*where to …?*
Ke mana anda pergi?	*Where are you going (to)?*
dari mana ...?	*where from …?*
Dari mana anda berasal?	*Where do you come from?*

These three questions are made up of a preposition (a word that indicates location) and **mana**. It is very important to note that, although these questions are made up of two components, these components cannot be separated as in the corresponding English sentences. For instance, in the last example above, notice how *where* can occur at the beginning of the phrase with the *from* at the end. This is not possible in Malay.

> ● **INSIGHT**
>
> You will find these questions easier to understand and use if you think of how they would appear in older style English: *To where are you going? From where do you come?* as this is what you are effectively saying in Malay.

As with most other question words, the above often occur with **-kah** giving us **di manakah**, **ke manakah** and **dari manakah**.

Exercise 7

Fill in the blanks with the appropriate question according to the meaning:

    a _____ dia masuk?

    b _____ dia belajar?

    c _____ meréka membawa bagasi itu?

    d _____ kami datang?

 Quick vocab

masuk	*to enter*
membawa	*bring/take*

4 Used on its own, **berapa?** means *how many?*

Berapa keréta?	*How many cars?*
Berapa kucing?	*How many cats?*

However, **berapa** is often combined with other words to create specific questions that ask about the quantity of something. In the Part two dialogue you were introduced to:

Berapa lama?	*How long?/For how long?*

> ● **INSIGHT**
>
> Note that **berapa lama?** can only be used to refer to time. If you want to ask *how long?* to refer to physical length the question **berapa panjang?** must be used.

This question is made up of **berapa** and **lama** which means *a long time*.

Similarly, **berapa kali?**, *how many times?*

Berapa kali saudara datang	*How many times have you*
ke Singapura?	*come to Singapore?*

 Quick vocab

datang	*to come*

Many useful questions can be formed with **berapa**. It is worth bearing this in mind as you work through the units as other questions using **berapa** will be presented in the appropriate units.

> ● **INSIGHT**
>
> The answer to a question with **berapa** will, more often than not, have a number in the answer.

Exercise 8

Complete these questions with **berapa lama** or **berapa kali** as appropriate:

    a _____ penerbangan dari London ke Singapura?
    b _____ anda makan nasi goréng?
    c _____ kita menunggu?
    d _____ dia tinggal di Malaysia?
    e _____ dia teléfon?

 Quick vocab

makan	*to eat*
nasi goréng	*fried rice*
teléfon	*to call/to make a phone call*

5 In Part One of this unit you were introduced to the question word **siapa** (or **siapakah**). When you ask for someone's name in English, you use *what?*, for example *What's your name?*. Malay, on the other hand, uses **siapa!**

Siapakah **nama anda?**	*What's your name?*
Siapa **nama orang itu?**	*What's the name of that person?*

But, if you are enquiring about the name of something other than a living being, you must use **apa**.

Apa **nama kampung ini?**	*What's this village called?*

 Quick vocab

kampung	*village*

6 Pernah and **tidak pernah** relate to the past in a specific way. From the English speaker's point of view, it is easier to grasp how to use **tidak pernah** first. **Tidak pernah** simply translates *never* as in such sentences as:

Saya *tidak pernah* **pergi ke Pulau Redang.**	*I have never been to Redang Island.*
Kami *tidak pernah* **melihat dia.**	*We have never seen her.*

Pernah expresses *ever* as in the English *Have you ever been to Redang Island?* However, whereas English only uses *ever* in the question form, Malay uses it in the postitive statement too. In this sense it expresses something you have done in the distant past, and can often be translated as *once* in English.

Saya *pernah* **pergi ke Bali.**	*I once went to Bali.*
Dia *pernah* **belajar memasak.**	*She once learnt to cook.*
Apa saudara *pernah* **ke Kelantan?**	*Have you ever (been) to Kelantan?*

● INSIGHT

Note that in the last example **pergi** can be omitted, as it is understood from the context which **ke** *to* creates. **Pergi** is often dropped. For example, in the dialogue, Encik Hanif asks **Saudari hendak ke mana?** The full form would be **Saudari hendak pergi ke mana?**

 Quick vocab

melihat	*to see*
memasak	*to cook*

Exercise 9

How would you say the following?

    a I have never seen that film (movie).
    b Have you ever been to Melaka?
    c We (use **kami**) once ate durian.
    d He once lived in America.

 Quick vocab

durian	*durian (see Unit 14)*

7 Selamat, a word connected with the idea of prosperity, welfare, happiness and salvation is used in many a Malay greeting. In addition to several set greetings, some of which you will find below, you can combine **selamat** with any verb to convey an idea of well-wishing in that particular action, etc. Here are some common ones you may find useful:

Selamat belajar!	*Enjoy your studies!*
Selamat makan!	*Enjoy your food!*
Selamat bekerja!	*Enjoy your work!*
Selamat berangkat!	*Have a good trip!*
Selamat hari jadi!	*Happy Birthday!*
Selamat malam!	*Good night!*
Selamat Hari Raya!	*Happy Eid!*
Selamat Menyambut Hari Krismas!	*Merry Christmas!*
Selamat jalan!	*Goodbye**
Selamat tinggal!	*Goodbye**
Selamat Tahun Baru!	*Happy New Year!*

● INSIGHT

*Why are there are two words for *goodbye* in Malay? If you are the one who is leaving, you say **Selamat tinggal** to whoever you are taking leave of. If you are the one staying, you wish the person leaving a happy journey with **Selamat jalan!**

Using Malay

Exercise 10

See if you can make these sentences in Malay:

    a They didn't arrive yesterday.
    b This isn't the flight to Kota Kinabalu.
    c I don't speak Arabic.
    d My wife isn't Singaporean.
    e That isn't an orang-utan. (English uses the same word as the Malay.)
    f Eman is not stubborn.

 Quick vocab

bahasa Arab	*Arabic*
keras kepala	*stubborn*

> ● **INSIGHT**
>
> **Orang-utan** is, in fact, a Malay word. **Orang** means *person* and **hutan** means *forest*. So **orang-utan** means *forest person*. This is not the only word we've adopted into English from Malay. For instance, **amok**, as in *to run amok*, is borrowed from the Malay **amuk**.

Exercise 11

Look at the following sentences. Use the rules above to determine whether the sentence uses **bukan** or **tidak** in the right way. If there is a mistake, correct it. Check your answer in the Key to the exercises.

    a Dia tidak orang Brazil.
    b Dia bukan pemain bola sépak.
    c Kami tidak bahagia.
    d Saya bukan bodoh.
    e Kelmarin meréka bukan datang.

Quick vocab

orang Brazil	*Brazilian*
pemain	*player*
bola sépak	*football*
bahagia	*happy*
bodoh	*stupid*

Exercise 12

Look at the answers. What were the questions?

a Sihat.

b Penerbangan sangat meletihkan.

c Ya, saya masih bujang.

d Nama saya Angela.

e Ya, saya pernah ke Miami.

f Meréka mahu tinggal di Miri cuma dua minggu.

g Tidak, saya bukan orang Thai.

Exercise 13

Over to you!

Imagine you are an Australian called Stuart from Canberra (**A**). One day you are out and about in your home town and you notice a foreign tourist having difficulty making herself understood (**B**). You notice that her guidebook is in Malay so you take the opportunity to practise the **bahasa Melayu** you learnt at school (**di sekolah**).

 03.05

A	*Are you Malaysian? How are you?*
B	Ya, khabar baik, terima kasih.
A	*Excuse me? What's your name?*
B	Nama saya Norsheela. Panggil saja Sheela.
A	*My name's Stuart. Just call me Stu.*
B	Maaf, bahasa Inggeris saya tidak lancar.
A	*Don't worry. I once learnt Bahasa Melayu at school.*
B	Bagus kalau begitu.
A	*Where are you staying?*
B	Saya tinggal di Hotél Hilton.
A	*How is Australia?*
B	Bagus sekali.
A	*How long will you stay in Canberra?*
B	Cuma 2 minggu.
A	*Have a nice holiday.*
B	Terima kasih. Sehingga berjumpa lagi.

 Quick vocab

bagus sekali	*great*
cuma	*just, only*

Test yourself

1. How do you say *How are you?* in Malay?
2. What does **orang Perancis** mean?
3. How would you refer to the English language in Malay?
4. What do **berbual** and **bertutur** need that **bercakap** doesn't?
5. What does **boléh** mean?
6. How would you say *I don't understand* in Malay?
7. What is unusual about the way you ask someone's name in Malay?
8. How should you use **bukan** and **tidak**?
9. Are adjectives placed after or before the noun in Malay?
10. What is the difference between **Selamat tinggal** and **Selamat jalan**?

At work and at school

In this unit you will learn how to:
▶ *talk about your job and ask about what other people do*
▶ *express your capabilities*
▶ *talk about education and study*

PART ONE

Dialogue

During his short stay in Malaysia, Stan needs a competent personal assistant to help him. One of the short-listed applicants for the job is Shanaz Salleh, whom Stan is interviewing.

 04.01

Shanaz	Selamat pagi, Tuan!
Stan	Selamat pagi, sila duduk! Saya perlu seorang setiausaha untuk membantu saya. Boléhkah saudari ceritakan sedikit tentang latar belakang pendidikan saudari?
Shanaz	Saya menerima pendidikan saya di Kolej Kesetiausahawan Antarabangsa di Kuala Lumpur.
Stan	Bilakah saudari tamat pengajian?
Shanaz	Lima tahun yang lalu.
Stan	Apa kemahiran saudari?
Shanaz	Saya boléh bertutur dalam tiga bahasa, iaitu Bahasa Inggeris, Perancis dan Jepun dengan baik. Saya juga boléh menaip dengan pantas.
Stan	Boléhkah saudari mengguna komputer?
Shanaz	Tentu boléh, Tuan. Saya juga boléh mengguna mesin faks dan e-mél.
Stan	Boléhkah saudari menguruskan segala surat-menyurat?
Shanaz	Boléh, saya mémang mahir dalam bidang itu.
Stan	Saudari masih bekerja di syarikat yang lain?
Shanaz	Ya, saya masih bekerja di Syarikat Oriental Exports sebagai seorang setiausaha.
Stan	Berapa gaji yang saudari harapkan?

Shanaz	Dua ribu ringgit sebulan, jika boléh.
Stan	Bila saudari boléh mula bekerja?
Shanaz	Pada bulan hadapan.
Stan	Saudari boléh bekerja sepenuh masa?
Shanaz	Maaf Tuan, bekerja sambilan sahaja, iaitu tiga hari dalam seminggu.
Stan	Baiklah kalau begitu. Saya akan pertimbangkan permohonan saudari dan beri jawapan dengan secepat mungkin.

 Quick vocab

duduk	to sit down
sila duduk	please sit down
perlu	to need
seorang	a (used with jobs)
setiausaha	secretary
untuk	for, (in order) to
ceritakan	to tell
tentang	about
belakang	behind
latar	background
pendidikan	education
menerima	to receive, to get
kolej	college
kesetiausahawan	secretarial
antarabangsa	international
tamat pengajian	to graduate
lima	five
tahun	year
lima tahun yang lalu	five years ago
kemahiran	skill(s)
iaitu	namely, that is to say
dengan baik	well
menaip	to type
pantas	brisk, quick
dengan pantas	quickly
mengguna	to use
komputer	computer
tentu	of course
tentu boléh	(here) of course I can
mesin faks	fax machine
menguruskan	to deal with, to handle
segala	all
surat-menyurat	correspondence

mahir	*adept, skilful*
dalam	*in, inside*
mahir dalam	*adept in*
bidang	*field (i.e. of expertise, etc.)*
bekerja	*to work*
lain	*other*
syarikat yang lain	*another company*
sebagai	*as*
gaji	*salary*
harapkan	*to expect*
dua ribu	*2,000*
ringgit	*ringgit (Malaysian currency)*
sebulan	*per month*
jika	*if*
jika boléh	*if possible*
mula	*to begin, to start*
bulan	*month*
pada bulan hadapan	*next month*
masa	*time*
sepenuh masa	*full time*
sambilan	*part time*
sahaja	*only*
seminggu	*a week*
pertimbangkan	*to consider*
permohonan	*application*
beri	*to give*
jawapan	*answer*
dengan secepat mungkin	*as soon as possible*
mungkin	*possible*

Translation

Shanaz	Good morning, Sir!
Stan	Good morning, please take a seat. I need a secretary to help me. Could you tell me a little about your educational background.
Shanaz	I received my education at the International Secretarial College in Kuala Lumpur.
Stan	When did you graduate?
Shanaz	Five years ago.
Stan	What are your skills?
Shanaz	I can speak three languages well, namely English, French and Japanese. I am also able to type fast.
Stan	Can you use a computer?

Shanaz	Of course I can, Sir. I can also use a fax machine and e-mail.
Stan	Can you handle all the correspondence?
Shanaz	(Yes) I can, I am particularly skilled in that field.
Stan	Are you still working for another company?
Shanaz	Yes, Sir, I'm still working for Oriental Express as a secretary.
Stan	What salary do you expect?
Shanaz	Two thousand per month, if possible.
Stan	When can you start work?
Shanaz	Next month.
Stan	Can you work full time?
Shanaz	I'm sorry, Sir, (but) I'm only able to work part time, that is, three days a week.
Stan	That's fine. I'll consider your application and give (you) an answer as soon as possible.

How the language works 1

1 Sila is a useful and polite word to use when urging someone to do something. It is one of the ways to say *please (do something)* in Malay. The form **silakan** also exists which takes the command to an even more polite level. Just combine it with a verb.

Sila duduk!	*Please sit down!*
Sila berdiri!	*Please stand up!*
Silakan cuci!	*Please wash!*
Silakan ikut saya!	*Please follow me!*

Exercise 1

Try forming **sila** or **silakan** phrases with the following word and then translate into English:

  a menyanyi
  b bercakap bahasa Melayu
  c minum
  d menari
  e masuk

 Quick vocab

berdiri	*to stand up*
cuci	*to wash*
ikut	*to follow*
menyanyi	*to sing*
menari	*to dance*

2 Boléh. In English the verb *can* has two slightly different meanings. It is used to express both ability, as in *I can play the violin* and permission, as in *Can I leave early today?* Just as in English, Malay needs just one word to express both meanings – **boléh**.

Saya *boléh* **hitung.**   *I can count.*

Meréka *boléh* **mengajar bahasa Sepanyol.**   *They can teach Spanish.*

Dia *boléh* **berhubung dengan baik.**   *He can communicate well.*

Saya *boléh* **jual produk ini.**   *I can sell this product.*

> ● **INSIGHT**
>
> **Mampu** is a good word to use when talking about your capabilities. Native speakers will be impressed to hear you using this!

 Quick vocab

hitung	*to count*
berhubung	*to communicate*
jual	*to sell*
produk	*product*

3 Remember also that, as an extension to the second meaning that we came across in the last unit, **boléh** can both be used to form phrases that make a request which corresponds to *Could you...?* in English, as in *Could you help me?* As in the dialogue, it more often than not occurs with the **-kah** in Malay, for example, **Boléhkah saudari mengguna komputer?**

4 You have already come across a way of indicating how an action is performed. Such a word is known as an adverb. It tells you more about the action expressed in the verb. Adverbs are usually formed by adding *-ly* to an adjective in English, for example: *quick → quickly*.

Look at these examples:

Saya bercakap bahasa Inggeris *dengan baik.*   *I speak English well.*

Dia mampu menaip *dengan cepat.*   *He can type quickly.*

You will see that in Malay adverbs are formed by **dengan** plus adjective. Adding any adjective to **dengan** has the same effect in Malay as adding *-ly* to a noun in English.

Exercise 2

How would you say the following?

     a Please drive carefully!

     b Please write accurately!

     c Please read slowly!

 Quick vocab

memandu	*to drive*
berhati-hati	*careful*

| tepat | accurate |
| perlahan-lahan | slow |

5 Job talk

 Quick vocab

doktor	doctor
doktor gigi	dentist
jururawat	nurse
ahli sains, saintis	scientist
arkitek	architect
mekanik	mechanic
pensyarah	lecturer
wartawan	journalist
pegawai kerajaan	public servant
peguam	lawyer
penulis	writer
pelukis	artist
penyanyi	singer
ahli muzik	musician
nelayan	fisherman
petani	farmer
jurufoto, jurugambar	photographer
tukang masak	chef
pelayan	waiter
suri rumah tangga	housewife

> ● **INSIGHT**
>
> The word **tukang** means *artisan* and features in several professions, especially the more 'traditional' ones like **tukang kayu** *carpenter* (**kayu** means *wood*), **tukang kunci** *locksmith* (**kunci** means *key*) and **tukang gunting** *barber* (**gunting** means *scissors*). The word **juru** also features in many professions and implies a skill, such as **jurulatih** *(sports) coach*, **jurubahasa** *interpreter*.

Apa *pekerjaan* anda?   *What's your job?/What do you do?*

When stating what job someone does, the word **seorang** is often inserted just before the job title:

Dia *seorang* **wartawan.**   *She's a journalist.*

Used in this way **seorang** corresponds to *a* or *an* in English. Although it is entirely optional, native speakers often prefer to include it.

Understanding Malay

Exercise 3

Using the dialogue from Part One say whether the following statements are true or false.

    a Shanaz menerima pendidikan di Kuala Lumpur.

    b Rita hanya mampu mengguna komputer dan e-mél.

    c Dia tidak boléh menguruskan surat-menyurat.

    d Dia mampu menaip dengan cepat.

    e Dia tidak boléh mula kerja minggu depan.

 Quick vocab

minggu depan   *next week*

Exercise 4

Imagine you work for an international employment agency. A company has asked you to find a sales person who is 30–55 years of age, has a university diploma, has at least five years' experience in sales and is computer literate. A Malay speaker is preferred but fluent English is a must. There are four people on your books who may be suitable. Read the information about each person and choose which one best fulfils the requirements the company is looking for.

Nama: *Nurul Lisa Roslan*
Umur: *30 tahun*
Warganegara: *Malaysia/Australia*
Pendidikan: *Kelulusan Universiti (Sarjana)*
Pengalaman kerja: *Pemasaran 4 tahun*
Kemahiran: *Komputer, Bahasa Inggeris*

Nama: *David Teng*
Umur: *40 tahun*
Warganegara: *Singapura*
Pendidikan: *Sarjana (Universiti Singapura)*
Pengalaman kerja: *Jualan dan pemasaran selama 10 tahun*
Kemahiran: *Komputer, Bahasa Inggeris (fasih)*

Nama: *Stephanie Marshall*
Umur: *36 tahun*
Warganegara: *Inggeris*
Pendidikan: *Diploma (Akademi)*
Pengalaman kerja: *Pemasaran 7 tahun*
Kemahiran: *Komputer, bahasa Inggeris, bahasa Perancis.*

Nama: *Dayang Sofia*
Umur: *31 tahun*
Warganegara: *Brunei Darussalam*
Pendidikan: *Ijazah (Universiti Brunei Darussalam)*

Pengalaman kerja: *Pemasaran 6 tahun*
Kemahiran: *Komputer, bahasa Inggeris dan bahasa Mandarin*

 Quick vocab

warganegara	*nationality*
universiti	*university*
pengalaman kerja	*work experience*
pemasaran	*marketing*
kemahiran	*skill*
sarjana	*master's degree*
jualan	*sales*
akademi	*academy*
bahasa Mandarin	*Mandarin*

PART TWO

Dialogue

Serena is taking Tom around her university, where she studies computer science.

 04.02

Serena	Tom, ini kampus saya. Kami ada dua kampus, A dan B. Kita sekarang berada di kampus A.
Tom	Di mana kampus B, pula?
Serena	Kampus B di Jalan Nuri, agak jauh dari sini, kira-kira satu jam. Saya boléh bawa kamu ke sana, jika mahu. Hari ini kamu kelihatan letih.
Tom	Mémang saya mahu. Saya boléh pergi hari ini.
Serena	Jomlah, kita ke sana sekarang.
(Di kampus B.)	
Tom	Di mana kelas kamu?
Serena	Di tingkat dua. Ikut saya.
Tom	Kamu belajar apa?
Serena	Komputer. Saya mahu jadi pengaturcara komputer.
(Meréka naik ke atas.)	
Serena	Ini kelas saya.
Tom	Kamu nak kerja dengan syarikat mana?
Serena	Syarikat swasta.
Tom	Di mana kamu nak cari pekerjaan?
Serena	Daripada iklan di surat khabar. Saya dah hantar butir-butir peribadi saya kepada satu syarikat swasta. Saya mahu dapatkan kerja sambilan.
Tom	Harap-harap kamu berjaya.

Quick vocab

kampus	*campus*
ada	*to have*
sekarang	*now*
berada	*to be (at a place)*
pula	*(here) again*
agak	*rather*
jauh	*far*
jauh dari sini	*far from here*
kira-kira	*about*
bawa	*to take*
kamu	*you*
mahu	*to want*
jika	*if*
jika mahu	*(here) if you want*
hari ini	*today*
kelihatan	*to look like/to seem*
Jomlah	*(popular slang) Let's go!*
kelas	*class*
tingkat	*floor, storey*
ikut saya	*follow me*
pengaturcara komputer	*computer programmer*
naik ke atas	*to go upstairs*
swasta	*private*
cari	*to look for*
pekerjaan	*job*
iklan	*advertisement*
surat khabar	*newspaper*
dah	*already (short for* **sudah***)*
hantar	*to send*
peribadi	*personal*
butir-butir peribadi	*curriculum vitae or personal details*
kepada	*to*
satu	*one, (here) a*
dapatkan	*to get*
harap-harap	*hopefully*
berjaya	*to succeed*
Harap-harap kamu berjaya	*I wish you luck, I hope you succeed*

> ● **INSIGHT**
>
> You've already met **akhbar** meaning *newspaper*. Another way to say this is **surat khabar**, which uses two Malay words you already know.

Translation

Serena	Tom, this is my campus. We have two campuses, A and B. Now we are at campus A.
Tom	Where is campus B again?
Serena	Campus B is on Jalan Nuri, rather far from here, about one hour. I can take you there if you want. Today you look so tired.
Tom	I really do want (to go). I can go there today.
Serena	Let's go there now (then)!
(At campus B.)	
Tom	Where is your class?
Serena	On the second floor. Follow me.
Tom	What do you study?
Serena	Computers. I want to be a programmer.
(They go upstairs.)	
Serena	This is my classroom.
Tom	Which company do you want to work for?
Serena	A private company.
Tom	Where can you find a job?
Serena	From an advert in the newspaper. I've already sent my CV to one private company. I want to get part-time work.
Tom	I wish you luck.

How the language works 2

1 In addition to the formal pronouns, there is an informal pronoun **kamu** *you* that is widely used between friends. Note, however, that it should only be used with people with whom you are on very familiar terms, or with people who are the same age or younger.

kamu cantik *you are beautiful*

In the dialogue, Tom and Serena are becoming much more familiar so they are starting to use **kamu**. It would be highly inappropriate to use **kamu** in a business environment or when you are unfamiliar with the speaker. If in doubt use **anda**, **saudara/saudari** or the title and name of the person you are addressing.

Kamu behaves just like most of the formal pronouns in that it can be placed after a noun to indicate possession:

kucing kamu *your cat*
rokok kamu *your cigarette*

However, when it is used to show possession it may be shortened to **-mu**. When shortened in this way it is added directly on to the end of the word it refers to:

kucingmu	*your cat*
rokokmu	*your cigarette*

Exercise 5

Use **-mu** to make the following phrases:

  a your camera
  b your spectacles
  c your key
  d your passport

 Quick vocab

rokok	*cigarette*
kamera	*camera*
cermin mata	*spectacles*
kunci	*key*

2 Tenses. In English, when you talk about what you are doing now, what you did yesterday and what you will do tomorrow, you convey the meaning through a change in the form of the verb you use, for example: *I am eating, I ate, I will eat*. The form of the verb is usually enough to indicate tense, i.e. when the action takes place. If you hear *I went* then you know immediately that the speaker is referring to the past. In fact, English has a very complex system of tenses. If you have bad memories of learning a foreign language before and struggling with the complications of learning the tenses, then you will be happy to hear that you are about to make a quantum leap in your study of Malay!

As Malay verbs do not indicate person, they do not indicate tense either. This means that, for instance, **pergi** can translate as *go, went, has been*, etc. depending on the context in which it occurs.

> ● **INSIGHT**
>
> This does not pose a translation problem for English speakers as your knowledge of English will automatically compensate and place the action in the correct time frame. You'll soon get the hang of it!

Malay has two ways of indicating tense: the first is by using a time expression which will give you a time frame and a tense for the verb.

Some basic units of time are:

hari	*day*
minggu	*week*
bulan	*month*
tahun	*year*

Adding either **depan**, **hadapan** or **akan datang** to any of these, or a day of the week or month puts the time unit into the future and automatically creates a future tense for anything you put with it and translates as *next* …:

tahun depan	*next year*
minggu akan datang	*next week*

Similarly, adding **yang lalu** (or just **lalu** in speech) to any of the time units mentioned above creates a past tense and translates as *last …* or *… ago*.

bulan lalu	*last month*

Note also:

hari ini	*today*
bésok or **ésok**	*tomorrow*
semalam	*yesterday*
kelmarin	*the day before yesterday (two days ago)*
dua hari yang lalu	*the day before yesterday (two days ago)*
dua hari yang akan datang	*the day after tomorrow*

When you are talking about events that happened in the very near past or future, usually the same day or in the same 24-hour period, you need to be aware of the usage of particular time expressions. These only occur with **pagi**, *morning*, **tengah hari**, *late morning to early afternoon*, **petang**, *late afternoon* and **malam**, *evening*.

> ● **INSIGHT**
>
> The time frames for these are the same as those indicated for the greetings in Unit 1.

With one or two exceptions **tadi** is used to refer to the past in this extremely limited time frame, and **nanti** is used to refer to the future.

Thus:

petang tadi	*yesterday evening*
pagi tadi	*this morning*
malam nanti	*tonight*
tengah hari nanti	*this afternoon*

You need to note the form **bésok pagi** (or **ésok pagi**) (rather than **pagi nanti**) for *tomorrow morning* as this is the only exception.

Note, finally, that if you are talking about something that will happen later on in the same time frame you are currently experiencing, for instance, it is evening and you want to talk about something that will happen on that same evening, the preferred form is **malam ini**. Note also **pagi ini**, etc.

Exercise 6

How would you say:

- **a** last year
- **b** next month
- **c** the year before last
- **d** last week
- **e** this afternoon?

The second way to indicate tense is by use of a tense marker. These are generally adverbs that, by the very nature of their meaning carry with them the idea of tense when used with a verb. For example, you have already met **sedang** which means *now*. When you combine **sedang** with a verb, it forms the equivalent of a continuous tense which is expressed by *to be … -ing* in English.

Saya mengajar biologi.	*I teach biology.*
Saya *sedang* **mengajar biologi.**	*I* **am teaching** *biology.*

You have also come across **sudah**, which you know means *already*, but when used as a tense marker indicates a past tense.

Meréka *sudah* **datang.**	*They* **have arrived**.*/They* **arrived**.

> ● **INSIGHT**
>
> **Sudah** is often shortened to just **dah** in speech, in the same way **hendak** is shortened to **nak**.

A tense marker with a similar meaning is **telah**. In spoken Malay, however, you will almost always use **sudah** because **telah** is considered highly formal. In writing, **telah** and **sudah** can be used interchangeably.

Saya *telah* **tamat universiti.**	*I* **have graduated** *from university.*

Note that if you have a time expression, you do not need a tense marker as the time period is already expressed:

Saya tamat universiti dua tahun yang lalu.	*I graduated from university two years ago.*

> ● **INSIGHT**
>
> As you might have started to notice, Malay likes to be as economical with words as possible!

Exercise 7

How would you say the following:

- **a** he wrote
- **b** they are typing
- **c** I am speaking
- **d** she read
- **e** are you studying? (Use **kamu**)

Subjects at school

pengurusan perniagaan	*business management*
kewangan	*finance*
perbankan	*banking*
pertanian	*agriculture*
alam sekitar	*environment*
sumber manusia	*human resources*
hubungan masyarakat	*human relationships (social studies)*
kejuruteraan	*engineering*
perakaunan	*accounting*
pelancongan	*tourism*
perguruan	*teaching*
perubatan	*medicine*
undang-undang	*law*
kemasyarakatan	*humanities*
seni bina	*architecture*
kimia	*chemistry*
biologi	*biology*
matematik	*mathematics*
geografi	*geography*
seni	*art*

Using Malay

Exercise 8

Match the pictures with the professions.

(i)

(ii)

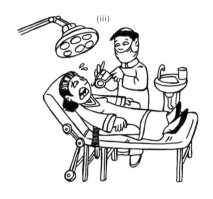

   a Dia seorang doktor gigi.
   b Dia seorang petani.
   c Faizal seorang nelayan.
   d Vikrama seorang pelukis.

Exercise 9

Read the sentences and fill in the blanks with appropriate words from the list that follows.

   a _____ dan _____ bekerja di hospital.
   b _____ mengurus anak dan suami di rumah.
   c Hotel itu mempunyai _____ terkenal.
   d Kami perlukan seorang _____ untuk merancang rumah baru kami.
   e Syarikat surat kabar itu memerlukan seorang _____

suri rumah tangga

doktor

jururawat

arkitek

tukang masak

wartawan

 Quick vocab

hospital	*hospital*
mempunyai	*to have*
mengurus	*to look after*
suami	*husband*
terkenal	*famous*
perlukan	*need*
merancang	*to design*

Exercise 10

Over to you!

A Malaysian (**A**) who runs a language school is looking for someone to help her teach English at her school. You (**B**) are being interviewed about the position.

 04.03

A	Apa pekerjaan anda sekarang?
B	*I am a language teacher.*
A	Apakah pengalaman anda?
B	*I have a lot of experience teaching English and I am fluent in three languages.*
A	Di mana anda belajar mengajar?
B	*At the International Language Institute.*
A	Berapa gaji yang anda harapkan?
B	*Two thousand dollars, if possible.*
A	Bila anda boléh mula bekerja?
B	*Next month.*
A	Harap-harap anda akan berjaya.

 Quick vocab

saya ada   *I have*

 Test yourself

1 Which word would you use when making a polite request?

2 What are the two meanings of **boléh**?

3 Which word can you use to express your abilities in a more impressive way?

4 How do you form an adverb in Malay?

5 Which word is often inserted before a job title in Malay?

6 How would you say *next month* in Malay? (three ways)

7 How would you say *tomorrow morning* in Malay? (Be careful!)

8 How would you create a continuous tense in Malay?

9 Which two words can be used to form a past tense in Malay?

10 When are tense markers unnecessary?

Meet the family

In this unit you will learn how to:
▶ *talk about members of your family*
▶ *express where things are in your house*
▶ *say the numbers 1 to 10*

PART ONE

Dialogue

Stan and Wong take the opportunity to get to know each other a little more during a coffee break in the company canteen.

 05.01

Stan	Encik Wong sudah berkeluarga, bukan?
Wong	Ya, Isteri saya dari Bandar Seri Begawan, Brunei. Kami ada 3 orang anak. Yang pertama lelaki dan masih di sekolah rendah. Yang kedua kembar perempuan. Meréka sungguh comél dan suka berjenaka.
Stan	Berapakah umur meréka?
Wong	Sepuluh tahun dan tujuh tahun. Encik Stan pula ada berapa orang anak?
Stan	Saya ada dua anak. Yang sulong perempuan, dan yang bongsu lelaki.
Wong	Berapakah umur meréka?
Stan	Lapan tahun dan enam tahun. Anak lelaki saya manja sekali.
Wong	Isteri Encik Stan bekerja?
Stan	Tidak. Dulu dia setiausaha, tapi sekarang suri rumah tangga. Menjaga anak-anak dan suami. Dia isteri yang baik. Isteri Encik Wong pula?
Wong	Dia seorang guru bahasa Inggeris. Tapi kami ada pembantu rumah untuk menjaga anak-anak.
Stan	Bagus kalau begitu. Isteri dan anak-anak saya akan datang minggu depan dari Singapura. Meréka ingin bertemu datuk, nénék dan sepupu-sepupunya.

Wong	Apakah datuknya masih bekerja?
Stan	Dia guru besar di Institusi Pengajian Tinggi dahulu, tapi kini sudah bersara. Isteri saya daripada keluarga besar. Adik-beradiknya terdiri daripada dua orang lelaki dan dua perempuan. Meréka semua sudah berkahwin.
Wong	Jangan lupa perkenalkan meréka, kalau meréka datang ke Bandar Seri Begawan. Saya akan jemput meréka untuk makan malam.
Stan	Sudah tentu, terima kasih.

 Quick vocab

bukan?	*(here) aren't you?*
ada	*to have*
pertama	*first*
lelaki	*boy*
sekolah	*school*
rendah	*low*
sekolah rendah	*primary school*
kedua	*second*
kembar	*twin*
perempuan	*girl*
sungguh	*really*
comél	*cute*
suka	*like*
berjenaka	*to joke around*
berapakah	*how many*
umur	*age*
berapakah umur?	*how old?*
sepuluh	*ten*
tujuh	*seven*
orang	*person*
anak	*child*
orang anak	*child, children*
sulong	*eldest, first-born*
bongsu	*youngest*
lapan	*eight*
enam	*six*
manja	*spoilt, pampered*
sekali	*very*
dulu	*before, formerly*
anak-anak	*children*
pembantu rumah	*maid*
menjaga	*to look after*

bagus	*good*
bagus kalau begitu	*so that's good*
ingin	*to want*
datuk	*grandfather*
nénék	*grandmother*
sepupu	*cousin*
sepupu-sepupunya	*their cousins*
guru besar	*principal*
Institusi Pengajian Tinggi	*Institute of Higher Education*
kini	*these days, nowadays*
bersara	*to retire, (here) retired*
adik	*younger sister or brother*
adik-beradik	*brothers and sisters*
terdiri daripada	*to consist of*
berkahwin	*married*
kalau	*if*
jemput	*to invite*
makan malam	*dinner*
sudah tentu	*sure*

● INSIGHT

Note that forms of address can be used with the first name in Malay, as in the dialogue: **Encik Stan**.

● INSIGHT

We will look at this later in the course, but the use of **orang,** as in **dua orang lelaki,** is a distinct feature of Malay, and most other East- or South-Asian languages. It is related to the **seorang** we met in the last unit. People are often counted in **'orang'**s, so two boys are often counted as **dua orang lelaki**. It is similar to the way we count cattle in 'heads' and hair in 'tufts'. There are other counting words for various categories of objects that we shall discuss fully in Unit 14.

Translation

Stan	Mr Wong, you're already married, aren't you?
Wong	Yes, my wife is from Bandar Seri Begawan, Brunei. We have three children. The first one is a boy and still at primary school. The second ones are twin girls. They are really cute and like to joke around.
Stan	How old are they?
Wong	Ten years and seven. How many children do you have?

Stan	I have two children. The first born is a girl and the youngest is a boy.
Wong	How old are they?
Stan	Eight and six. The boy is very spoilt.
Wong	Does your wife work?
Stan	No. She used to be a secretary but now she's just a housewife. She looks after her children and husband. She is a good wife. Does your wife work?
Wong	She is an English teacher. But we have a housemaid to look after the children.
Stan	That's good. My wife and children will arrive next week from Singapore. They want to see their grandfather, grandmother and cousins.
Wong	Does their grandfather still work?
Stan	He used to be a senior lecturer at a Higher Education Institute, but these days he is retired. My wife is from a big family. She has two brothers and two sisters. They are all already married.
Wong	Don't forget to introduce them (to me) if they come to Bandar Seri Begawan. I will invite them for dinner.
Stan	Sure! Thank you.

How the language works 1

1 In spoken English we add phrases like ... *don't you?, ... isn't she?* to the end of statements to form what are known as question tags. In English, the tag changes depending on the content of the statement it refers to, for instance, *she speaks Malay, doesn't she? They were at the airport, weren't they?*

In Malay you only need to use one tag, **bukan?**, which is often shortened just to **kan?** in more casual speech:

Meréka sudah berangkat ke Sabah, *bukan***?**	*They've already left for Sabah,* **haven't they**?
Anda mahu membeli keréta, *bukan***?**	*You want to buy a car,* **don't you**?

It is very important, however, to note that you must always use **bukan** (or **kan**) when you are adding a question tag to a negative statement, even when you have used **tidak** in the statement already according to the rules given in Unit 3. **Tidak** can never be used as a question tag.

Meréka *tidak* **datang,** *bukan***?**	*They didn't come,* **did they**?
Dia *tidak* **marah,** *kan***?**	*She isn't angry,* **is she**?

Exercise 1

Turn these statements into questions using question tags, then translate them, noting the simplicity of the Malay question tags compared to the English ones.

    a Dia sedang tidur.

    b Itu salah.

    c Meréka bukan askar.

 Quick vocab

berangkat	*to leave for*
marah	*angry*
salah	*wrong*
askar	*soldier(s)*

2 Sangat and **sekali** are both used to translate *very*. However, each is used in a different position in relation to the word you want to refer to. When you use **sangat** you need to place it before the word it refers to but when you use **sekali** you need to place it after the word. You can use these with adjectives or adverbs. Study the following examples:

sangat **kacak**	*very handsome*
kacak *sekali*	*very handsome*
dengan cepat *sekali*	*very fast*

 Quick vocab

kacak	*handsome*

Exercise 2

Give the Malay for the following. Give both forms where possible:

    a very dark

    b very wide

    c very good

    d extremely strong

    e extremely tired

 Quick vocab

gelap	*dark*
luas	*wide*
bagus	*good*
kuat	*strong (physically)*
penat	*tired*

3 Numbers.

 05.02

Numbers 0 to 10 form the basis for all the numbers that come after so learning them thoroughly now will really pay off later.

Quick vocab

kosong	*zero*
satu	*one*
dua	*two*
tiga	*three*
empat	*four*
lima	*five*
enam	*six*
tujuh	*seven*
lapan	*eight*
sembilan	*nine*
sepuluh	*ten*

Note also the so-called ordinal numbers:

Quick vocab

pertama	*first*
kedua	*second*
ketiga	*third*

> ● INSIGHT
>
> After **pertama**, adding **ke-** to any number will form the ordinal.

4 In this unit we have come across the word **yang** which has several important uses in Malay, some of which will be examined here and some in later units.

▶ **Yang** corresponds to *the one which (is)*, *the one who (is)*, *the ones who (are)* and *the ones which (are)* in English. It can refer to things as well as people.

Yang sulong perempuan.	*The (one who is) first born is a girl.*
Yang lelaki berumur 7 tahun.	*The one who is male is 7 years old.*
Mahu yang kecil? Tidak, yang besar.	*Do you want the small one (i.e. the one that is small)? No, the big one (the one that is big).*
Anda perlu yang ini? Tidak, yang lain.	*Do you need this one (the one that is this)? No, another one (the one that is other).*
Saya mahu yang itu.	*I want that one.*
Sepupu Eva yang menolong saya.	*The one who helped me is Eva's cousin.*

▶ By extension, **yang** can be used, as in the dialogue, with ordinal numbers meaning *the first one*, *the second one*, etc.:

Yang pertama lelaki.	*The first one (i.e. the one who is first) is male.*
Yang ketiga sudah siap.	*The third one is ready.*

 **Quick vocab**

perlu	*to need*
menolong	*to help*
siap	*ready*

▶ **Dia isteri yang baik**. It is very common for Malay speakers to insert **yang** between the noun and the adjective, even though it may not seem necessary given the rules for noun + adjective you learnt in Unit 3. It is sometimes used by the speaker to stress the quality expressed by the adjective in relation to the noun it refers to. It could be used by the speaker to add emotional emphasis, creating a meaning such as *She is a good wife*, stressing the quality *good*, although you will hear it used naturally and regularly by Malay speakers simply as a speech habit and not always to add emphasis.

5 Talking about your family.

ayah	*father*
ibu	*mother*
anak lelaki	*son*
anak perempuan	*daughter*
datuk	*grandfather*
nénék	*grandmother*
pak cik	*uncle*
mak cik	*aunt*
suami	*husband*
isteri	*wife*

Many family words in Malay are not gender specific:

abang or **kakak**	*older brother/sister*
adik	*younger brother/sister*
ipar	*brother/sister-in-law*
anak	*child/son/daughter*
cucu	*grandchild/grandson/granddaughter*
sepupu	*cousin*
anak saudara	*niece/nephew*
mertua	*father/mother-in-law*
kembar	*twin(s)*
budak	*child*

This is not usually a problem as either context will tell you or you may already be aware of the gender of the person the speaker is referring to. When clarification is needed **lelaki** is applied to all the words above to indicate a male, and **perempuan** is applied to indicate a female.

Lelaki and **perempuan** can also be used with **anak** or **budak**, both meaning *child*, to mean *boy* or *girl* or with **orang**, *person* to indicate *man* or *woman*, although **perempuan** or **lelaki** alone can also mean *woman* or *man* respectively.

Orang tua means *parent* or *parents*. *Grandparents* is rendered by **datuk-nénék** in Malay.

> ● **INSIGHT**
>
> **Orang tua** literally means *old person* or *old people*, but it is really only used to refer to parent or parents. If you want to say *old person* or *old people* you need to use that **yang** we talked about earlier to make the distinction: **orang yang tua**. To take this a stage further, **mertua** means *father-* or *mother-in-law*. **Bapa mertua** refers to *father-in-law* and **ibu mertua** refers to *mother-in-law*, and is used to indicate *father* or *mother* specifically.

Exercise 3

Write the gender specific forms of the following:

  a granddaughter
  b father-in-law
  c nephew
  d older sister

6 There are two words in Malay to express what you have, namely **ada** or **mempunyai**. They can be used interchangeably but **ada** is the more common of the two.

Saya *ada* **anak kembar.**	*I have twins.*
Saya *mempunyai* **anak kembar.**	*I have twins.*
Kami *mempunyai* **rumah yang cantik.**	*We have a nice house.*

Siapa can mean *whose?* but with this meaning the word order is important. In this case **siapa** must immediately follow the noun it is referring to, as an adjective does:

Gelas *siapa* **ini?**	*Whose glass is this?*
Rumah *siapa* **itu?**	*Whose house is that?*

 Quick vocab

gelas	*glass*

7 -nya. Another Malay word with many uses is **-nya**. It is very commonly used as an alternative to **dia** or **meréka** when they occur as possessive pronouns (*his/her/their*). **-nya** cannot occur as a separate word in a sentence. Instead, it is attached to the end of the word or words it refers to to create one word (like **-mu** in Unit 3).

permainan dia	*his toy*
permainan + nya = permainannya	*his toy*
rumah besar meréka	*their big house*
rumah besar + nya = rumah besarnya	*their big house*

(Note in the last example, the **-nya** is attached to the adjective as the noun and the adjective in this case form a single unit. If you attach the **-nya** to the **rumah**, as in **rumahnya besar**, it would change the meaning to *their house is big*).

Exercise 4

Give the alternative forms of the following:

- **a jam tangan dia** *(her watch)*
- **b sekolah rendah meréka** *(their elementary school)*
- **c kebun meréka** *(their garden)*
- **d alat CD dia** *(her CD player)*
- **e Anak saudara perempuan dia comél sekali.** *(His niece is very cute.)*

 Quick vocab

kebun	*garden*
alat CD	*CD player*

The important point to remember when using **-nya** is that it has to refer back to something already mentioned or a context that has already been established.

Kakak saya akan tiba ésok.	*My elder sister is arriving tomorrow.*
Isterinya bekerja di biro pengiklanan.	*His wife works in an advertising bureau.*

The context you establish does not have to be verbal. You could just as easily point to someone and say, *His wife works in advertising* and use **-nya** as above.

 Quick vocab

biro	*bureau*
pengiklanan	*advertising*

8 Saya akan jemput meréka untuk makan malam. *I will invite them to dinner.* **Meréka** means *they*, but it also means *them*. In English, some of the personal pronouns change to *me*, *him*, *her*, *us* and *them* when they occur as objects (when they are on the receiving end of the action) or when they occur after words like *for*, *to*, etc. In Malay they remain the same, with one exception:

Kami kenal meréka.	*We know* **them**.
Stan menolong kami.	*Stan helps* **us**.

Potential confusion arises because **dia** is used to refer to both males and females. For example, **Kami melihat dia** means *We saw him*, but it can also mean *We saw her*. The context of the situation will usually tell you which.

The exception occurs in sentences such as ***He*** *knows* ***her*** or ***She*** *knows* ***him*** because you cannot have **dia** for both the subject (the person who is doing the action, in this case knowing) and the object (here the one who is being known).

In such a situation you must use **-nya** for the object pronoun and attach it to the verb:

Dia kenal + nya = Dia kenalnya.	*He knows her, etc.*

Exercise 5

How would you say the following?

   a We are waiting for them.
   b She phoned me.
   c They disturbed him.
   d He loves her.
   e We went with them.

 Quick vocab

kenal	*to know*
menelefon	*to telephone*
mengganggu	*to disturb*
mencintai	*to love*

9 Berapakah umur anda? *How old are you?* There are two ways of expressing age in Malay.

▶ The first uses **umur** which is a noun, therefore you need to use a pronoun or a name after **umur**, which means *age*:

Umur Maria 10 tahun.	*Maria is 10.*
Umurnya 10 tahun.	*She's 10.*

▶ The second uses a verb **berumur** which is a verb meaning *to be X years old*. As it is a verb the pronoun or name occurs in front:

Maria berumur 10 tahun.	*Maria is 10 years old.*
Dia berumur 10 tahun.	*She is 10 years old.*

Exercise 6

Give the alternative forms of the following:

   a Kembar saya berumur empat tahun.
   b Umur Angie sembilan tahun.
   c Yang sulong berumur tiga tahun.
   d Umur adik lelakinya lima tahun.

▶ The use of **umur** above is similar in construction to the use of **nama** in **Nama saya …**, *My name is …* As with **umur** there is an alternative way to give someone's name in Malay which uses a verb **bernama** – *to be called*, which we also met in Unit 1, Part Two.

Nama saya Ratna.	*My name's Ratna.*
Saya bernama Ratna.	*I am called Ratna.*

> **● INSIGHT**
>
> It is easy to see that the verbs **berumur** and **bernama** are formed from **umur** and **nama** respectively. This is a common feature of Malay which we will look at in more depth in a later unit.

10 Dulu (also **dahulu**) means *formerly* but it can also function as a tense marker to indicate *used to* as in *She used to be a teacher*. **Dulu dia seorang guru. Dulu** can occur first in the sentence or after the subject of the sentence.

Dulu kami tinggal di Pulau Pinang.	*We used to live in Penang.*
Dulu dia miskin.	*She used to be poor.*
Kami dulu sering jumpa janji di tempat ini.	*We often used to go dating in this place.*

 Quick vocab

miskin	*poor*
sering	*often*
jumpa janji	*to go dating*

11 The other tense marker you have met in this unit is **akan** which always indicates a future action or event. Unlike **dulu** it is used purely as a tense marker and translates *will*, *shall* and *to be going to …* in English.

Meréka akan pergi ke sesuatu tempat.	*They will go somewhere.*
Amy akan jemput nénék di stésen bas.	*Amy will pick grandma up at the bus station.*

 Quick vocab

sesuatu tempat	*somewhere*
jemput	*to pick up*
stésen bas	*bus station*

Understanding Malay

Exercise 7

True or false? Answer the following questions based on Dialogue 1.

    a Isteri Encik Wong suri rumah tangga berasal dari Brunei.
    b Stan mempunyai dua anak lelaki.
    c Anak-anak Encik Wong berumur 10 tahun and 7 tahun.
    d Isteri Stan masih bekerja sebagai seorang setiausaha.
    e Isteri Encik Wong seorang guru bahasa Perancis.
    f Keluarga Stan akan datang minggu depan.
    g Semua adik-beradiknya sudah berkeluarga.

 Quick vocab

sebagai	*as*
semua	*all*

Exercise 8

05.03

First familiarize yourself with the vocabulary. Look at the five pictures of families (**a–e**), and choose which picture fits with what each person says about his or her family. If you are not using the recording, treat this as a reading exercise.

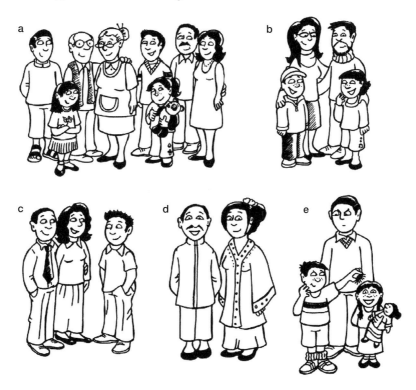

 Quick vocab

pegawai	*employee*
kerajaan	*government*
pegawai kerajaan	*civil servant*
pelajar	*student*
bersekolah	*to go to school*
duda	*widower*
bercerai	*to be divorced, to get divorced*
berdua	*both*
murid	*pupil (of primary school age)*
pengurus	*manager*
peréka	*designer, inventor*
fesyen	*fashion*
peréka fesyen	*fashion designer*
pakaian	*clothes*
pakaian kanak-kanak	*children's clothes*

menuntut	*studying*
Pulau Pinang	*Penang (Island)*
tunggal	*only, single*
anak tunggal	*only child*
butik	*boutique*
pensyarah	*lecturer*
mekanik	*mechanic*
sebuah	*a*
béngkel	*workshop*
sebuah béngkel keréta	*a car repair garage*
tukang jahit baju	*tailor*

PART TWO

Dialogue

Serena wants to introduce Tom to some real Malaysian hospitality so she invites him to stay with her grandmother who lives in the suburbs of Kuala Lumpur.

 05.04

Serena	Nék, ini kawan saya Tom. Dia akan tinggal dengan kita di sini selama beberapa hari.
Nénék	Selamat datang, Tom. Saya sudah siapkan bilik.
Tom	Terima kasih. Tak payah susah-susah, nénék.
Nénék	Tidak mengapa. Saya ada banyak bilik kerana saya ada tujuh anak. Tapi sekarang semua anak saya sudah kahwin. Saya tinggal seorang dengan pembantu. Di sini ada banyak bilik kosong.
Tom	Rumah nénék ada berapa bilik?
Nénék	Lima bilik. Bilik saya paling besar. Dulu saya tidur dengan suami saya di sini, tapi dia meninggal dunia dua tahun yang lalu.
Tom	Ini bilik siapa?
Nénék	Ini bilik anak sulong saya. Oh, ya. Serena akan tunjukkan bilik-bilik yang lain. Buatlah seperti rumah sendiri. Jangan malu-malu.
Serena	Jangan risau Nék. Mari ikut saya, Tom. Kita mula dari belakang. Ini dapur, di sebelahnya bilik makan. Yang depan itu bilik tamu.
Tom	Buku-buku siapa itu?
Serena	Oh, itu buku-buku nénék. Dia memang gemar membaca. Kalau suka, kamu boléh pinjam daripada nénék.

Tom	Terima kasih.
Serena	Itu bilik saya dan bilik kamu di sebelah.
Tom	Oh ya. Di mana bilik mandi?
Serena	Maaf, saya terlupa. Ada 2 bilik mandi, satu di tingkat atas dan satu lagi di tingkat bawah. Tapi bilik-bilik mandi ini berlainan dengan bilik mandi di luar negeri. Kami mandi mengguna gayung.
Tom	Menarik sekali.
Serena	Saya harap kamu akan selésa tinggal di sini.

 Quick vocab

beberapa hari	*a few days*
siapkan	*to prepare*
bilik	*room*
tak	*(short for* **tidak***)*
tak payah susah-susah	*don't go to any trouble*
banyak	*a lot of*
kerana	*because*
kahwin	*married*
seorang	*(here) alone*
pembantu	*maid*
kosong	*vacant, empty*
paling besar	*biggest*
dunia	*world*
meninggal dunia	*passed away, died* (lit. *to leave the world*)
tunjukkan	*to show (someone something)*
yang lain	*other*
buatlah	*make*
seperti	*like, similar to*
sendiri	*oneself (here) yourself*
buatlah seperti rumah sendiri	*make yourself at home*
malu	*shy*
jangan malu-malu	*don't be shy*
risau	*anxious, worry*
jangan risau	*don't worry*
mari	*let's (alternative to* **biar***)*
mari ikut saya	*(please) follow me*
belakang	*(here) the rear*
dapur	*kitchen*
di sebelah	*next to*
di sebelahnya	*next to it*
depan	*in front of*
yang depan itu	*the one in front of that*
tamu	*guest*

bilik tamu	*guest room*
gemar	*to be fond of*
kalau	*if*
suka	*to like*
kalau suka	*if you want*
pinjam	*to borrow*
bilik mandi	*bathroom*
terlupa	*to forget*
atas	*above*
tingkat	*floor, storey*
tingkat atas	*upstairs*
bawah	*below*
tingkat bawah	*downstairs*
berlainan dengan	*different from*
di luar negeri	*abroad*
gayung	*scoop*

● INSIGHT

Luar negeri, meaning *'abroad'* is composed of **luar**, meaning *outside*, and **negeri**, which means *country*. So *abroad* in Malay is literally *outside the country*. Another word you'll come across in this course, which can also be translated as *country*, is **negara**. The difference? **Negara** tends to refer to *state*.

Translation

Serena	Grandma, this is my friend, Tom. He's going to be staying with us here for a few days.
Grandmother	Welcome, Tom. I have already prepared a room (for you).
Tom	Thank you. Don't trouble yourself.
Grandmother	It's no problem. I have a lot of rooms because I have seven children. But now all my children are married. I live alone with a maid. There are a lot of unused rooms here.
Tom	How many rooms do you (does your house) have?
Grandmother	Five (rooms). My room is the biggest. My husband and I used to sleep there but he died two years ago.
Tom	Whose room is this?
Grandmother	This is my eldest son's room. By the way, Serena will show you the other rooms. Make yourself at home. Don't be shy.

Serena	Don't worry, Grandma. Come on, Tom, follow me. We'll start from the rear. This is the kitchen and next to it is the dining room. The one in front of that is the living room.
Tom	Whose books are those?
Serena	Oh, those are grandma's books. She is really fond of reading. If you like, you can borrow (them) from Grandma.
Tom	Thank you.
Serena	That is my room and your room is next to it.
Tom	By the way, where is the bathroom?
Serena	Sorry, I forgot. There are two bathrooms, one upstairs and one downstairs. But these bathrooms are different from bathrooms abroad. We take a shower using a scoop.
Tom	(That's) very interesting.
Serena	I hope you will feel at home here.

How the language works 2

1 anak-anak, *children*, **buku-buku**, *books*.

▶ When we talk about something being plural we mean that we are talking about more than one thing. In English we usually indicate a plural by adding *-s* or *-es* to the singular form: *bus*, *buses*, etc. In Malay the noun is simply doubled to create a plural:

kedai	*shop*
kedai-kedai	*shops*

▶ If you need to make a plural of a noun that is modified by another noun (see Unit 2) note that only the main noun is doubled:

rak buku	*bookcase*
rak-rak buku	*bookcases*

▶ Having said all this, plural forms are nowhere near as common in Malay as they are in English. In fact, plurals are only really used in Malay when it is not obvious from the context that more than one thing is intended. Thus, if you use a number or a word that indicates a quantity, you do not need to double the noun:

empat orang	*four people*
banyak anak	*a lot of children*

This also applies to **berapa**. Where we always use a plural in English when we ask *How many?* you only need to use the singular form in Malay:

Berapa orang?	*How many people?*

Exercise 9

Rewrite these sentences making the plural form of the word indicated in brackets. When doing this exercise, pay attention to the meaning of the sentence. Do you need to double the noun or just leave it as it is? Could the sentence be ambiguous if you do not use a double plural? Where you decide to use double plurals, indicate what the sentence would mean if you had not doubled the noun.

    a (Anak) meréka pergi ke sekolah di désa itu.
    b Saya mempunyai empat (saudara perempuan).
    c Berapa (buku) yang anda pinjam?
    d Sukakah kamu (filem) Stephen Spielberg?
    e Di mana (beg) saya?

 Quick vocab

désa	*village*
sukakah kamu	*do you like?*
beg	*bag*

2 As with *who?* in English, **siapa** combines with other words to form questions like:

who for?	**untuk siapa?**
who to?	**kepada siapa?**
who with?	**dengan siapa?**
who from?	**daripada siapa?**

As you have probably noticed, **dari** also means *from*. What is the difference? **Daripada** should be used when it means *from* a person. **Dari** is used for place and time. Look at these examples:

Dia berasal dari Brunei.	*She is from Brunei.*
Surat ini daripada ibu.	*This letter is from mother.*

However, as with **ke mana?** and **dari mana?** in Unit 3, the main difference in usage is that the components of the Malay questions cannot be separated. For example, in modern English it is usual to say **Who** *did he do it* **for**? or **Who** *did you go* **with**?, splitting the two parts of the question. The Malay questions, however, follow the pattern of older hyper-perfect English forms (**For whom** *did he do it?*, **With whom** *did you go?*) Thinking of these questions in this way will help you greatly in formulating this type of question in Malay. Compare the following:

Daripada siapa **surat ini?**	*Who is this letter from?*
Dengan siapa **meréka bermain bola sépak?**	*Who do they play football with?*
Untuk siapa **kita masak?**	*Who do we cook for?*
Kepada siapa **kamu menulis surat?**	*Who did you write the letter to?*

 Quick vocab

bermain bola sépak	*to play football (soccer)*
masak	*to cook*

Exercise 10

Add **untuk siapa**, **daripada siapa**, **kepada siapa** and **dengan siapa** to complete the following questions (use each question only once):

    a _____ meréka pergi ke pésta?

    b _____ bungkusan ini?

    c _____ kita menyanyi?

    d _____ kami mengirim surat?

 Quick vocab

pésta	*party*
bungkusan	*present, parcel*

In the same way, certain other questions can be formed with **apa**:

what with?	**dengan apa?**
what for?	**untuk apa?**

Again, the two components cannot be separated and they correspond to the older English forms *with what?* and *for what?*

Kamu sedang menulis *dengan apa***?**	**What** *are you writing* **with***?*
Kamu memanaskan makanan *dengan apa***?**	**What** *do you heat the meal* **with***?*
Kita membayarnya *dengan apa***?**	**What** *do we pay for it* **with***?*
Untuk apa **kita datang ke sini?**	**What** *did we come here* **for***?*
Wang ini *untuk apa***?**	**What** *is this money* **for***?*

 Quick vocab

memanaskan	*to heat something up*
membayar	*to pay for*
wang	*money*

> ● **INSIGHT**
>
> **Di sini** and **ke sini** translate into English as *here*, and **di sana** and **ke sana** translate as *there*, so what's the difference? **Di** is used when what is being talked about is static; **ke** is used when movement is involved or implied. This applies to many expressions.

3 Malay uses the following words to express static location: **depan** *front*, **belakang** *back*, **atas** *on*, **bawah** *under*, **antara** *between*, **dalam** *inside*, **luar** *outside*, **samping** *side* and **sebelah**, which also means *side*.

All these words can be combined with **di** to form the following expressions:

di depan	*in front of*
di belakang	*behind*
di bawah	*below*
di antara	*in between*

di dalam	inside
di luar	outside
di samping	beside, next to
di sebelah	beside, next to

Jakét keselamatan di bawah tempat duduk.	*Life-jacket is under the seat.*
Meréka tinggal di sebelah rumah kami.	*They live next door to us.*

Di sebelah combines with **kiri**, *left* and **kanan**, *right*, to form:

di sebelah kiri	*on the left-hand side*
di sebelah kanan	*on the right-hand side*
Di Inggeris kami mengemudi di sebelah kiri.	*In England we drive on the left.*

 Quick vocab

jakét keselamatan	*life-jacket*
tempat duduk	*seat*
mengemudi	*to drive*

Using Malay

Exercise 11

Look at the picture below and answer the questions that follow.

a Siapa anak lelaki di depan Ai Lin?

b Siapa anak perempuan di depan Jefri?

c Siapa anak perempuan di sebelah kanan Jefri?

d Siapa anak lelaki di antara Evon dan Benni?

e Siapa anak lelaki di belakang Lee Keong?

f Siapa anak perempuan di samping Ahmisha?

Exercise 12

Look at the picture of the house and answer the following questions.

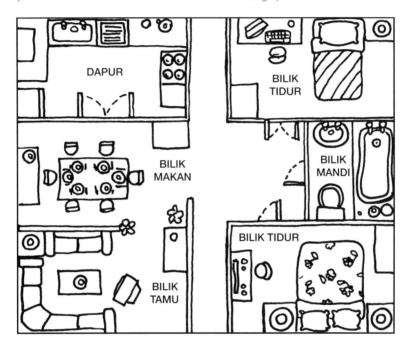

a Bilik apa di belakang rumah, sebelah kiri?

b Bilik apa di sebelah dapur?

c Bilik apa di depan bilik makan?

d Bilik apa di antara dapur dan bilik keluarga?

 Quick vocab

dapur	*kitchen*
bilik tidur	*bedroom*
bilik makan	*dining room*

Exercise 13

Look at the picture of the buildings. Complete the following sentences with **di antara**, **di sebelah kanan**, **di sebelah kiri**, **di depan** or **di belakang** according to the location of the buildings mentioned in relation to each other.

Makmal

Dewan Sekolah

Pejabat Guru Besar

Bilik Guru

Bilik Kelas 1

Bilik Kelas 3

Pejabat
Pentadbiran

Bilik Kelas 2

a Perpustakaan ada _____ bilik kelas 1.

b Makmal ada _____ perpustakaan dan dewan sekolah.

c Pejabat guru besar sekolah ada _____ bilik kelas 3.

d Pejabat pentadbiran ada _____ bilik kelas 2.

e Bilik guru ada _____ bilik kelas 1.

 Quick vocab

perpustakaan	*library*
ada	*(here) is*
makmal	*laboratory*
guru besar	*head teacher/principal*
besar	*big*
pejabat	*office*
pejabat pentadbiran	*administration office*
dewan sekolah	*school hall*
bilik guru	*staff room*
bilik kelas	*classroom*

Exercise 14

Over to you!

You (**B**) are on vacation in Malaysia and your friend has invited you to stay with her family. When you arrive at your friend's house, you find that dinner has been prepared and you waste no time in getting to know your friend's mother (**A**) who is eager to find out more about you!

05.05

A	Saya sudah siapkan makanan untuk kamu. Jangan malu-malu!
B	*Thank you. Don't trouble yourself.*
A	Apakah kamu sudah berkeluarga?
B	*Sure. I have two children.*
A	Berapakah umur meréka?
B	*The first one is seven and the second is four.*
A	Ini bilik kamu, di dalamnya ada bilik mandi.
B	*Where is the kitchen?*
A	Di belakang dekat bilik makan. Buatlah seperti rumah sendiri.
B	*Thank you. Whose room is that?*
A	Ini bilik saya. Mudah-mudahan kamu selésa tinggal di sini.

 Quick vocab

dekat	*close to, near*

 Test yourself

1 Which one word is used as a question tag in Malay?

2 Which comes before the adjective: **sangat** or **sekali**?

3 How do you form an ordinal number from 2 onwards?

4 How would you translate *the one who*?

5 Which two ways do you know to say *have* in Malay?

6 What does **-nya** mean, and how does it function?

7 What are the two different ways to express your name and age?

8 How do you express *used to* in Malay?

9 How does Malay form plurals?

10 Why is it often unnecessary to express plurals in Malay?

Sightseeing

In this unit you will learn how to:

▸ *ask about what there is to see and do*
▸ *express existence*
▸ *use numbers 1 to 99*
▸ *tell the time*
▸ *say the days of the week*

PART ONE

Dialogue

The Davies family are planning a trip to Brunei Darussalam during their stay in Singapore. Stan and Sue-Ann are in a travel agent's making enquiries.

 06.01

Pegawai	Selamat pagi, Puan! Boléh saya bantu?
Puan Sue-Ann	Ya. Kami ingin melawat Bandar Seri Begawan, di Brunei Darussalam. Ada apa yang boléh kami lihat dan lakukan di sana?
Pegawai	Puan boléh melawat banyak tempat yang menarik di sana seperti tempat bersejarah.
Puan Sue-Ann	Boléhkah Encik berikan beberapa cadangan?
Pegawai	Boléh. Puan boléh melawat Kampong Ayer, sebuah perkampungan unik yang dikenali sebagai 'Venice Timur', Taman Permainan Jerudong, dan juga Taman Negara Ulu Temburong.
Puan Sue-Ann	Ada pakéj percutian yang boléh saya beli?
Pegawai	Ada pakéj untuk 3 hari, 5 hari dan ada juga 7 hari.
Puan Sue-Ann	Bagaimana pula dengan hotél?
Pegawai	Puan boléh pilih sama ada hotél di tepi pantai atau di bandar.
Puan Sue-Ann	Oh ya, ada restoran-restoran makanan tradisional yang bagus dan selésa di sana?
Stan	Isteri saya ni mémang suka mencuba masakan yang baru.

Pegawai	Ada beberapa restoran yang besar dan terkenal di bandar. Puan nak tinggal berapa lama di sana?
Puan Sue-Ann	Satu minggu. Ada pakéj percutian yang murah dan bagus?
Pegawai	Ada, tapi ia tidak termasuk makanan. Ini ada beberapa brosur pakéj percutian.
Puan Sue-Ann	Naik pesawat apa ke sana?
Pegawai	Puan akan menaiki pesawat Royal Brunei Airlines.
Puan Sue-Ann	Baiklah. Terima kasih atas bantuan Encik. Kami akan berbincang dahulu sebelum membuat keputusan. Pukul berapa pejabat ini tutup?
Pegawai	Pukul 5 petang. Oh ya, ini kad nama saya. Puan boléh hubungi saya untuk keterangan yang lebih lanjut.

 Quick vocab

ingin	*to want*
melawat	*to visit*
lihat	*to see*
lakukan	*to do*
tempat	*place*
bersejarah	*historical*
berikan	*to give, (here) to offer*
cadangan	*suggestion*
sebuah	*a*
perkampungan	*settlement*
unik	*unique*
dikenali sebagai	*known as*
taman	*garden*
permainan	*game (play or sports)*
negara	*country*
pakéj percutian	*package holiday*
beli	*to buy*
pilih	*to choose*
sama ada	*either (of two choices)*
tepi pantai	*seaside*
bandar	*city*
restoran	*restaurant*
makanan	*food*
tradisional	*traditional*
mencuba	*to try*
masakan	*cooking, food*
ni	*short for* **ini**
mémang	*indeed, really*
terkenal	*well-known*

murah	*low-cost*
ia	*it*
termasuk	*included*
tidak termasuk makanan	*food is not included*
brosur	*brochure*
tentang	*about*
naik	*to take some form of transport*
pesawat	*aeroplane*
menaiki	*to travel on/by*
atas	*for*
bantuan	*help*
berbincang	*to discuss*
dahulu	*(here) further*
sebelum	*before*
membuat	*to make*
keputusan	*decision*
pukul berapa	*what time?*
pejabat	*office*
tutup	*to close*
pukul 5	*at 5 (o'clock)*
kad nama	*business card*
hubungi	*to contact*
keterangan	*explanation, information*
lanjut	*continuous*
lebih lanjut	*(here) further*
keterangan yang lebih lanjut	*further information*

> ● **INSIGHT**
>
> Although **unik** has the same meaning as in English, it has also come to refer to something excellent which is not necessarily unique.

Translation

Employee	Good morning, Madam! May I help you?
Sue-Ann	Yes, we would like to visit Bandar Seri Begawan, in Brunei Darussalam. What can we see and do there?
Employee	You can visit a lot of interesting places there such as historical places.
Sue-Ann	Could you give (us) some suggestions?
Employee	Sure. You can visit Kampong Ayer, a unique group of villages known as 'Venice Timur' (Venice of the East), Jerudong Park and also Ulu Temburong National Park.
Sue-Ann	Is there a package tour I can buy?

Employee	There are 3 day, 5 day and also 7 day packages.
Sue-Ann	What about hotels?
Employee	You can choose between hotels by the sea or in the city.
Sue-Ann	Oh yes, are there good and cosy traditional food restaurants there?
Stan	My wife really likes to try new foods.
Employee	There are a few big, traditional restaurants in the city. How long do you intend to stay?
Sue-Ann	One week. Is there a good, low-cost package holiday?
Employee	There is, but meals are not included. Here are a few brochures about the package holidays.
Sue-Ann	Who shall we fly with?
Employee	You will go with Royal Brunei Airlines.
Sue-Ann	Right. Thank you for your help. We will discuss it further before making a decision. What time does this office close?
Employee	At 5 p.m. By the way, here is my business card. You can contact me for further information.

How the language works 1

1 To express the existence of something in Malay you only need to use one word, **ada**. This translates both *there is* and *there are* in English.

Ada **pancutan di pusat bandar.**	*There is a fountain in the city centre.*
Ada **bunga-bunga di taman itu.**	*There are flowers in that garden.*

To ask about the existence of something you can simply use **ada...?**

Ada **balai polis di sini?**	*Is there a police station here?*
Ada **penerbangan yang murah?**	*Are there (any) cheap flights?*

To ask *Is there anything else* or *Are there any other…?* **Apakah ada…?** tends to be used, usually with …**lain** which means *other*.

Apakah *ada* **barang lain yang dijual?**	*Are there any other goods being sold?*
Apakah *ada* **makanan lain yang dihidangkan?**	*Is there any other food being served?*

> ● **INSIGHT**
> Remember that **ada** also means *to have*, and can also translate *is* with location words. The context will tell you which.

Finally, as **ada** is a verb, it is negated with **tidak**. It translates *there is no* and *there are no/there aren't any*.

Tidak *ada* **mentéga di peti sejuk.**   *There is no butter in the fridge.*

Tidak *ada* **ikan di sungai ini.**   *There aren't any fish in this river.*

> ● **INSIGHT**
>
> As with **berapa** and other quantity words, you do not need to indicate plurals when using **tidak ada** as we do with the English equivalent.

Tidak ada bunga.   *There aren't any flowers.*

 Quick vocab

pancutan	*fountain*
pusat bandar	*city centre*
bunga-bunga	*flowers*
balai polis	*police station*
barang	*goods*
dijual	*to be sold*
dihidangkan	*to be served*
mentéga	*butter*
peti sejuk	*fridge*
sungai	*river*

Exercise 1

Form the following sentences in Malay.

    a There is a souvenir shop.
    b There are some traditional restaurants.
    c Are there other cakes in this shop?
    d There aren't any hotels.
    e Is there any information?
    f Is there a sports centre?
    g There isn't an art gallery.

 Quick vocab

kedai cenderamata	*souvenir shop*
kuih	*cake*
pusat sukan	*sports centre*
balai	*station*
balai seni	*art gallery*

2 More on using **yang**. When a noun is described by two or more adjectives in English we simply list them in order before the noun, as in *a **beautiful**, **friendly** flight attendant* and ***large**, **romantic** restaurants*. Notice how these phrases are represented in Malay: **pramugari**

yang ramah dan cantik and **restoran yang besar dan romantik**. You will notice that the two adjectives, which still follow the noun, are separated by **yang** and **dan** so you end up with phrases which more literally translate as *a flight attendant who is beautiful and friendly* and *restaurants which are large and romantic*.

From this you can see that the pattern is:

noun **yang** *first adjective* **dan** *second adjective*

bandar *yang* damai *dan* indah

a peaceful, beautiful city

pésta *yang* meriah *dan* ramai

a lively, crowded party

(If you need to have three adjectives to describe the same noun (as in) *a friendly, beautiful, slim flight attendant* or *large, romantic, cheap restaurants* you simply place two of the adjectives together after the *yang* and the third after the *dan*.

pramugari *yang* ramah, cantik *dan* langsing
restoran *yang* besar, romantik *dan* murah

In theory, if you want to add even more adjectives to describe one noun you can amass all but one in between the **yang** and **dan**, being sure to leave one to place after the **dan**. You might find it useful to think of it in the same way we list adjectives in English:

*She was beautiful, charming, loveable, honest **and** cute.*

A final, but important point to note is that the above applies to true adjectives only and not to nouns or verbs acting as adjectives (refer back to Unit 2):

restoran Malaysia yang romantik,   *romantic, excellent, cheap*
  terbaik dan murah   *Malaysian restaurants*

 Quick vocab

pramugari	*air hostess, flight attendant*
damai	*peaceful*
indah	*beautiful (of places)*
meriah	*lively*
ramai	*crowded*
langsing	*slim*
terbaik	*excellent*

> ● **INSIGHT**
>
> **Pramugari** refers specifically to female air crew; a male air crew member, i.e. *an air steward*, is **pramugara**.

Exercise 2

Form the following phrases in Malay.

    a a long, boring film

    b keen, clever children

    c a long, tiring journey

    d a lively, crowded, expensive holiday resort

    e a big, comfortable, stylish room

 Quick vocab

panjang	*long*
bosan	*boring*
bersemangat	*enthusiastic, keen*
pandai	*clever*
perjalanan	*journey*
tempat peranginan	*holiday resort*
mahal	*expensive*
moden	*stylish*

3 Telling the time. First, you will need to know the numbers up to 60, although if you have learnt the numbers 1 to 10 from the last unit, it is very easy to form numbers up to 99. **Sepuluh**, as you know, means *ten*, but it also means *one ten*. The **se-** only indicates something in the singular or to do with the number one.

The numbers 11 to 19 are formed with **-belas**:

sebelas	*11*	**enam belas**	*16*
dua belas	*12*	**tujuh belas**	*17*
tiga belas	*13*	**lapan belas**	*18*
empat belas	*14*	**sembilan belas**	*19*
lima belas	*15*		

As the *-teens* were formed with **-belas**, the *-ties*, that is 20, 30, 40 etc., are formed with **puluh**. Thus:

dua puluh	*20*
tiga puluh	*30*
empat puluh	*40, etc.*

Note that to make compound numbers you use the same pattern as in English, i.e. take 40, **empat puluh** and add 1, **satu** making:

empat puluh satu	*41*

Exercise 3

Write out the following numbers in Malay.

    a 54

    b 78

    c 81

    d 99

There are two ways of telling the time in Malay, as in English. To answer the question **Pukul berapa?**, *What time is it?*, you always start with **pukul** in the reply.

To express the *o'clock* start with **pukul** and add the number for the hour to it:

Pukul satu.	*It's 1 o'clock.*
Pukul lima.	*It's 5 o'clock.*

> **● INSIGHT**
>
> It is important to know that **pukul** + number for the hour forms the basis for telling the time in Malay. Minutes past and to the hour come after this base.

To express minutes *past* the hour, simply add the number of minutes to **pukul**, which begins all expressions of telling the time. For example, *20 past nine* is expressed as *nine twenty* or **pukul sembilan dua puluh minit.**

Pukul dua sepuluh minit.	*It's ten past 2.*
Pukul empat lima belas minit.	*It's 15 minutes past four.*

Minutes to the hour are expressed as minutes past the last hour, in other words, like looking at the face of a digital clock!

For example:

Pukul sembilan lima puluh minit.	*It's ten to ten or It's nine 50.*
Pukul tujuh lima puluh lima minit.	*It's five to eight or It's seven 55.*

Quarter past and *quarter to* can also be expressed using **suku**, which means *quarter*. The words *past* and *to* are omitted:

Pukul lima suku.	*It's quarter past five.*
Pukul dua tiga suku.	*It's quarter to three or It's two 45.*

As you can see, **suku** alone is used to mean *quarter past*, and **tiga suku** refers to *three quarters past* (or *quarter to the next hour*).

Half past is expressed using **setengah**. Note that **minit** does not need to be included with **setengah.**

Pukul enam *setengah*.	*It's half past six.*
Pukul lapan *setengah*.	*It's half past eight.*

Exercise 4

Write the following times in Malay.

    a It's 7 o'clock.
    b It's half past four.
    c It's 9.45.
    d It's quarter past ten.
    e It's quarter to two.

a.m. can be expressed by adding **pagi** and *p.m.* can be expressed by adding **tengah hari**, **petang** or **malam** after the time. Which one you use will depend on the way the day is divided according to Malaysian ways. Refer to Unit 1 for specific details of each time frame.

Resépsi perkahwinan bermula pukul sepuluh pagi.	*The wedding reception starts at 10 a.m.*
Pesawat dari Sydney mendarat pada pukul 6 petang.	*The aircraft from Sydney lands at 6 p.m.*
Pertunjukan berakhir pada pukul 11 malam.	*The show finishes at 11 p.m.*
Dia selalu pergi ke pejabat pada pukul 6.30 pagi.	*He always goes to the office at 6.30 a.m.*

 Quick vocab

resépsi	*reception*
perkahwinan	*wedding*
bermula	*to begin*
mendarat	*to land*
berakhir	*to finish*
selalu	*always*

The 24-hour clock is used in Malay with more frequency than you might expect to find in your home country. You will see it used on invitations and in TV programme listings, etc. It is formed exactly as in English, with 18.20, for example, being expressed as *eighteen twenty*.

Pesawat Malaysia Airlines ke London akan berlepas pada pukul lapan belas dua puluh minit.	*The Malaysia Airlines flight to London will take off at 18.20.*
Berita terakhir di TV ada pada pukul dua puluh satu tiga puluh minit.	*The last news on TV is at 21.30.*

 Quick vocab

berlepas	*to take off*
berita	*news*
terakhir	*the last*

06.02

The days of the week in Malay are as follows:

Isnin	*Monday*
Selasa	*Tuesday*
Rabu	*Wednesday*
Khamis	*Thursday*
Jumaat	*Friday*
Sabtu	*Saturday*
Ahad	*Sunday*

You can use the days of the week as they stand, but colloquially, Malay speakers prefer to express them by adding each to **hari** which means *day*. So they say:

hari Isnin	*Monday*
hari Selasa	*Tuesday*
hari Rabu	*Wednesday, etc.*

Examples of usage

Hari ini hari apa?	*What day is it today?*
Hari ini hari Isnin.	*Today is Monday.*
Semalam hari apa?	*What day was it yesterday?*
Semalam hari Ahad.	*Yesterday was Sunday.*
Ésok hari apa?	*What day is it tomorrow?*
Ésok hari Selasa.	*Tomorrow is Tuesday.*
Lusa hari apa?	*What day is it the day after tomorrow?*
Lusa hari Rabu.	*The day after tomorrow is Wednesday.*

> **●INSIGHT**
> Capital letters are used for days of the week in Malay, as they are in English.

 Quick vocab

hari ini	*today*
lusa	*the day after tomorrow*
dua hari yang lalu	*the day before yesterday*

Exercise 5

Answer the questions using short sentences as in the examples above.

    a Semalam hari Khamis. Hari ini hari apa?
    b Hari ini hari Rabu. Ésok hari apa?
    c Dua hari yang lalu Isnin. Lusa hari apa?
    d Lusa hari Jumaat. Ésok hari apa?

To say *on* a certain day of the week Malay uses **pada**. Note that to be correct you should include **hari** if you use **pada**. Thus:

pada hari Selasa	*on Tuesday*

In spoken Malay, however, **pada** is almost always omitted, so **hari Selasa** can also mean *on Tuesday*.

When you ask the question *On what day?* you can say either **pada hari apa?** or just **hari apa**?

Hari apa dia datang?	*On what day is he coming?*

5 Ada apa yang boléh kami lihat dan lakukan di sana. Under certain circumstances, when you want to ask *what?*, it is necessary to insert **yang** after the question word **apa**, creating the question form **apa yang?** When you are going to make a sentence in Malay using **apa**, where we use *what?*, ask yourself whether you can replace *what* with the phrase *What is it that...?* for example, *What (is it that) we can do there?* and this will show you whether **yang** needs to be inserted.

Look at the following examples:

Apa yang boléh saya lakukan di tempat itu?	*What may I do in that place?*
Apa yang boléh meréka buat untuk kita?	*What can they do for us?*
Apa yang sedang dia tulis sekarang?	*What is she writing now?*

 Quick vocab

buat	*to do*

You may also notice that an inversion occurs with **kami boléh** becoming **boléh kami**. This is because a verb should directly follow **yang**. Although some speakers do not adhere to this rule, it is bad form not to do so.

In the same way, **siapa** may also be followed by **yang**. The question form **siapa yang** is used when *Who?* is followed by a verb, for instance, when you want to ask *Who lives here?* You cannot use **siapa** alone in this type of question. As with **apa yang** it may also help if you consider whether *Who?* can be replaced by *Who is it that...?*: *Who (is it that) speaks French?*

Look at these examples.

Siapa yang mempunyai peta Pulau Redang?	*Who has a map of Redang (Island)?*
Siapa yang mengarang buku itu?	*Who wrote that book?*
Siapa yang nak mendaki gunung ésok?	*Who wants to go mountain climbing tomorrow?*

> ● **INSIGHT**
>
> You'll notice, in the examples above, that **mengarang** and **mendaki** are **me-** verbs, both of which also have shorter forms of **garang** and **daki** with the same meaning. In all of these examples, it is the person doing the action (i.e. the subject of the verb) being referred to. However, when **siapa yang** refers to the receiver of the action (i.e. the object of the verb) only the shorter (base) form can be used. **Siapa yang dia tolong?** *Who does she help?* In correct English this should be *Whom does she help?* That gives you the clue – if it is *whom* in English then you should not use the **me-** verb.

Quick vocab

peta	*map*
pulau	*island*
mengarang	*to write, compose*
mendaki	*climb*
gunung	*mountain*

6 When you make phrases such as *The man **who** sells fruit* and *The building **which** is behind the museum*, the parts of the phrases in bold are both rendered by **yang** in Malay.

Orang yang menjual buah-buahan, ayah saya.	*The man who sells fruit is my father.*
Gedung yang terletak di belakang muzium, kedutaan.	*The building which is located behind the museum is the embassy.*

> ● **INSIGHT**
>
> Notice the comma in the Malay sentence. It indicates a slight pause that you need to take when saying this sentence. Can you spot the reason? **Musium kedutaan** without the pause means *the embassy museum!* This leaves what appears to be an unfinished sentence – *The building that is located behind the embassy museum…* Remember that *is* is not usually translated in Malay. Remember that we commonly drop these words in spoken English, so you may need to bear this in mind when creating Malay sentences, as the **yang** will always be needed in such sentences in Malay. *The cake you bought* should really be *the cake which you bought*. Thinking of it in this way will indicate that you need **yang** in Malay: **Kuih yang kamu beli.**

Quick vocab

kedutaan	*embassy*
buah-buahan	*fruit*
gedung	*building*
muzium	*museum*
menjual	*to sell*

Exercise 6

Try writing the following in Malay.

   a The house he built.
   b The town we visited.
   c The girl who used to work here.

Understanding Malay

Exercise 7

Read or listen to the dialogue once again and say whether these statements are true or false.

- **a** Puan Sue-Ann mahu maklumat tentang Sarawak.
- **b** Ada tiga pakéj percutian yang Puan Sue-Ann boléh pilih.
- **c** Isteri Stan suka mencuba masakan yang baru.
- **d** Ada pakéj percutian yang murah dan bagus dan juga termasuk makanan.
- **e** Pejabat percutian tutup pukul enam petang.

Exercise 8

Look at the times on the watches and match them to the correct time phrases in Malay.

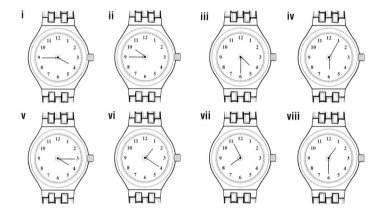

- **a** Pukul empat setengah
- **b** Pukul tiga empat suku
- **c** Pukul tujuh lima puluh lima minit
- **d** Pukul satu dua puluh minit
- **e** Pukul enam lima minit
- **f** Pukul dua belas setengah
- **g** Pukul sembilan empat puluh lima minit
- **h** Pukul tiga suku

PART TWO

Dialogue

Serena and Tom are in a tourist information centre in Melaka asking about things to do.

 06.03

Serena	Cik, boléh kami dapatkan sedikit maklumat tentang Melaka?
Kerani	Tentu sekali. Ada banyak tempat yang menarik untuk pelancong.
Serena	Mari kita bermula dari Bandar Melaka.
Kerani	Baiklah. Di sana ada Kota A Famosa, Bangunan Stadhuys dan Perkampungan Portugis.
Tom	Apa itu Kota A Famosa?
Kerani	Kota ini ialah sebuah kubu yang dibina oleh orang Portugis. Kalau anda berdiri di atas bukit di belakang kota ini, anda boléh melihat seluruh kota Melaka.
Serena	Kalau saya tak silap, ada terowong bawah tanah di sana.
Kerani	Betul sekali. Setiap hari Ahad, tempat itu selalu penuh dengan pelancong.
Serena	Selain itu, apa tempat lagi yang menarik?
Kerani	Perkampungan Portugis. Perkampungan orang Portugis ini juga terkenal dengan nama 'Mini Lisbon'.
Tom	Menarik sekali. Apa lagi yang boléh kami lihat?
Kerani	Anda boléh pergi ke Taman Mini Malaysia. Anda boléh lihat semua rumah tradisional negeri-negeri di Malaysia.
Kerani	Anda boléh pergi ke rumah-rumah beribadat, muzium maritime, Perigi Hang Tuah, Bukit China, Bangunan Stadhuys, zoo dan Jalan Jonker. Kedai-kedai di Jalan Jonker menjual barang-barang antik dan menarik. Ia kira-kira 20 minit dari Kota A Formosa.
Tom	Saya dah tidak sabar lagi.
Kerani	Sila ambil brosur-brosur ini pulang.
Serena	Terima kasih atas bantuan anda.

 Quick vocab

Cik	*Miss*
dapatkan	*to get*
maklumat	*information*

kerani	*clerk*
ialah	*is, are*
kubu	*fort*
dibina	*is built/to be built*
oléh	*by*
Portugis	*Portuguese*
berdiri	*to stand*
bukit	*hill*
seluruh	*the whole*
silap	*mistaken*
kalau saya tak silap	*if I'm not mistaken*
terowong	*tunnel*
tanah	*ground*
bawah tanah	*underground*
betul sekali	*that's right*
terkenal	*famous, well-known*
terkenal dengan	*known as*
penuh dengan	*full of*
negeri	*country*
beribadat	*to worship*
rumah beribadat	*house of worship*
muzium maritime	*maritime museum*
perigi	*well, shaft*
zoo	*zoo*
ambil	*to take*
antik	*antique*
sabar	*patient*
saya dah tidak sabar lagi	*I can hardly wait*
terima kasih atas	*thank you for*
atas	*for*

Serena	Sir, could we have some information about Melaka?
Clerk	Of course. There are lots of places for tourists.
Serena	Let's start from Bandar Melaka.
Clerk	OK. There is A Famosa, The Stadhuys Building and the Portuguese Settlement.
Tom	What is A Famosa?
Clerk	This city was built by the Portuguese. If you stand on the hill at the rear of the fort, you can see the whole city of Melaka.
Serena	If I am not mistaken, there is an underground tunnel there.
Clerk	That's right. Every Sunday that place is full of tourists.

Serena	Apart from that, are there any more interesting places?
Clerk	Portuguese Settlement. This Portuguese settlement is also known as 'Mini Lisbon'.
Tom	That's very interesting. What else can we see?
Clerk	You can go to the Mini Malaysia Park. You can see all the traditional houses of the states in Malaysia. You can go to the houses of worship, the maritime museum, the Well of Hang Tuah, China Hill, The Stadhuys Building, the zoo and Jonker Street. The shops in Jonker Street sell interesting antique goods. It is about 20 minutes from A Famosa.
Tom	I can hardly wait.
Clerk	Please take these brochures away (with you).
Serena	Thanks for your help.

How the language works 2

1 To say *what* + noun, as in *what day?* or *what flight?* Malay uses **apa**, but with this meaning, **apa** follows the noun it refers to. For example:

hari *apa*	**what** *day?*
penerbangan *apa***?**	**what** *flight?*
Bilik *apa* **ini?**	**What** *room is this?*
Ini bilik makan.	*It's the dining room.*

Exercise 9

How would you say the following in Malay?

    a What flower is this?
    b What programme is that?
    c What language is this?

2 Lagi is a useful word with various uses in Malay, two of which we will look at here.

▶ With a positive statement or question, **lagi** means *further, more* or *again*.

Ada apa *lagi***?**	*What* **else***?*
Silakan ulang itu *lagi*.	*Please repeat that* **again***.*
Berapa jam *lagi* **kita harus tunggu?**	*How* **many** *more hours should we wait?*

Exercise 10

How would you say the following in Malay?

    a Do you want some more?
    b I must take a bath again.

▶ With a negative statement or question, it means *not...any more* or *not...any longer*.

Dia bukan guru *lagi*.   *She's **not** a teacher **any more**.*

Dia bukan teman lelaki saya *lagi*.   *He is **not** my boyfriend **any more**.*

Saya bukan pemilik syarikat itu *lagi*.   *I am **not** the owner of that company **any more**.*

 Quick vocab

teman lelaki   *boyfriend*

pemilik   *owner*

Exercise 11

Give the following sentences in Malay.

a She is not a dancer any more.

b He is not rich any more.

 Quick vocab

kaya   *rich*

3 Terima kasih atas..., *Thank you for...* Notice that when you express *thanks for* something in Malay *for* is rendered by **atas** and not by **untuk**, as you might expect.

Terima kasih atas bantuannya.   *Thanks for the help.*

Using Malay

Exercise 12

Reconstruct these sentences so that they make sense starting with the word in **bold** in each case.

a hari Abad – **kami** Kelantan – ke – hendak – pergi – pada.

b ada-seperti – air panas – kolam renang – restoran – banyak kemudahan – **di Poring**.

c pusat kota – **dari** – memakan masa – jam – dua – ke sana

 Quick vocab

kolam renang   *swimming pool*

kemudahan   *amenities*

memakan masa   *take time*

Exercise 13

Read the schedule Mr Davies' secretary made for him, then answer the questions below in Malay.

Isnin   *10.15 temu janji dengan Encik Nathan*

               11.00 mengambil tiket

               14.40 temu janji dengan Encik Rustam

Selasa   *15.45 ke lapangan terbang/berangkat ke Singapura dengan Malaysia Airlines*

Rabu	*12.10 makan tengah hari dengan Puan Adelina*
Khamis	*09.25 menjemput Encik Davies dari Singapura*
Jumaat	*08.30 mesyuarat pekerja-pekerja*

 Quick vocab

temu janji	*appointment*
mengambil	*to get*
menjemput	*to pick up, to fetch*
pekerja	*employee*

   a Pukul berapa Encik Davies harus mengambil tiket?

   b Pukul berapa ada janji dengan Encik Rustam?

   c Pukul berapa Encik Davies makan tengah hari dengan Puan Adelina?

   d Hari apa Encik Davies pulang dari Singapura?

   e Pukul berapa ada mesyuarat pekerja-pekerja?

Exercise 14

Over to you!

You (**B**) are in a travel agent asking the assistant for information about Kuala Lumpur.

 06.04

A	Selamat pagi. Boléh saya bantu?
B	*Yes, I need some information about Kuala Lumpur.*
A	Tentu. Kami ada pakéj percutian lima hari.
B	*What can I see there?*
A	Ada taman orkid, tasik, taman burung, muzium, tempat membeli-belah dan lain-lain lagi.
B	*Is there a great nightlife?*
A	Ya.
B	*With what airline can I get there?*
A	Dengan penerbangan Malaysia Airlines.
B	*Are meals included?*
A	Ya. Pakéj ini sudah termasuk tikét penerbangan, hotél dan lawatan.
B	*How much does it cost?*
A	Lima ratus dolar Amérika. Ini brosur dan senarai harga untuk anda bawa pulang.
B	*Thank you for your information.*

Quick vocab

orkid	*orchid*
tasik	*lake*
burung	*bird*
membeli-belah	*shopping*
lain-lain lagi	*more besides*
hiburan malam	*night life*
sangat baik	*great*
lawatan	*excursion*
bawa pulang	*to take away*

Test yourself

1 How do you say *there is* or *there are* in Malay?

2 What do you need to do to form the -teens in Malay?

3 How do you form the -ties as in 30, 40 etc.?

4 Which word do you always need to include when telling the time?

5 What are the two different ways to express *quarter past* and *half past*?

6 How would you say *on Wednesday* in Malay?

7 How do you use **apa yang** and **siapa yang**?

8 How would you say *what day?* in Malay?

9 What does **lagi** mean in positive and negative sentences?

10 In the Malay expression for *thank you for*, what word translates *for*?

Invitations

In this unit you will learn how to:

▶ *make, accept and decline an invitation*
▶ *give reasons*
▶ *say the months*

PART ONE

Dialogue

Wong invites Stan and his family over to his house for dinner, but unfortunately Stan's family already has other plans.

 07.01

Wong	Saya dan isteri saya ingin menjemput anda sekeluarga untuk makan malam pada hari Sabtu ini.
Stan	Terima kasih, tapi sayang sekali kami tidak boléh pergi. Kebetulan kami merancang untuk pergi ke Pulau Langkawi pada hari Sabtu ini.
Wong	Bila anda akan pulang dari Pulau Langkawi?
Stan	Kami pulang pada hari Isnin pagi.
Wong	Kalau begitu, datanglah ke rumah saya pada hari Jumaat malam.
Stan	Hm...Maaf sekali lagi. Saya terpaksa menghantar anak saya ke hospital. Bagaimana pula pada Sabtu tengah hari? Saya tidak ada apa-apa rancangan.
Wong	Baiklah. Saya pun rasa hari Sabtu mémang tepat. Anda suka makanan pedas?
Stan	Saya makan apa saja, tidak ada masalah. Isteri dan anak-anak saya suka sekali makanan pedas.
Wong	Bagus. Isteri saya akan masak sambal udang. Oh ya, anak-anak selésa tinggal di sini?
Stan	Tentu sekali. Meréka sudah ada banyak teman dan suka bergaul dengan meréka.
Wong	Sampaikan salam saya kepada meréka.
Stan	Terima kasih. Kami akan datang pada pukul 12 tengah hari.

Quick vocab

menjemput	*to invite*
sekeluarga	*one family*
anda sekeluarga	*you and your family*
sayang sekali	*unfortunately*
kebetulan	*as it happens, by chance*
merancang	*to plan*
pulang	*to return home*
kalau begitu	*in that case*
datanglah	*please come (here: come over)*
terpaksa	*to have to*
menghantar	*to take, to convey*
apa-apa	*(here) any*
rancangan	*plans*
pun	*also*
rasa	*to feel, to think*
tepat	*perfect (of time)*
pedas	*spicy*
apa saja	*anything*
masalah	*problem*
tidak ada masalah	*(it's) no problem*
masak	*to cook*
sambal	*a type of chilli salsa*
udang	*shrimp, prawn*
bergaul	*to socialize, to spend time together*
sampaikan salam saya kepada meréka	*give them my regards*

● **INSIGHT**

Note that **merancang** *to plan to* is followed by **untuk** *in order to*, which may sound odd in English, but is perfectly fine in Malay.

Translation

Wong	My wife and I want to invite you and your family for dinner this Saturday.
Stan	Thank you, but unfortunately we can't go. By coincidence we planned to go to Langkawi this Saturday.
Wong	When will you come back from Langkawi?
Stan	We will come back on Monday morning.
Wong	In that case, come over to my house on Friday evening.

Stan	Hm…, Sorry again. I have to take my child to hospital. How about on Saturday afternoon? I don't have any plans.
Wong	That's fine. I also think Saturday is convenient. Do you like spicy food?
Stan	I eat anything. It's not a problem. My wife and children like spicy food a lot.
Wong	Great. My wife will make a prawn sambal. By the way, have your children settled in here?
Stan	Of course. They already have a lot of friends and like to spend time with them.
Wong	Give them my regards.
Stan	Thank you. We will be there at 12.

● INSIGHT

Notice that where we say **Langkawi**, Malay refers to it as **Pulau Langkawi**, *Langkawi Island*. Similarly, **Pulau Penang**, **Pulau Sumatera**, etc.

How the language works 1

1 When dealing with numbers we came across **se-** prefixed to numbers that indicated *one* such as **sepuluh** meaning *ten* or, literally, *one ten*.

A further but very common usage of the **se-** prefix with nouns is to indicate *the same*, for example, **sepejabat**, *the same office*.

Kami bekerja *sepejabat*.   *We work in the* **same office**.

● INSIGHT

Note that with this type of usage **di** *in* is not required.

Exercise 1

Use two more important similar expressions: **sekelas**, *in the same class* and **seumur**, *to be the same age* to make these two sentences:

    a Kami _____ ada ujian. *We have a test in the same class.*
    b Dia _____ dengan saya. *She is the same age as me.*

 Quick vocab

ujian   *test*

Se- can also mean *all* or *the whole (of)*:

Saya ingin menjemput saudara   *I would like to invite you and* **all**
   sekeluarga **ke pésta.**   **your family** *to a party.*

2 To ask *why?* in Malay use **kenapa?** or **mengapa?** They both mean *why?* but **kenapa?** is the form widely used in conversation. **Mengapa?** is preferred in writing.

Unlike other question words, which may appear in various positions, these question words can only occur at the beginning of the sentence. Thus:

Kenapa dia marah?	*Why is he angry?*
Kenapa keréta itu berhenti?	*Why did that car stop?*
Kenapa kamu tidak minum?	*Why don't you drink?*
Kenapa meréka ketawa?	*Why are they laughing?*
Kenapa kamu tidak meneléfon?	*Why don't you call?*

 Quick vocab

ketawa	*to laugh*

Of course, to answer this question you will need the word **kerana** which means *because*. It can be used just like *because* in English as the answer to **kenapa?** (**mengapa?**)

Kenapa kamu tidak datang ke tempat tinggal saya semalam?	*Why didn't you come over to my place yesterday?*
Kerana saya sibuk.	*Because I was busy.*
Mengapa dia sedih?	*Why is she sad?*
Kerana dia baru saja putus hubungan dengan teman lelakinya.	*Because she has just broken up with her boyfriend.*

 Quick vocab

tempat tinggal	*place (where someone lives)*
sedih	*sad*
baru saja	*to have just*
putus hubungan	*to break up*
teman lelaki	*boyfriend*

Kerana can also be used independently as in:

Kerana sibuk dia lupa meneléfon isterinya.	*Because he was busy, he forgot to phone his wife.*

3 In Unit 4 we came across **sila** and **silakan** as ways to form polite and formal commands. In this unit you have met another form of command, a much softer command that is formed by adding **-lah** to a verb, as in **datanglah**, *come over*. In the dialogue Stan and Wong have become friends so the formality needed for the interview situation in Unit 4 is no longer appropriate. The **lah** form is more like a gentle urging rather than a command.

4 **Sampaikan salam saya kepada meréka**, *Give them my regards.* Look at the way this useful phrase is structured in Malay. **Sampaikan salam**, *pass greetings*, **saya**, *of me*, **kepada meréka**, *to them*.

Exercise 2

How would you say the following?

- **a** Give her my regards.
- **b** Give Sue our regards.
- **c** Give them our regards.
- **d** Give them regards from me and my family.

5 An introduction to word bases. English has a vast vocabulary. This is due, in part, to the fact that the English vocabulary makes use of root words from several different languages. This often means that parts of speech (i.e., nouns, verbs, adjectives, etc.) referring to related concepts bear no relation to each other. Malay vocabulary, on the other hand, tends to build related words, or words that relate to a single topic area, around the same root.

Compare the Malay with the English in the following words, all related to the topic of teaching and learning. Note the ever-present base **ajar** in the Malay, and no similar roots in the English translations we have used to illustrate this vital difference between the two languages.

 Quick vocab

belajar	to learn
mengajar	to teach
pelajar	student
pelajar**an**	lesson
pengajar	instructor
terpelajar	educated

To describe how words are built up in Malay we will regularly be referring to three basic concepts:

- ▶ **prefix** – this is a bit added to the beginning of a word, such as the *im-* in *impossible* in English.
- ▶ **suffix** – this is a bit added on to the end of a word. You have already come across the Malay possessive **-mu** (Unit 5) and **-nya** (Unit 5). These are technically known as suffixes.
- ▶ **base word** – this is the word in its simplest form to which prefixes or suffixes may be added. A base word may be a noun, a verb or an adjective.

● INSIGHT

These may be called *root words* in some textbooks or dictionaries.

A prefix or a suffix, or a combination of both, added to a base word, can create related vocabulary. There is often a pattern whereby a specific prefix or suffix creates a new and particular part of speech. This happens in English too. For example, some verbs, with the suffix *-ion* added create a related noun, the meaning of which is derived from the verb. For example, *to suggest* is the verb, but when we add *-ion* we end up with the noun *suggestion*. In Malay the addition of prefixes and suffixes to base words is an integral part of how the vocabulary is built up, and there is often a definite pattern to the resulting words created.

An ability to see how words are built up from their bases will not only help you learn related vocabulary more easily, but it will also give you a better chance of deducing the meaning of new words you may come across. At this stage it is better just to notice how the prefixes and suffixes affect the base word. You will soon begin to get a feel for the patterns in which prefixes and suffixes modify the base and create a word with a separate meaning.

From now on base words are included next to modified words in the vocabulary sections. They appear in brackets followed by *n*, *v* and *a* to indicate whether the base word is a noun, verb or adjective. Base words from all units appear in the glossary in a similar fashion.

Understanding Malay

Exercise 3

True or false? Read the following questions based upon the dialogue and decide which are true and which are false.

   a Wong mahu menjemput Stan sekeluarga untuk makan malam.
   b Stan pulang dari Pulau Langkawi hari Jumaat.
   c Stan tidak suka makanan pedas.
   d Anak-anak Stan mempunyai banyak teman.
   e Stan sekeluarga akan datang hari Sabtu pukul 11 tengah hari.
   f Stan menghantar anaknya ke hospital hari Jumaat.
   g Pada hari Sabtu Stan sangat sibuk.

Exercise 4

Match up the questions with the correct answers.

   1 Kenapa kamu sakit perut?
   2 Mengapa dia terlambat?
   3 Mengapa bajunya basah?
   4 Kenapa polis menangkapnya?
   5 Kenapa kamu tidak membalas surat saya?
   6 Mengapa dia gagal dalam ujian itu?

a Kerana saya sibuk.

b Kerana tidak belajar.

c Kerana makan terlalu banyak cili.

d Kerana kerétanya rosak.

e Kerana tidak mempunyai lésén memandu.

f Kerana hujan.

 Quick vocab

basah	*wet*
menangkap (tangkap v.**)**	*to catch*
membalas (balas v.**) surat**	*to answer a letter*
baju	*clothes*
gagal	*fail*
cili	*chilli*
ujian	*test*
rosak	*broken down*
lésén memandu	*driving licence*
hujan	*rain*

PART TWO

Dialogue

Serena has received a telephone call from a friend inviting her to go to a night club. She is wondering whether Tom would like to go too...

 07.02

Serena	Tom, teman saya ajak saya ke disko malam nanti. Kamu mahu ikut?
Tom	Tentu. Saya mahu minum wain dan mencari teman berbual.
Serena	Ya, sambil menyelam minum air.
Tom	Ada gula ada semut.
Serena	Inilah sifat lelaki!
Tom	Saya bergurau saja. Harga minuman di sana mahal?
Serena	Saya tidak tahu. Tapi saya rasa tidak begitu mahal. Jangan risau. Dia akan belanja kita.
Tom	Terima kasih. Naik apa ke sana?
Serena	Dengan keréta. Dia akan jemput kita pada pukul 10 malam.
Tom	Siapa yang pergi?
Serena	Kita bertiga, saya, kamu dan Roni.
Tom	Perlu bayar untuk masuk?

Serena	Tidak, kita cuma bayar minuman.
Tom	Apakah itu disko yang popular di sini?
Serena	Ya, tempat anak-anak muda berkumpul.
Tom	Bagaimana muzik di sana?
Serena	Ada macam-macam rentak lagu. Ada 'persembahan live' oleh penyanyi dari luar negeri.
Tom	Yakah?
Serena	Benar. Kamu harus berpakaian kemas.

 Quick vocab

ajak	*to invite*
disko	*disco*
malam nanti	*tonight*
ikut	*to follow, (here) to come*
wain	*wine*
teman berbual	*social friends*
sambil	*while*
menyelam (selam *v.***)**	*to dive*
Sambil menyelam minum air	*To drink water while you are diving (proverb similar in meaning to: to kill two birds with one stone)*
gula	*sugar*
semut	*ant*
Ada gula ada semut	*Where there's sugar there are ants (proverb)*
sifat	*nature*
Inilah sifat lelaki!	*Typical man!*
bergurau (gurau *n.***)**	*to joke*
harga	*price*
minuman (minum *v.***)**	*drinks*
bertiga	*three of us*
perlu	*necessary, it is necessary*
bayar	*to pay for*
belanja	*(here) to treat*
popular	*popular*
muda	*young*
berkumpul (kumpul *v.***)**	*to gather, to hang out*
muzik	*music*
macam-macam	*various, different sorts of*
rentak lagu	*types of songs*
rentak	*rhythm*
persembahan (sembah *n.***)**	*show*
persembahan live	*live show*
penyanyi (nyanyi *v.***)**	*singer*
luar negeri	*abroad*

yakah?	*really?*
benar	*true, it's true*
harus	*should*
berpakaian (pakai *v.***)**	*to dress, to get dressed*
kemas	*neat, tidy*
berpakaian kemas	*to dress well*

Translation

Serena	Tom, my friend has invited me to a disco this evening. Do you want to come?
Tom	Of course. I want to drink wine and find friends to talk to.
Serena	Yes, kill two birds with one stone.
Tom	Where there is sugar there are ants.
Serena	Typical man!
Tom	I'm just joking. Are the drinks expensive there?
Serena	I don't know. But I don't think they are too expensive. Don't worry. He will treat us.
Tom	Thanks. How are we going there?
Serena	By car. He will pick us up at ten.
Tom	Who is going?
Serena	There (will be) three of us: me, you and Roni.
Tom	Do (we) need to pay to get in?
Serena	No, we just pay for drinks.
Tom	Is it a popular disco around here?
Serena	Yes, it's the place (where) young people get together.
Tom	What is the music like there?
Serena	There are various types of songs. There are live shows with singers from foreign countries.
Tom	Really?
Serena	(Yes, it's) true. You have to dress well.

How the language works 2

1 bertiga, *three of us*. From *two* onwards, you can specify a group by prefixing the number with **ber-**

dua	*two*	**berdua**	*as a pair*
empat	*four*	**berempat**	*in a group of four*

When we say *in a group of three* or *the four of them*, etc., we usually only include the number for a specific purpose, such as to stress the number of people in the group. Otherwise we normally just say *together*. Malay, on the other hand, tends always to be specific in this situation, as long as the group is small, and, of course, as long as you know how many people are in the group. These **ber-** + number words are usually used with a pronoun as in the following examples:

Meréka selalu bertiga.   *They are always together (i.e. the three of them).*

Kami berdua pergi bercuti ke   *The two of us went on holiday to*
Pulau Pangkor di Pérak.   *Pangkor Island in Perak.*

Meréka berlima keluar untuk   *The five of them went out for*
makan malam di restoran yang   *dinner to that new restaurant in*
baru di pusat bandar.   *the town centre.*

Exercise 5

Form the following sentences in Malay.

- **a** They came together (in a pair).
- **b** The three of us are good friends.
- **c** The ten of us climbed Mount Kinabalu.

 Quick vocab

bercuti (cuti *n.***)**	*to be on holiday*
bersahabat (sahabat *n.***)**	*to be friends*
bersahabat dengan baik	*to be good friends*
mendaki (daki *v.***)**	*to climb*
Gunung Kinabalu	*Mount Kinabalu*

If you know the number in the group you should try and be specific by using language such as that just discussed. If you do not know the number, you can use **bersama-sama** to mean *together*.

Meréka selalu bersama-sama.   *They are always together.*

Meréka makan malam bersama-sama.   *They have dinner together.*

If you want to express *together with* use **bersama dengan**.

Saya berenang bersama   *I swim together with him at*
dengan dia di tepi pantai.   *the beach.*

Ibu itu bekerja keras bersama   *That woman, together with her*
dengan anak-anaknya.   *children, works hard.*

2 Months of the year

 07.03

Januari *January*		**Julai** *July*	
Februari *February*		**Ogos** *August*	
Mac *March*		**September** *September*	
April *April*		**Oktober** *October*	
Mei *May*		**November** *November*	
Jun *June*		**Disember** *December*	

In the same way **hari** is used with days of the week, **bulan** which means *month* (and also, incidentally, means *moon*) occurs before the name of the month when you wish to express *in* + month, which also uses **pada**. **Pada** is always used with time. For example: **pada bulan Mei**, *in May*.

> ● **INSIGHT**
>
> In speech it is common to drop the **pada** when the meaning is understood, so **bulan Mei** can also mean *in May*.

3 Verb + **-an**. Many nouns ending in **-an** are created from verb base words. Their meaning is closely related to the verb they come from.

pakai	*to wear*
pakaian	*clothes*
makan	*to eat*
makanan	*food*
beli	*to buy*
belian	*purchases*

Exercise 6

Note the meanings of the verb bases on the left. Look at the nouns created from the respective verbs on the right and see if you can deduce the meanings:

a	**minum** *to drink*	**minuman**
b	**jawab** *to reply*	**jawapan***
c	**main** *to play*	**mainan**
d	**pilih** *to choose*	**pilihan**
e	**beli** *to buy*	**belian**
f	**hibur** *to entertain*	**hiburan**
g	**kerja** *to work*	**pekerjaan**
h	**fikir** *to think*	**fikiran**

(*This is subject to a spelling change.)

A few noun bases and verb bases also have the suffix **-an** applied to them, which makes other nouns, although the meaning created by the suffix is not always as easy to see as with verb base **-an** nouns.

With noun bases the meaning of the suffixed noun tends to be an extension of the noun base:

laut *sea*	**lautan** *ocean/seas*
gambar *picture*	**gambaran** *description*
rambut *hair*	**rambutan** *a hairy type of fruit*
duri *thorn*	**durian** *a spiky kind of fruit*

With adjective bases the noun created reflects the quality expressed by the adjective:

kotor *dirty*   **kotoran** *dirt/rubbish/trash*

manis *sweet*   **manisan** *sweets*

pahit *bitter*   **pahitan** *bitterness*

Using Malay

Exercise 7

Look at the texts and fill in the invitations accordingly.

a Asiah akan menjemput Riana dan Ramona ke rumah saya di No. 9. Jalan Melati, Kuala Lumpur untuk meraikan jamuan hari jadinya pada 24 haribulan Jun, pukul 4 petang.

> *JAMUAN HARI JADI:* ....
>
> *Tempat:* ....
>
> *Masa:* ....
>
> *Tetamu jemputan:* ....

b Serena ingin menjemput Tom ke majlis perkahwinan Nurliza pada malam Sabtu, 7 haribulan Jun, pukul 7 malam di Déwan Suria.

> *MAJLI SAKAD NIKAH:* ....
>
> *Tempat:* ....
>
> *Tarikh:* ....
>
> *Masa:* ....

c Saya akan menjemput ibu-bapa saya untuk menghadiri upacara ijazah di kampus Universiti Sains Antarabangsa, pada hari Isnin, 9 haribulan Jun, pukul 10 pagi.

> *UPACARA IJAZAH:* ....
>
> *Tempat:* ....
>
> *Tarikh:* ....
>
> *Masa:* ....

d Kami akan menjemput rakan-rakan sekelas ke Pésta Tahun Baru di Johor Bahru pada 31 Disember, hari Khamis pukul 8 malam.

```
PÉSTA TAHUN BARU

Tarikh: ...................................................................................................

Hari: .....................................................................................................

Masa: ...................................................................................................
```

 Quick vocab

jamuan	*feast, festival, party*
hari jadi	*birthday*
meraikan (raya *v.***)**	*to celebrate*
tetamu	*guest*
jemputan	*invitation*
tetamu jemputan	*the person invited*
majlis	*ceremony*
perkahwinan	*marriage*
haribulan	*date*
akad nikah	*marriage vows*
tarikh	*date*
ibu-bapa	*mum and dad*
menghadiri (hadir *v.***)**	*to attend*
upacara	*ceremony*
ijazah	*degree*
upacara ijazah	*graduation ceremony*
rakan	*friend*
rakan sekelas	*classmate*
tahun baru	*new year*

Exercise 8

Over to you!

Your Singaporean friend (**A**) has decided to invite you (**B**) out for dinner at the Terrace Hotel Restaurant. Respond in Malay as indicated.

07.04

A	Saya ingin menjemput anda bersama isteri untuk makan malam.
B	*Thank you. When?*
A	Ésok pada pukul tujuh di Restaurant Hotél Terrace.
B	*OK (use **boléh**). I don't have work tomorrow.*
A	Apakah anda dan isteri suka minum wain?
B	*I'm sorry. We are not used (to it).*
A	Jangan risau, saya akan dapatkan minuman jus atau minuman tanpa beralkohol.
B	*Thank you. See you then!*
A	Sampaikan salam kepada isteri.

Quick vocab

wain	*wine*
biasa	*to be used to*
dapatkan	*to get*
tanpa	*without*
minuman jus	*fruit juice*
minuman tanpa beralkohol	*alcohol-free drinks*

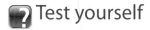 # Test yourself

1 What does **se-** mean when added to a noun?

2 Which two words can mean *Why?* and which is the more conversational one?

3 How do you form a gentle command in Malay?

4 What is the difference between a prefix and a suffix?

5 How would you say *in a group of five* in Malay?

6 How would you say *together with* in Malay?

7 How would you say *in August* in Malay?

8 From what are nouns with the suffix **-an** derived?

9 What effect does **-an** have on noun bases?

10 What does a noun resulting from **-an** mean when applied to adjective bases?

Directions

In this unit you will learn how to:
▶ *ask for directions*
▶ *understand the directions you are given*

PART ONE

Dialogue 1

Stan and his family finally decided to book a package tour offered by the travel agency. On the way to pick up the voucher from the office, Stan gets lost and has to ask a passer-by for help.

 08.01

Stan	Maaf. Encik, tumpang tanya … di mana Pejabat Pelancongan Holiday Tours?
Pejalan kaki	Boléh saya tahu alamatnya? Di jalan mana?
Stan	Di Jalan Bunga Melor. Apa nama jalan ini?
Pejalan kaki	Oh, ini Jalan Bunga Raya.
Stan	Bagaimana nak ke sana?
Pejalan kaki	Ia dekat sekali. Jalan terus ikut jalan ini hingga sampai ke lampu isyarat dan bélok kanan. Kira-kira 50 meter, ada hotel … Pejabat pelancongan itu ada di sebelahnya.
Stan	Ia dekat panggung wayang?
Pejalan kaki	Betul sekali. Pejabat itu terletak di antara panggung wayang dan hotél.
Stan	Terima kasih banyak-banyak.

 Quick vocab

tumpang tanya	*do you mind if I ask you…?*
perjalan kaki	*pedestrian, passer-by*
boléh saya tahu	*could you let me know…?*
alamat	*address*
jalan	*street*
di jalan mana?	*on what street?*
bagaimana nak ke sana?	*how do I get there?*
terus	*straight on*
hingga	*until*

sampai	*to reach*
hingga sampai	*until you reach*
lampu	*lamp*
isyarat	*sign*
lampu isyarat	*traffic signal, traffic light*
bélok	*to turn*
bélok kanan	*turn right*
kira-kira	*about*
pelancongan (lancong n.**)**	*tourism*
pejabat pelancongan	*travel agency*
panggung	*stage*
panggung wayang	*puppet theatre*
terletak (letak n.**)**	*to be situated*
banyak-banyak	*a great deal, a lot*
terima kasih banyak-banyak	*thanks a million*

● INSIGHT

Panggung wayang is a *stage* (**panggung**) featuring shows with two-dimensional puppets (**wayang**), depicting stories such as the Ramayana, an Indian epic, and accompanied by a gamelan orchestra. The puppets can be made of leather (**wayang kulit**) or wood (**wayang kayu**). Nowadays the expression **panggung wayang** also refers to a *cinema*.

Translation

Stan	Excuse me (Sir), do you mind my asking…where is the Holiday Tours travel agency?
Passer-by	Could you tell me the address? What street?
Stan	Bunga Melor Street. What's the name of this street?
Passer-by	Oh, this is Bunga Raya Street.
Stan	How do I get there?
Passer-by	It is really near. Take this street, walk straight on until you reach the traffic lights, then turn right. About 50 metres, there is a hotel. The travel agency is next to it.
Stan	Is it by the puppet theatre?
Passer-by	That's right. That office is between the theatre and the hotel.
Stan	Thanks a million.

How the language works 1

1 When you need to ask for directions to a place in Malay, you can use **di mana?** or **di manakah?**, *where is?* or you could use the phrase **Bagaimana menuju ke?** or **bagaimana boléh saya ke?**

Di mana Menara Kembar Petronas?

Bagaimana menuju ke Menara Kembar Petronas?

Bagaimana boléh saya pergi ke Stésen Sentral?

Where are the Petronas Twin Towers?

How do I get to the Petronas Twin Towers?

How do I get to Central Station?

> **● INSIGHT**
>
> If you need to stop a passer-by, after you have said **maaf**, *excuse me*, it is polite to request information with the useful phrase **tumpang tanya ...?**, *may I ask you...?*

Exercise 1

Ask how to get to the following places.

- **a** Hotél Mandarin Pacific
- **b** KLIA (Kuala Lumpur International Airport)
- **c** Menara Genesis

Understanding Malay

Exercise 2

Answer the following true/false questions based on the dialogue.

- **a** Stan hendak pergi ke Pejabat Pelancongan Holiday Tours.
- **b** Stan tersesat di Jalan Sultan.
- **c** Pejabat pelancongan ada di Jalan Malaya.
- **d** Pejabat itu ada di antara hotél dan panggung wayang.
- **e** Selepas lampu isyarat, Stan mesti bélok kiri, kira-kira 50 meter.
- **f** Pejabat pelancongan Holiday Tours tidak jauh.

 Quick vocab

tersesat (sesat *a.***)**	*lost*
mesti	*must*

Exercise 3

 08.02

First familiarize yourself with the vocabulary. Listen to each short dialogue which features someone asking the way to a place. For each dialogue, circle the place the person is trying to get to. If you are not using the recording, turn to the transcript at the back of the book and treat this as a reading exercise.

a Taman Burung – Taman Orkid – Taman Rama-rama
b Muzium Negara – Tugu Negara – Bangunan Parlimen
c Stésen LRT Universiti – Stésen LRT Bangsar – Stésen LRT Bandaraya
d Akuarium Tunku Abdul Rahman – Masjid Negara – Zoo Negara
e Hotél Vistana – Hotél Milah – Plaza Raya

 Quick vocab

persimpangan (simpang *n.*)	*crossroads*
tugu	*monument*
maksud	*to mean*
kondominium	*condominium*
maksudkan (maksud *v.*)	*to mean*
zoo negara	*national zoo*
hujung	*end*
tersilap (silap *a.*)	*to be mistaken*
bulatan (bulat *a.*)	*roundabout*

> ● **INSIGHT**
> LRT stands for Light Rail Transit, and refers to Kuala Lumpur's efficient monorail system.

PART TWO

Dialogue

Serena cannot accompany Tom to the bank so she gives him directions to the People's Bank. Somehow he still manages to get lost …

 08.03

Pejalan kaki	Saudara kelihatan keliru. Boléh saya bantu?
Tom	Ya, saya tersesat.
Pejalan kaki	Mahu pergi ke mana?
Tom	Saya mahu pergi ke People's Bank di Jalan Sultan. Bagaimana boléh saya ke sana?
Pejalan kaki	Kalau berjalan kaki agak jauh.
Tom	Tak mengapa. Saya suka jalan kaki.
Pejalan kaki	Ikut jalan ini dan jalan terus hingga sampai ke bulatan dan bélok kanan. Jalan terus sampai ke satu persimpangan. Bank terletak di antara tiga bangunan dari persimpangan.

Tom	Sukar saya nak ingat. Boléh anda tunjukkan di peta ini?
Pejalan kaki	Mari saya lihat. Sekarang kamu di sini dan ini People's Bank yang dicari.
Tom	Terima kasih kerana membantu.
Pejalan kaki	Tidak apa-apa. Kalau malu bertanya nanti sesat jalan.

 Quick vocab

kelihatan (lihat v.**)**	*to seem*
keliru	*confused*
berjalan (jalan n.**)**	*to walk*
jalan kaki/berjalan kaki	*go on foot*
tak mengapa	*no problem*
jalan terus	*keep walking*
sukar	*difficult*
ingat	*to remember*
dicari (cari v.**)**	*to be looked for (here: you are looking for)*
kerana	*because of (here: for)*
bertanya (tanya n.**)**	*to ask*
Malu bertanya nanti sesat di jalan	a proverb meaning *If you're too shy to ask you will get lost in the street*. It can be used in other contexts too.

Translation

Passer-by	You look confused. Can I help you?
Tom	Yes. I'm lost.
Passer-by	Where do you want to go?
Tom	I want to go to the People's Bank on Sultan Street. How do I get there?
Passer-by	It's a little far on foot.
Tom	No problem. I like walking.
Passer-by	Follow this road, straight on until you come to a roundabout, then turn right. Keep walking until you come to a cross roads. (The) Bank is located three buildings from the crossroads.
Tom	It's difficult for me to remember. Could you point to it on this map?
Passer-by	Let me see. You are here and this is the People's Bank you are looking for (that is being looked for).
Tom	Thank you for helping (me).
Passer-by	No problem. If you don't ask, you don't get.

How the language works 2

1 Most Malay words beginning with **ber-** and **me-** are verbs. These prefixes can be applied to noun, adjective and verb bases.

When **ber-** and **me-** occur as prefixes to a verb root, they often have no particular function and express the same meaning as the verb base. Some verbs of this type are:

▶ *with* **ber-**

berhenti *to stop*	(from **henti** *to stop*)
berbelanja *to spend*	(from **belanja** *to spend*)
bertanya *to ask a question*	(from **tanya** *to ask a question*)
bermain *to play*	(from **main** *to play*)
bertukar *to change*	(from **tukar** *to change*)

> ● **INSIGHT**
>
> It is best to learn these verbs with the **ber-** prefix as a single unit, as this is the form you will almost always use.

Note that there are some cases where, owing to sound changes, **ber-** changes slightly. Such exceptions are:

bekerja *to work*	(from **kerja** *to work*)
berenang *to swim*	(from **renang** *to swim*)
belayar *to sail*	(from **layar** *to sail*)

▶ *with* **me-**

membeli *to buy*	(from **beli** *to buy*)
melihat *to see*	(from **lihat** *to see*)
mendengar *to hear*	(from **dengar** *to hear*)
mencari *to look for*	(from **cari** *to look for*)
menjual *to sell*	(from **jual** *to sell*)

(The **me-** prefix creates certain sound changes which will be dealt with in a later unit.)

Some verb bases, that are verbs in their own right, occur with **me-** which creates a verb with a different meaning, usually related. Some common ones are:

menunggu *to expect*	(from **tunggu** *to wait*)
meninggal *to leave*	(from **tinggal** *to stay or to live*)
menarik *to attract*	(from **tarik** *to pull*)
mendapat *to get*	(from **dapat** *to be able*)
membangun *to build*	(from **bangun** *to waken up or to get up*)

Care needs to be taken with a few verb bases as they can exist with either the **ber-** or the **me-** prefix, which create verbs with different meanings. For example:

membuat *to make*　　**berbuat** *to do*　　(from **buat** *to make/do*)

melepas *to let go*　　**berlepas** *to depart*　　(from **lepas** *to let go/depart*)

Using Malay

Exercise 4

Look at the map, then fill in the passages with the words specified in each section.

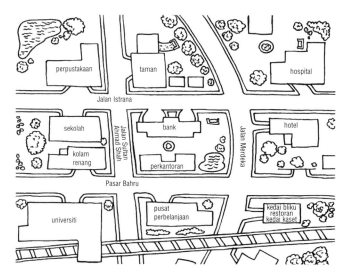

a　Use **terus**, **antara**, **menyeberang**, **bélok** to complete this text.

Bagaimana saya ke restoran dari perpustakaan?

Jalan _____ ke Jalan Istana, kemudian _____ jalan. _____ kiri, restoran ada di _____ kedai buku dan kedai kasét.

b　Use **belok**, **kéluar**, **belakang**, **terus**, **menyeberang** to complete this text.

Bagaimana saya ke kolam berenang dari restoran?

Ketika kamu _____ dari restoran _____ kanan. Jalan _____ ke Jalan. Jalan Pasar Baru dan _____ jalan. Kolam berenang ada di _____ sekolah.

c　Use **terus**, **bélok**, **sudut**, **keluar** to complete this text.

Bagaimana saya ke hospital dari taman?

Pertama _____ taman ke Jalan Sultan Ahmad Shah, kemudian _____ kanan. Jalan _____ sampai kamu bertemu Jalan Istana. Hospital ada di _____.

Exercise 5

Over to you!

 Quick vocab

pertama	*first of all*
kemudian	*then*
kedai buku	*bookshop*
kasét	*tape/cassette*

You (**B**) are wandering the streets looking for a post office. A passer-by (**A**) can see that you are lost so she offers to help you…

 08.04

A	Saudara kelihatan keliru. Boléh saya bantu?
B	*I'm lost. I want to go to a post office.*
A	Mudah sekali. Ikut jalan raya ini terus hingga sampai persimpangan dan bélok kiri. Pejabat pos terletak di sebelah kiri jalan.
B	*Is it (that) near the LRT Station?*
A	Tepat sekali. Juga ada McDonalds di sebelahnya.
B	*Could you point it out on this map? Where are we now?*
A	Tentu. Kita sekarang ada di Jalan Petaling. Ini pejabat pos di sebelah McDonalds.
B	*Thanks a million.*

 Quick vocab

mudah	*simple*	**di samping kiri**	*on the left-hand side*
jalan raya	*main road*	**tepat sekali**	*that's right*
		tepat	*accurate*

Test yourself

1. What are the four different ways to ask for directions in Malay?
2. What useful phrase should you use when stopping someone and asking for information?
3. True or false: when **ber-** is applied to a verb it always alters the meaning.
4. How should you aim to remember **ber-** verbs?
5. What is unusual about the **ber-** prefix when used with *to work* and *to swim*?
6. What other common verb prefix did you learn in this unit?
7. Do verbs with the **me-** prefix always have the same meaning as the verb base?
8. What is the difference between **melepas** and **berlepas**?
9. What is the difference between **berbuat** and **membuat**?
10. How would you say *on the right-hand side* in Malay?

Changing money

In this unit you will learn how to:

▶ *change money*
▶ *understand and express high numbers*
▶ *express distance, weight, height, etc.*

PART ONE

Dialogue

Sue-Ann has been so busy shopping that she did not realize she was running out of Singaporean currency until she was getting ready to pay…

 09.01

Puan Sue-Ann	Maaf Pak cik, wang saya tidak cukup. Boléh saya bayar dengan dolar América?
Pekedai	Maaf Puan, kami hanya menerima wang dolar Singapura. Tapi di seberang jalan ada pengurup wang. Atau Puan boléh tukar di bank di sebelah kanan kedai buku itu.
Puan Sue-Ann	Baiklah, tolong simpan barang ini. Nanti saya akan kembali?
(In the bureau de change.)	
Puan Sue-Ann	Selamat pagi, boléh saya tukar dolar kepada dolar Singapura?
Pengurup wang	Ya, dolar Amérikalah Puan?
Puan Sue-Ann	Ya, betul. Berapakah kadar pertukaran untuk hari ini?
Pengurup wang	Satu dolar América adalah sama dengan 1.5 dolar Singapura. Puan nak tukar berapa banyak?
Puan Sue-Ann	500 dolar. Berapa dalam dolar Singapura?
Pengurup wang	500 kali 1.5 dolar sama dengan 750.00 dolar Singapura.
Puan Sue-Ann	Tolong berikan dalam wang kertas lima puluh dan sepuluh dolar.
Pengurup wang	Sila hitung semula.
Puan Sue-Ann	Ya, betul. Terima kasih.

Quick vocab

wang	*money*
cukup	*enough*
bayar	*to pay*
dolar	*dollar*
pekedai (kedai *n.***)**	*shopkeeper*
menerima	*to accept*
di seberang jalan	*across the road*
pengurup wang	*money changer, bureau de change*
tukar	*to change*
simpan	*to keep, (here) to keep to one side*
barang	*goods*
kadar pertukaran	*exchange rate*
adalah	*is, are*
sama dengan	*equal to, the same as*
beri	*to give*
berikan	*to give (something) to (someone)*
kertas	*paper*
wang kertas	*bank note*
semula	*again*

> ● **INSIGHT**
>
> Although *is/are* does not need to be translated in Malay, it can be translated using **adalah**. This is more commonly found in written, rather than spoken, Malay. It is similar in usage to **ialah**.

Translation

Sue-Ann	I'm sorry, I don't have enough money. Can I pay in US dollars?
Shop assistant	Sorry, Madam, we only accept Singaporean dollars. But across the road there is a bureau de change. Or you can change (money) in the bank to the left-hand side of that bookshop.
Sue-Ann	OK, please keep my goods (to one side). I'll be back later.
Sue-Ann	Good morning, can I change dollars into Singapore dollars?
Clerk	Yes, US dollars, Madam?
Sue-Ann	Yes. What's today's rate?
Clerk	It's one US dollar to 1.5 Singaporean dollars. How much do you want to change?
Sue-Ann	500 dollars. How much (is that) in Singapore dollars?

Clerk	500 times 1.5 dollars, that's 750 Singapore dollars.
Sue-Ann	Please give it to me in 50s and then some ten dollar bills.
Clerk	Please count your money again.
Sue-Ann	Yes, it's correct. Thank you.

How the language works 1

1 When shopping and changing money you will need to know some fairly high numbers, which are not difficult to learn once you have mastered 1 to 10.

> ● **INSIGHT**
>
> If your travels take you as far as Indonesia, which uses the same number system as in Malaysia with just one variation – **lapan** is expressed as **delapan** – you will need to know how to form and understand numbers into the millions, so they are worth learning here.
>
> You already know that to form the -*teens* you follow the number by **belas** and to make the -*ties* you need to use **puluh**. It is just as simple to form *hundreds, thousands* and *millions*.

▶ For *hundreds* use **ratus:**

dua ratus	*200*
lima ratus empat	*504*

▶ For *thousands* use **ribu:**

lapan ribu	*8,000*
enam ribu empat ratus dua belas	*6,412*

▶ For *millions* use **juta:**

empat juta	*4 million*
tujuh juta empat ratus ribu	*7,400,000*

▶ Note that numbers that refer to *one* or *a* (as in *1 million* or *a million*) are different and are formed with the prefix **se-** which means *one*.

seratus	*100*
seribu	*1,000*
sejuta	*1 million*

Exercise 1

Write the following numbers in words (note that where we separate parts of a big number with commas in English, Malay does the same thing too):

a 19,432

b 2,865,714

c 3,197

d 8,600,111

e 25,155,613

2 Years are formed in the same way as the numbers above. They follow the word **tahun** which means *year*.

2005	**tahun dua ribu lima**
1492	**tahun empat belas sembilan puluh dua**
1945	**tahun sembilan belas empat puluh lima**

> **●INSIGHT**
>
> As with days and weeks, **pada** can be used to express *in* with years, although it is not obligatory; furthermore, it is rarely used in spoken Malay.

3 Adding the suffix **-an** to **puluh**, **ratus**, **ribu** and **juta** gives you *tens*, *hundreds*, *thousands* and *millions*.

Ratusan anak muda akan ambil bahagian dalam maraton amal.	*Hundreds of young people will take part in the charity marathon.*
Ribuan tikus besar menyerang sawah padi.	*Thousands of rats attacked the rice field.*

 Quick vocab

ambil bahagian dalam	*to take part in*
maraton	*marathon*
amal	*charity*
tikus	*mouse*
tikus besar	*rat*
menyerang (serang *n.***)**	*to attack*
sawah padi	*rice field*

Understanding Malay

Exercise 2

Answer the following true/false questions based on the dialogue.

a Puan Sue-Ann tidak mempunyai cukup dolar Singapura untuk membeli-belah.
b Pekedai hanya menerima wang tunai.
c Puan Sue-Ann akan kembali ke kedai setelah menukar wang.
d Bank ada di seberang jalan.
e Pengurup wang ada di sebelah kanan kedai buku.
f Puan Sue-Ann ingin menukar wang sebanyak 500 dolar Amérika.

 Quick vocab

wang tunai	*cash, ready money*
setelah	*after*
sebanyak	*as much as, to the amount of*

Exercise 3

09.02

You are going to hear numbers being called out in a lottery game. Check off the numbers for each of the players as you hear them and note down who wins first, second and third by getting all four numbers. The empty card is for you to play. Choose four numbers between 1 and 100. **Semoga berjaya!** (*Good luck!*)

Harry

30	38
25	69

Michael

12	52
79	13

Arvinder

61	70
9	45

Xiao Ling

36	24
91	83

Ravin

99	17
22	50

PART TWO

Dialogue

Tom is looking for somewhere to change his money so that he can go shopping for souvenirs.

09.03

Tom	Serena, kamu tahu keluarkan wang dengan kad kredit di sini?
Serena	Ya. Ada mesin ATM di luar.
Tom	Serena, kad kredit saya ditelan mesin ATM. Boléh bantu saya? Saya cuma ada sedikit pound sterling.
Serena	Jangan risau. Saya akan uruskan kad kredit kamu di bank dan kamu boléh tukar wang di sana. Kalau tidak cukup, saya akan pinjamkan kamu wang.
Pegawai	Boléh saya bantu Encik?
Tom	Ya, saya mahu tukar wang pound sterling kepada ringgit. Berapa kadar pertukaran hari ini?
Pegawai	1 pound sterling sama dengan 8 ringgit. Kadar hari ini lebih bagus daripada semalam.
Tom	Untung sekali. Saya mahu tukar 30 pound sterling saja.
Pegawai	Baik, jumlahnya RM240.00.
Tom	Wow! … banyak sekali. Kayalah saya!

Pegawai	Encik mahu wang kecil atau wang besar?
Tom	Tolong beri saya wang kertas 100 ringgit dan bakinya pula dalam beberapa kepingan 10 ringgit.
Pegawai	Baiklah. Ini semua wangnya. Jangan lupa untuk hitung semula.

 Quick vocab

keluarkan	*to get (something) out, to withdraw (something)*
kad kredit	*credit card*
mesin ATM	*ATM machine, cashpoint machine*
ditelan (telan *v.*)	*to be swallowed*
uruskan	*to deal with, to sort out*
pinjamkan (pinjam *v.*)	*to lend*
lebih bagus	*better*
daripada	*(here) than*
semalam	*yesterday*
untung	*luck*
untung sekali!	*what luck!*
jumlah	*amount, total*
kayalah saya	*I'm rich!*
wang kecil	*small money*
wang besar	*big money*
baki	*remainder*
kepingan	*piece*

Translation

Tom	Serena, do you know how to withdraw money with a credit card here?
Serena	Yes. There's an ATM machine outside.
Tom	Serena, my credit card has been swallowed by the ATM machine. Can you help me? I only have a little pound sterling (a few pounds).
Serena	Don't worry. I will sort out your credit card in the bank and you can change money there. If (you) don't have enough, I can lend you money.
Clerk	May I help you, Sir?
Tom	Yes, I want to change pound sterling into ringgit. What's today's rate?
Clerk	(It's) 1 pound sterling to 8 ringgit. Today's rate is better than yesterday's.
Tom	What luck! I want to change just 30 pounds.
Clerk	Ok, the total is 240.00 ringgit.

Tom	Wow! That's a lot. I'm rich!
Clerk	Would you like (it in) small money or big money?
Tom	Please give me 100 ringgit notes and the rest in 10 ringgit pieces.
Clerk	Right. Here's (all) your money. Don't forget to count (it) again.

How the language works 2

1 So far we have seen how **-nya** is used to mean *his* or *her*. It is frequently used where we would use *the* or *your* in English in sentences such as:

Bagaimana penerbangan*nya*?	*How was **the** flight? or How was **your** flight?*
Bagaimana kelas*nya*?	*How was **the** class? or How was **your** class?*
Ini kamus*nya*.	*This is **the** dictionary. or This is **your** dictionary.*

It is especially used in this way to refer back to something that has been previously mentioned, or a situation that is understood by both speakers. In the first example, it could be that you are being met by someone at the airport who asks you how your flight was, knowing that you have just arrived on a plane. The second example could be asked by someone who knows that you have just had a class. As you can see from the third example the usage of **-nya** in this way is not restricted to questions. This person may have borrowed your dictionary and is returning it, he or she might be handing you a book that was the subject of a previous conversation meaning *This is the dictionary I told you about*. There could be many situations that would warrant the use of **-nya** by a Malay speaker, but what all these situations have in common is that they refer to a situation or something previously known or understood by both speakers.

Similarly, in the dialogue, the clerk says **Ini semua wangnya** as a situation has been created whereby, due to a previous interaction, Tom is waiting for money so the clerk says *Here is the money* (that you have been waiting for).

> ● **INSIGHT**
>
> This use of **-nya** is very common and, even though it may take a little time to get used to, you will start to get a feel for how it is used as you hear it used by Malay speakers or see it used in the dialogues. In the above examples it is not wrong to say **Bagaimana penerbangan kamu?** or **Ini kamus** in the same situations. It just so happens that native Malay speech tends to use **-nya** in such cases.

By extension, you will notice that all the phrases that ask about prices and fares use **-nya**:

Berapa harganya?	*How much does it cost?*
Berapa tambangnya?	*What's the fare?*

In the same way, **-nya** is also used with weight and measure words. It refers to these words in such a way as to mean, for example, *its length is 45 centimetres* where we would say *it is 45 centimetres long* in English. Such measure words are mostly formed from an adjective to which **-nya** is attached.

panjang   *long*
Panjangnya **45 sentimeter.**   *it is 45 centimetres long.*
tebal   *thick*
Buku itu tebalnya **300 muka surat.**   *That book is 300 pages thick.*

An exception is **kelajuannya** which is formed from the noun **kelajuan** *speed*:
Kelajuannya 70 km per jam. *Its speed is 70 km per hour.*
Sentimeter *centimetre.*

Quick vocab

muka surat   *page*
per jam   *per hour*

Exercise 4

Use the adjectives in the vocabulary section beneath the exercise to express the following:

 a It weighs 56 kilos.
 b It is 45 centimetres high.
 c It is 100 metres wide.
 d It is 2 metres deep.
 e It takes 7 hours.

Quick vocab

berat   *heavy/weight*
tinggi   *high/tall*
lébar   *wide*
dalam   *deep*
lama   *long*
sentimeter   *centimetre*
meter   *metre*

The adjectives above combine with **berapa** to form questions related to measure:

Berapa tinggi?   *How tall?*

> ● **INSIGHT**
> Make sure you do not confuse **lama** and **panjang** as they both translate *long* in English. **Lama** refers to a length of time only, whereas **panjang** refers to physical distance only.

Berapa lama penerbangan dari Kuala Lumpur ke Kota Kinabalu?	*How long is the flight from Kuala Lumpur to Kota Kinabalu?*
Berapa panjang méja itu?	*How long is that table?*

2 The **ber-** and **me-** prefixes with noun bases.

▶ With **ber-**:

Many verbs in Malay are nouns that have been modified by means of a prefix. You have already come across this in Units 1 and 8 when you met **berumur** and **bernama**. For example, when **sukan**, which means *sport*, occurs with **ber-** the result is the verb **bersukan** which means *to play sport*. In the same way, **rehat**, *(a) rest* becomes **berehat** *to rest*, and **bahasa** which means *language* becomes **berbahasa** *to speak (such and such a language)*.

● INSIGHT

In the final example notice how the noun and the meaning of the noun become absorbed into the verb. You already know that **bahasa Inggeris** means *(the) English (language)*, **berbahasa Inggeris** means *to speak English*. It is an alternative to **bercakap bahasa Inggeris**.

Many **ber-** + noun verbs can be translated into English as *to be…* or *to have…* .

akal *intelligence*	**berakal *to be*** *intelligent*
cuti *holiday*	**bercuti *to be*** *on holiday*
pendapat *opinion*	**berpendapat *to be*** *of the opinion*
teman *friend*	**berteman *to be*** *with a friend (i.e. to have a friend)*
isteri *wife*	**beristeri *to have*** *a wife (i.e. to be married)*
anak *child*	**beranak *to have*** *children*

Ber- used in this way can create expressions such as:

Dia berkaki panjang.	*He has long legs.* (**kaki panjang** *long legs*)
bangunan bertingkat empat	*a four storey building (a building that has 4 storeys)*

 Quick vocab

kaki	*leg*
bangunan	*building*

Exercise 5

Look at the nouns in the left-hand column noting the meaning. See if you can find suitable English meanings for the verbs on the right that use the nouns as a base.

a	**puasa** *fast (as in a religious fast)*	**berpuasa**
b	**gerak** *movement*	**bergerak**
c	**keluarga** *family*	**berkeluarga**

▶ With **me-**:

tari *dance*	**menari** *to dance*
ala *net*	**menjala** *to net*
bungkus *parcel*	**membungkus** *to wrap up*
gunting *scissors*	**menggunting** *to cut with scissors*

> ● **INSIGHT**
>
> You will notice that, in some cases, when the **me-** prefix is added to create a verb, the noun (which has now become the base) undergoes a change in spelling and, therefore, pronunciation. Such sound changes are for ease of pronunciation (from a Malay point of view) and will be dealt with in more detail in Unit 16. For now, just concentrate on the meaning of the prefixed verbs.

Exercise 6

See if you can deduce the meanings of the **me-** verbs in the right-hand column created from the nouns in the left-hand column. You may find that with **me-** + noun verbs, the meanings are a little less easy to deduce than with the **ber-** + noun verbs.

a	**potong** *slice*	**memotong**
b	**dayung** *paddle*	**mendayung**
c	**cukai** *tax*	**mencukai**

Using Malay

Exercise 7

Read the English for the following facts about Malaysia. Rewrite the Malay sentences inserting the Malay form of the number in words.

a *The population of Malaysia is 25 million.*
Penduduk Malaysia _____ orang.

b *Mount Kinabalu is 4,100 metres high.*
Gunung Kinabalu tingginya _____ meter.

c *Malaysia gained independence in 1957.*
Malaysia memperoléh kemerdékaan pada tahun _____.

d *Sarawak has a population of 2 million people.*
Penduduk Sarawak _____ orang.

e *Malaysia is made up of 13 states.*
Malaysia terdiri daripada _____ negeri.

f *The Portuguese arrived in Malacca in 1511.*
Orang Portugis tiba di Melaka pada tahun _____.

g *Kuala Lumpur International Airport (KLIA) was first opened in 1998.*
Kuala Lumpur International Airport (KLIA) mula dibuka pada _____.

h *Petronas Twin Towers are 452 metres tall.*
Ketinggian Petronas Twin Towers ialah _____ meter.

i *Genting Highlands is 2,000 metres above sea level.*
Genting Highlands ialah _____ meter tinggi dari aras laut.

j *The Kenyir Lake covers an area of 369 square kilometres.*
Tasik Kenyir meliputi kawasan seluas _____ kilometer persegi.

k *Langkawi is made up of 99 islands.*
Pulau Langkawi terdiri daripada _____ pulau.

l *The Malay Peninsula has a land area of 131,805 square kilometres.*
Semenanjung Malaysia seluas _____ kilometer persegi.

m *The Rejang River in Sarawak is 567 kilometres long.*
Sungai Rejang di Sarawak adalah sepanjang _____ kilometer.

 Quick vocab

penduduk (duduk *v.***)**	*population*
memperoléh (oléh *n.***)**	*to gain*
kemerdékaan (merdéka *n.***)**	*independence*
terdiri daripada	*to be made up of, to be composed of, comprises*
dibuka (buka *v.***)**	*to be opened*
aras laut	*sea level*
meliputi (liput *n.***)**	*to cover, to include*
kawasan	*area*
seluas	*as wide as*
semenanjung	*peninsula*
persegi	*square*
sepanjang	*length*

Exercise 8

Over to you!

You (**A**) want to change some money.

 09.04

A	*Hello. Can I change dollars into ringgit?*
B	Dolar apa? Dolar Amérika?
A	*No, Singapore dollars.*
B	Tentu.
A	*What's the rate?*
B	Satu dolar sama dengan RM2.50. Mahu tukar berapa?
A	*1,000 dollars. I'd like some small change, please.*
B	Ini wangnya. Sila hitung semula.

Test yourself

1 How would you form *hundreds* in Malay?

2 How would you form *thousands*?

3 How would you form *millions*?

4 What prefix is used with numbers to mean *one* as in *one thousand*?

5 How do you express years in Malay?

6 What effect does the suffix **-an** have on number words such as **ratus** and **juta**?

7 What further use of -**nya** did you learn in this unit?

8 In what kind of expressions is **-nya** usually found?

9 When **ber-** is added to a noun base, what is often the resulting meaning?

10 What is the effect of adding **me-** to a noun base?

Getting around

In this unit you will learn how to:
▶ *buy tickets for journeys*
▶ *talk about using various modes of transport*
▶ *use more time expressions*

PART ONE

Dialogue

Stan and his family would like to travel from Kuala Lumpur to Kuching by plane. Stan approaches a taxi driver to take him to the travel agency.

 10.01

Stan	Teksi ini ada meter?
Pemandu	Ya, Encik.
Stan	Tolong hantarkan saya ke Worldwide Tours di Jalan Amansari.
Pemandu	Kita sudah sampai, Encik. Mahu saya tunggu di sini?
Stan	Boléh, tunggu sekejap saja, tapi dilarang letak keréta di sini.
Pemandu	Saya akan kembali dalam masa 30 minit lagi.
(In the agency.)	
Stan	Saya mahu beli tikét penerbangan ke Kuching.
Kerani	Tikét satu jalan atau tikét pulang-balik, Encik?
Stan	Tikét satu jalan. Berapa harganya dari Kuala Lumpur ke Kuching?
Pegawai	Kelas ekonomi atau bisnés?
Stan	Ekonomi saja.
Pegawai	Harga tikét untuk kelas ekonomi RM262.00 sahaja. Untuk berapa orang?
Stan	Untuk empat orang. Ada tawaran tikét khas yang murah?
Pegawai	Ya, kami ada tikét untuk kumpulan, untuk masa satu bulan, tetapi tidak boléh tukar tarikh atau déstinasi.
Stan	Ada peraturan lain?
Pegawai	Ya, tidak boléh kembalikan wang.
Stan	Berapa kali penerbangan ke Kuching?
Pegawai	Setiap hari, 7 kali seminggu.

Stan	Masa penerbangan?
Pegawai	Pukul 8.50 dan pukul 10.15.
Stan	Berapa jam ke sana?
Pegawai	Hanya 1 jam 45 minit.
Stan	Pukul berapa saya harus ke lapangan terbang?
Pegawai	Satu jam sebelum bertolak.
Stan	Baik. Tolong buat tempahan untuk empat orang pada minggu depan.
Pegawai	Jangan lupa untuk mengésahkan tikét anda.
Stan	Tentu sekali. Boléh saya dapatkan tempat duduk di sebelah tingkap?
Pegawai	Saya cuba.

 Quick vocab

hantarkan saya ke…	*take me to…*
sampai	*to arrive*
mahu saya tunggu?	*do you want me to wait?*
sekejap	*moment*
dilarang (larang *v.***)**	*it is forbidden, not allowed*
letak keréta	*to park a car*
dalam masa 30 lagi	*in another 30 minutes*
tikét	*ticket*
tikét satu jalan	*one-way ticket*
tikét pulang-balik	*return ticket*
berapa harganya?	*how much is the cost* or *how much is the fare?*
kelas	*class*
ekonomi	*economy*
bisnés	*business*
sahaja	*only*
untuk berapa orang?	*for how many people?*
tawaran (tawar *v.***)**	*bargain*
khas	*special*
kumpulan (kumpul *v.***)**	*group*
masa	*time, (here) validity*
déstinasi	*destination*
peraturan (atur *v.***)**	*restriction, regulation*
tidak boléh kembalikan wang	*non-refundable*
berapa kali?	*how many times?, (here) how frequent?*
seminggu	*a week*
berapa jam?	*how many hours?*
sebelum	*before*
bertolak (tolak *v.***)**	*to leave*
buat	*make*
tempahan (tempah *v.***)**	*reservation, booking*

jangan lupa untuk	*don't forget to*
mengésahkan (sah *v.*)	*to authenticate, (here) to confirm or reconfirm, to prove*
boléh saya dapatkan	*could I have?, could you give me?*
dapatkan	*to get*
tingkap	*window*
tempat duduk di sebelah tingkap	*a window seat*

Translation

Stan	Does this taxi have a meter?
Driver	Yes, Sir.
Stan	Please take me to Worldwide Tours on Amansari Street.
Driver	We're here, Sir. Do you want me to wait?
Stan	OK, I'll only be a moment, but it is forbidden to park here.
Driver	I'll come back in 30 minutes.
(In the agency.)	
Stan	I want to buy an air ticket to Kuching.
Employee	A one-way ticket or a return, Sir?
Stan	A one-way ticket. What's the fare from Kuala Lumpur to Kuching?
Employee	Economy or business class?
Stan	Just economy.
Employee	The price for economy class ticket is 262 ringgit. For how many people?
Stan	For four people. Is there a special bargain ticket (that is cheap)?
Employee	Yes, we have a group ticket that is valid for one month, but you cannot change the date or destination.
Stan	Are there (any) other restrictions?
Employee	Yes, it is non-refundable.
Stan	How frequent is the flight to Kuching?
Employee	Every day, seven times a week.
Stan	The flight time?
Employee	At 8.50 and at 10.15.
Stan	How many hours (does it take) to (get) there?
Employee	Just 1 hour 45 minutes.
Stan	At what time should I be at the airport?
Employee	One hour before departure.
Stan	OK, please make a booking for four people (for) next week.
Employee	Don't forget to reconfirm your ticket.
Stan	Sure. Can I reserve a seat by a window?
Employee	I'll see what I can do.

How the language works 1

1 When asking *what's the price?*, *how much is it?*, *how much does it cost?*, etc., in Malay this is usually rendered by **berapa(kah) harga(nya)**. (The **-nya** is optional.) There is an exception to this. Although **harga** is used generally to ask about the cost of something, the word **tambang** is, however, more commonly used to mean *fare* where transportation is concerned.

Berapa tambang bas dari Melaka ke Singapura?	*How much is the bus fare from Melaka to Singapore?*
Tambang bas sekolah akan bertambah pada bulan Ogos.	*The school bus fare will increase in the month of August.*
Berapa tambangnya ke Putrajaya?	*What's the cost to Putrajaya?*

 Quick vocab

bertambah (tambah v.**)**	*to increase*

Exercise 1

How would you ask:

    a What the fare is to Penang?

    b How much is it from Bangsar to KLIA (Kuala Lumpur International Airport)?

2 A key phrase to use when asking for anything is **Boléh saya dapatkan …?** *May I have …?*

Other useful phrases to use when asking for something are:

Boléh saya minta…?	*May I request…?*
Boléh beri saya…?	*Could you give me…?*

Three other useful phrases to use when asking for services occur in the dialogue:

Tolong, hantarkan saya ke…	*Please take me to…*
Tolong sediakan…	*Please prepare…*
Tolong, buat saya…	*Please make/do for me…*

Tolong *please* should always be placed before the request in Malay.

3 **Dilarang** + verb is used to state that something is forbidden. You will come across it regularly in official signs telling you not to do something:

DILARANG MEROKOK	*NO SMOKING*
DILARANG MELETAK KERÉTA	*NO PARKING*

 Quick vocab

merokok	*to smoke*
meletak (letak *v.***)**	*to park*

4 You have already come across **lagi** meaning *further* or *more* with verbs in Unit 6. With periods of time, it has another important and distinct meaning: it translates ***in*** *a certain period of time* where that means *after* a certain period of time has passed. For example:

Saya akan beritahu kamu sepuluh minit lagi.	*I'll let you know in ten minutes.*
Meréka akan pulang dari pelayaran persiaran keliling dunia dua bulan lagi.	*They will come back from their world cruise in two months.*

 Quick vocab

pelayaran persiaran	*cruise*
keliling	*around*
dunia	*world*

Exercise 2

Form the following time periods:

    a in seven months

    b in 55 minutes

    c in three weeks

5 English also uses *in* to refer to the time it takes to complete an action, as in *I will complete this exercise in ten minutes* in other words *it will take me ten minutes to complete this exercise*. Note that Malay does not use **lagi** in this case. In this situation **dalam masa** translates *in*.

Saya akan menyelesaikan latihan ini *dalam masa* **sepuluh minit.**	*I will complete this exercise in ten minutes (within the space of ten minutes).*

 Quick vocab

menyelesaikan (selesai *v.***)**	*to finish*
latihan	*exercise*

6 Durations of time such as **hari**, **minggu**, **bulan** etc., take the prefix **se-** with the specific meaning of *a* as in *once a month* etc.

minggu *week*	**seminggu** *a week*	
Berapa kali seminggu?	*How many times a week?*	

bulan *month*	**sebulan** *a month*
Pulau ini menerima	*This island receives*
4,000 pelawat sebulan.	*4,000 visitors a month.*

Exercise 3

Prefix these time expressions with **se-** then make the phrases that follow:

hari	*day*
tahun	*year*
abad	*century*

   a twice a year

   b three times a day

   c once a century

7 *If* and *when*. To make a question with *when?* you already know that you must use **bila(kah)?** In English we also use *when* in sentences where it is not a question such as ***When** I was young I used to eat ice cream* or *Remember to give her this book **when** you see her.* You cannot use **bila** in this type of sentence.

When translating *when* you also need to consider whether you are talking about an event in the future or the past.

To express *when* in the past in Malay, **semasa** or **ketika** is used. **Semasa** is used more in the spoken language while **ketika** tends to be more used in written language. This usage often corresponds to *while* in English, as in ***while** I was waiting for the bus…*

Dia datang ke rumah saya *semasa* **saya**	*He came to my house **when** I was*
sedang menonton TV.	*watching TV.*
Ketika **abangnya bernikah,**	***When** her brother got married,*
dia di London.	*she was in London.*
Ibu meneléfon saya *ketika*	*Mother called me **when** I was*
saya sedang makan.	*eating.*

To express *when* in the future, you must use **kalau** or **jika**, both of which also mean *if*.

Tolong beritahu kami *kalau*	*Please tell us **when** we get there.*
sudah sampai.	
Jika **saya lulus ujian, saya akan**	***If** I pass the exams I will have*
buat jamuan.	*a party.*
Kalau **saya jutawan, saya akan beri**	***When** I become a millionaire,*
sumbangan kepada orang miskin.	*I will give charity to the poor.*

 **Quick vocab**

jutawan (juta *n.***)**	*millionaire*
sumbangan (sumbang *v.***)**	*charity*

A word needs to be said about the tense structure in sentences such as the one above. As **kalau** and **jika** have two meanings (*when* and *if*) this sentence could also mean *If I were a millionaire, I would give charity to the poor*. Note that in *if* sentences of this type, **akan** still needs to be included where it replaced *would* in English.

> ● INSIGHT
>
> **Akan**, as you know, normally means *will* but in this type of construction it corresponds to *would*.

Understanding Malay

Exercise 4

Read or listen to the dialogue again and say whether the following statements are true or false.

   a Teksi yang Stan mahu naik tidak ada meter.
   b Pemandu teksi bersedia menunggu Stan.
   c Stan dan keluarga membeli tikét kelas bisnés.
   d Stan membeli lima tikét.
   e Stan dan keluarganya harus tiba di lapangan terbang satu jam sebelum berlepas.
   f Stan meminta tempat duduk dekat di lorong.

 Quick vocab

bersedia (sedia *a.***)**	*to be ready to, to be willing to*
berlepas (lepas *v.***)**	*departure*
meminta (minta *v.***)**	*to request*
lorong	*aisle (street, alley)*

Exercise 5

The following expressions refer to things you are being told not to do. Look at the signs below and write the number of the expression next to the corresponding sign.

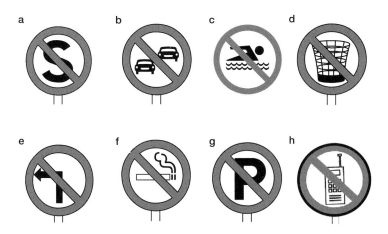

i Dilarang Memotong

ii Dilarang Masuk

iii Dilarang Bélok Kiri

iv Dilarang Mengguna Teléfon Mudah Alih

v Dilarang Membuang Sampah

vi Dilarang Berenang

vii Dilarang Merokok

viii Dilarang Meletak Keréta

 Quick vocab

memotong (potong v.)	to overtake
masuk	to enter
mengguna (guna v.)	to use
teléfon mudah alih	mobile phone
membuang (buang v.)	to throw
sampah	rubbish, trash
merokok (rokok n.)	to smoke
berhenti (henti v.)	to stop

> ● INSIGHT
>
> Mobile phone in Malay is literally *a telephone* **teléfon,** *it's convenient* **mudah**, *to move around* **alih**.

PART TWO

Dialogue

Tom and Serena are planning to go to Singapore by train. They are discussing how to get to the railway station.

 10.02

Tom	Kita ke stésen keréta api naik apa?
Serena	Kita naik bas saja.
Tom	Di mana nak menunggunya?
Serena	Ada perhentian bas di depan bangunan itu.
Tom	Berapa minit bas akan berlalu?
Serena	Setiap 5 minit.
Tom	Bas nombor berapa akan pergi ke stésen?
Serena	Bas nombor 68.
Tom	Bas yang itukah?
Serena	Bukan yang berwarna perang. Itu basnya.

(On the bus.)

Tom	Kita ada di mana sekarang? Tolong beritahu saya kalau sudah sampai.
Serena	Kita ada di Jalan Bunga Melor. 15 minit lagi sampailah.
Tom	Lihat tu! Ada kemalangan.
Serena	Patutlah jalan raya sesak sekali.

(To the conductor.)

Serena	Berhenti Encik, kami mahu turun di sini.

(At the railway station.)

Serena	Eh Tom, cepatlah! Kita ke tingkap jual tikét. Kami mahu beli tikét keréta api ke Singapura. Berapa harganya?
Pegawai	Harganya 60 ringgit.
Tom	Berapa lama perjalanannya?
Pegawai	6 jam.
Serena	Pukul berapa keréta api bertolak?
Pegawai	Pukul 4 petang.
Tom	Di mana kami harus tukar keréta api?
Pegawai	Keréta api ini terus ke Singapura.
Tom	Boléh kami dapat tempat duduk sebelah tingkap?
Pegawai	Oh maaf, sudah penuh.
Tom	Apa nama stésen di Singapura?
Pegawai	Namanya Stésen Tanjung Pagar.
Serena	Baik. Saya rasa lega, semuanya dah selesai.
Pegawai	Jangan léwat sampai tertinggal keréta api.

 Quick vocab

stésen	*station*
keréta api	*train*
perhentian (henti *v.***)**	*(a) stop*
berlalu (lalu *v.***)**	*to pass*
nombor	*number*
berwarna (warna *n.***)**	*to be coloured*
perang	*brown*
beritahu (tahu *v.***)**	*to let (someone) know*
ada	*to be*
tu	*short for* **itu** *(colloquial)*
kemalangan (malang *a.***)**	*accident*
patutlah	*that's the reason* or *that's why*
turun	*to get off or out of a vehicle*
cepatlah	*hurry up, quick!*
terus	*direct*
penuh	*full, (here) booked*

lega	*free from anxiety, relieved*
dah	*short for* **sudah** *(conversational usage)*
selesai	*to finish, to complete*
léwat	*late*
tertinggal (tinggal *v.***)**	*to miss*

Translation

Tom	How shall we get to the station?
Serena	We just take the bus.
Tom	Where do we wait for it?
Serena	There's a bus stop in front of that building.
Tom	How many minutes before the bus comes?
Serena	Every five minutes.
Tom	What number bus goes to the station?
Serena	Bus number 68.
Tom	Is it that one?
Serena	It's not the brown one. That's the bus there.
(On the bus.)	
Tom	Where are we now? Please tell me when we're there.
Serena	We're on Bunga Melor Street. (Another) 15 minutes before we arrive.
Tom	Look at that! There has been an accident.
Serena	That's the reason the main road is so congested.
(To the conductor.)	
Serena	Stop. We want to get off here.
(At the railway station.)	
Serena	Hey Tom, get a move on! Let's get to the ticket window. We want to buy train tickets to Singapore. What's the fare?
Clerk	It's 60 ringgit.
Tom	How long is the journey?
Clerk	Six hours.
Serena	What time does the train leave?
Clerk	At four in the afternoon.
Tom	Where do we have to change trains?
Clerk	This train is direct to Singapore.
Tom	Could we have seats next to the window.
Clerk	Oh, I'm sorry. They are all taken.
Tom	What's the name of the station in Singapore?
Clerk	The station is called Tanjung Pagar station.
Serena	Great. I can relax now, everything is sorted out.
Clerk	Don't be late (or) you'll miss the train.

How the language works 2

1 Naik apa ke…?, *How shall we go to…?*

The most common way to express going by some form of transport is by using the verb
naik + vehicle word.

naik keréta	*to go by car*
naik keréta api	*to go by train*

Some words for vehicles you have not yet met are:

motorsikal	*motorbike*
béca	*trishaw, rickshaw*
féri	*ferry*
sampan	*small boat*
kapal	*ship*
kapal terbang	*plane*

> ● INSIGHT
>
> **Kapal terbang** is literally a *flying vessel*, i.e. *plane*. You have already met the other word
> for *plane*, **pesawat**.

Naik is the most common way to say how you are going somewhere, although you can also
express it using **dengan** where we use *by* in English. So you can say, for example:

Meréka suka pergi ke sana dengan bas.	*They like going there by bus.*
Pagi ini ayah saya datang dari	*This morning my father came from*
pasar dengan keréta.	*the market by car.*

 Quick vocab

pasar	*market*

In theory, you can add the prefix **ber-** to any form of transport, thus creating a verb meaning
to go by that mode of transport. So **naik keréta api** would become **berkeréta api**. In
practice, however, only two of these forms are common in colloquial language: **berkuda**,
to go by horse, and **berbasikal**, *to go by bike*, which is very common. For all other forms of
transport it is more natural to use **naik**:

Ramesh berbasikal ke universiti	*Ramesh cycles to the university*
setiap hari.	*every day.*

> ● INSIGHT
>
> As well as meaning *to ride* (a form of transport), colloquially **naik** can mean *to get on*
> one, and its opposite, **turun**, can mean *to get off*. For example, **Saya asyik naik turun**
> **bas saja hari ini!** *I've been getting on and off buses all day!* (referring to a journey of many
> buses to reach the destination).

Finally, *to go on foot* is expressed by **berjalan kaki** in Malay.

Mari kita berjalan kaki ke   *Let's walk to the cinema.*
  panggung wayang.

 Quick vocab

panggung wayang   *cinema*

2 The last question word you will meet in this course is **yang mana** meaning *which*. It can be used on its own to ask *which one?* or it can be used to mean *which* + noun, in which case it follows the noun it refers to, like an adjective.

Exercise 6

Can you now say the following?

  a which bag
  b which idea

The important thing to note when using **yang mana** is that it is asking about a choice given a set of alternatives. It differs in usage from noun + **apa** which asks about the *type* of something.

Look at these two examples:

Filem apa yang kamu tonton?   *What films do you watch? (i.e., what kind of films)*
Filem yang mana kamu suka?   *Which film do you like? (given that*
                                            you have a choice of two or more)

3 Prefix **me-** with suffix **-i**. Verbs with **me- -i** are created from noun, adjective, adverb and verb bases.

tahu *to know*	**mengetahui** *to comprehend*
cinta *love*	**mencintai** *to love*
kurang *less*	**mengurangi** *to reduce*
faham *understanding*	**memahami** *to understand*

Most of these verbs imply an action towards someone or something, or a closing of distance between two things. With these verbs there is always an object. For example:

naik *to go up*	**menaiki** *to climb*
dahulu *previous*	**mendahului** *to overtake*
dekat *close*	**mendekati** *to draw close to*

Using Malay

Exercise 7

Choose words and phrases from the dialogues in this unit to complete the following:

a Bas _____ ke pusat bandar?

b _____ duduk dekat pintu keluar?

c _____ tempahan untuk dua orang ke Pulau Pinang!

d _____ saya ke Jalan Orchard.

e _____ tambangnya dari Singapura ke Kuala Lumpur?

f _____ penerbangannya?

g Jangan sampai _____ pesawat!

h _____ kita ke Kuantan.

 Quick vocab

pintu keluar   *exit*

Exercise 8

Over to you!

You (**A**) are a student called Daniel Johnson. You have gone to the travel agent (**B**) to book a flight to Melbourne.

 10.03

A	*I would like to book a seat to Melbourne. Economy class.*
B	Bila tarikhnya?
A	*Next week (on) 15 September. What's the fare?*
B	1,800.00 ringgit untuk tikét pulang-balik.
A	*How long is the flight to Melbourne from Kuala Lumpur?*
B	Lebih kurang 6 jam.
A	*Good. Please make a reservation for me under the name of Daniel Johnson. Can I have a window seat?*
B	Saya cuba.

 Quick vocab

duduk dekat tingkap   *a window seat*

Test yourself

1 Which word is usually used to talk about fares?
2 How would you say *May I have?* in Malay?
3 What should you do if you see a sign with **Dilarang** on it?
4 What does **lagi** mean with time expressions?
5 What is the difference in usage between **lagi** and **dalam masa?**
6 What does **se-** mean when added to a time word such as **hari?**
7 How do you express *when* to refer to both past and future events?
8 What is the most common way to express *to go by* some form of transport?
9 What prefix can also be used to express *to go by* some form of transport?
10 What does **yang mana** mean?

11 *Checking in*

In this unit you will learn how to:

▶ *get rooms in a hotel*
▶ *ask about services*
▶ *say what you usually do*

PART ONE

Dialogue

Stan and his family have arrived at Poring Hot Springs, a hot spring and health resort at Kota Kinabalu, Sabah. They have not made a reservation so Stan is trying to negotiate rooms for his family.

 11.01

Stan	Selamat tengah hari. Ada bilik kosong?
Pegawai	Tunggu sebentar…ya, ada. Berapa bilik?
Stan	Dua bilik. Satu katil twin dan satu katil kelamin untuk saya dan isteri.
Pegawai	Untuk berapa malam?
Stan	Saya masih belum tahu untuk berapa malam.
Pegawai	Baiklah, saya akan sediakan untuk satu malam dahulu.
Stan	Berapa harganya untuk satu malam?
Pegawai	Untuk harga sebilik RM250.00.
Stan	Dengan sarapan pagi sekalikah?
Pegawai	Ya, Encik.
Stan	Boléhkah anda berikan bilik penghubung supaya mudah kami mengawasi anak-anak. Boléh dapatkan bilik yang menghadap ke gunung?
Pegawai	Tentu boléh. Encik nak bayar dengan kad kredit atau tunai?
Stan	Kad kredit. Boléh kami tengok biliknya dahulu?
Pegawai	Boléh. Tolong isikan nama, alamat, nombor pasport dan tanda tangan pada borang ini, Encik.
Stan	Baik. Apakah kemudahan yang ada di sini?
Pegawai	Kolam renang dengan air panas yang dibuka 24 jam.
Stan	Bagus sekali. Kami sekeluarga suka berenang setiap minggu. Ada karaoké? Anak perempuan saya suka menyanyi.

Pegawai	Ya. Ada setiap malam. Selain itu, kami juga menyediakan bufét hidangan istiméwa masakan Sabah pada setiap malam Sabtu.
Stan	Apakah ada yang lain? Seperti urut? Setiap kali saya ke Kuala Lumpur, saya selalu pergi ke rumah urut.
Pegawai	Ada, Encik. Teléfon saja Concierge, dan meréka akan sediakan untuk Encik. Ini kunci bilik dan kupon untuk sarapan pagi dari pukul 8 sampai 10.30 pagi. Selamat beristirehat.

 Quick vocab

kosong	*empty*
bilik kosong	*vacancies*
katil twin	*twin bed*
katil kelamin	*queen-sized bed, double bed*
berapa malam?	*how many nights?*
sediakan	*to prepare*
dahulu	*at first*
sebilik	*for one room, per room*
sekali	*(here) too, inclusive*
penghubung (hubung v.**)**	*link*
bilik penghubung	*connecting rooms*
supaya	*so that*
mengawasi (awas n.**)**	*to keep an eye on*
menghadap (hadap v.**) ke**	*to look out onto*
téngok	*to take a look at*
isikan (isi n.**)**	*to fill in*
tanda tangan	*signature*
borang	*form, document*
kemudahan (mudah a.**)**	*amenity*
air panas	*hot water* (or specifically *hot spring*)
berenang (renang n.**)**	*to swim*
selain itu	*apart from that*
menyediakan (sedia a.**)**	*to prepare*
bufét	*buffet*
hidangan	*dish, i.e. food*
istiméwa	*special*
hidangan istiméwa	*(culinary) specialities*
masakan	*cookery, cuisine*
urut	*massage*
rumah urut	*massage parlour*
kupon	*coupon*
sarapan pagi	*breakfast*

Translation

Stan	Good afternoon. Are there (any) vacancies?
Employee	Wait a moment…yes, there are. How many rooms (do you want)?
Stan	Two. One twin bedroom and one double room for my wife and me.
Employee	For how many nights?
Stan	I don't know how many nights yet.
Employee	OK, I will prepare (it) for one night at first.
Stan	What's the rate for one night?
Employee	The cost per room is 250 ringgit.
Stan	(Is that) with breakfast?
Employee	Yes, Sir.
Stan	Could (we) have connecting rooms, so that we can watch over our children? Can you give (us) a view of the mountains?
Employee	Certainly. How would you like to pay, by credit card or cash?
Stan	Credit card. Can we take a look at the room beforehand?
Employee	Certainly. Please fill in (your) name, address, passport number and signature on this form, Sir.
Stan	OK. What amenities do you have here?
Employee	(We have) a swimming pool with a hot spring open 24 hours.
Stan	That's great. My family and I usually go swimming every Sunday. Do you have karaoke? My young daughter likes to sing.
Employee	Yes. (There is) every evening. Apart from that we can also put on a buffet of culinary specialities from Sabah every Saturday evening.
Stan	Is there anything else, like massage? Every time I (come) to Kuala Lumpur, I always go to a massage parlour.
Employee	Yes, there is. Just telephone the concierge, and they can arrange (it) for you. This is the room key and the coupon for breakfast from 8 to 10.30 a.m.. Have a nice stay.

How the language works 1

1 Did you notice the use of **beri(kan)** in this dialogue? Two more phrases you might find useful when making requests are **Apa boléh dapatkan?**, *May I have…?* and **Apa boléh beri?**, *May I have…?*

Apa boléh dapatkan **bilik yang**   *Can I have a room that looks out*
  menghadap ke kolam renang?   *onto the swimming pool?*

> ● **INSIGHT**
>
> Note also that **menghadap ke** is used to express *looks out onto* or *with a view of* in Malay.

2 Position of question words. In Units 1 to 10 you have been gradually introduced to all the question words you will need to know to function in everyday Malay. You will have noticed that some question words occur in various positions in the sentence, while others, namely **kenapa** and **mengapa**, must always occur as the first word in the sentence. **Apa** is also an exception, as you will see below.

Although it is quite possible to place the other question words first in the sentence, there is a rule governing where the question word should occur, if you want to mimic authentic Malay speech.

To find where the question word should be placed, you first need to think of the question as it would be if it were a statement that already has the answer to the question in it. For example, if you want to ask *where does she come from?* a possible answer could be *she comes from New York*, in Malay **Dia berasal dari New York**. The question word occupies the same position in the question as the thing it asks about in the corresponding statement. Therefore **dari mana** replaces **dari New York** giving you the completed question, **Dia berasal dari mana?**

> ● **INSIGHT**
>
> Remember, also, that Malay speakers like to add the suffix **kah** to make questions so the question may also be **Dia berasal dari New Yorkkah?** in Malay.

Look at the following questions:

Siapa **pergi ke London?**   **Who** *is going to London?*
Yati pergi ke *mana***?**   **Where** *is Yati going?*

The two questions above could both be based on the sentence **Yati pergi** *ke London*, *Yati is going to London*. The first question asks *who* so **siapa** replaces **Yati**. The second asks where **Yati** is going, so **ke mana** replaces **ke London**.

Exercise 1

Make four questions using the sentence below based upon the words in italics and numbered in each case:

Tahun lalu	Rosa	bercuti	dengan sepupunya	di Genting Highlands.
1	2		3	4

Possible complications arise with **apa** because, as you know from Unit 2, **apa** not only means *what?*, but it also functions as a question marker. As a question marker **apa** must occur at the begining of the sentence.

When you are using **apa** with the intended meaning of *what?* you need to follow the positioning rules above, otherwise what you say might be ambiguous. Look at the following examples in which **apa** has different functions:

Apa **anda minum?**	*Are you drinking?*
Anda minum *apa*?	*What are you drinking?*
Apa **kamu sedang makan?**	*Are you eating?*
Kamu sedang makan *apa*?	*What are you eating?*

Two question words that you learnt in Unit 6, **apa yang** and **siapa yang**, are always used at the beginning of the sentence and are exceptional to the rules of question word order. Many questions asking *what?* or *who(m)?* can be expressed both ways:

Dia kenal *siapa*?	*Who(m) does she know?*
Siapa **yang dia kenal?**	*Who(m) does she know?*

In addition, when **apa** + noun occurs, as in Unit 6, it is treated as a single unit and is not subject to the positioning rules.

Exercise 2

Translate the following pairs of questions, paying particular attention to how the different position of **apa** affects the meaning.

- **a** **i** Apa dia makan?
  - **ii** Dia makan apa?
- **b** **i** Apa nak pesan?
  - **ii** Nak pesan apa?
- **c** **i** Apa kamu baca?
  - **ii** Kamu baca apa?

Understanding Malay

Exercise 3

Using the dialogue, say whether the following sentences are true or false.

- **a** Hotél masih ada bilik yang kosong.
- **b** Harga hotél belum termasuk sarapan pagi.
- **c** Stan membayar dengan wang tunai.

   d Kolam renang air panas dibuka 24 jam.

   e Stan meminta bilik yang menghadap ke pantai.

   f Sarapan pagi bermula dari pukul 7 sampai pukul 10.30.

Exercise 4

Read and fill in the following form. Try to work out what the form is asking before checking with the vocabulary section below.

NAMA ....

ALAMAT ....

TARIKH LAHIR ....

TEMPAT LAHIR ....

UMUR ....

JANTINA ....

TARAF PERKAHWINAN ....

KEWARGANEGARAAN ....

AGAMA ....

PEKERJAAN ....

NOMBOR PASPORT ....

TUJUAN LAWATAN ....

TÉMPOH TINGGAL ....

TANDA TANGAN ....

 Quick vocab

tarikh lahir	*date of birth*
tempat lahir	*place of birth*
jantina	*sex*
lelaki	*male*
wanita	*female*
taraf perkahwinan	*marital status*
kewarganegaraan	*nationality*
belum berkahwin	*not married*
berkahwin	*married*
bercerai	*divorced*
janda	*widow*
duda	*widower*
tujuan lawatan	*reason for visit*
bisnés	*business*
bercuti	*holiday*
melancong	*sightseeing*
melawat keluarga	*visiting relatives*

belajar	*(here) studying*
dalam transit	*in transit, stop-over*
témpoh tinggal	*length of stay*
tanda tangan	*signature*

(The words above appear as you would use them on a form such as this.)

PART TWO

Dialogue

Serena and Tom check in to a hotel at which they have already booked rooms by telephone.

 11.02

Tom	Selamat tengah hari, kami mahu daftar masuk di atas nama Tom Black dan Serena Danker yang kami tempah kelmarin.
Pegawai	Tunggu sebentar. Biar saya semak di komputer. Betul sekali, dua bilik standard atas nama Encik Tom Black dan Cik Serena Danker.
Tom	Terima kasih. Di sini ada pusat kesihatan? Saya biasanya bersenam setiap tengah hari.
Pegawai	Ada, juga kolam renang, sauna dan mandi wap.
Tom	Menarik sekali. Saya biasanya bangun pukul 8 pagi. Kita boléh berenang, sauna dan bersarapan pagi.
Serena	Bagus rancangan kamu. Bagaimana pula pada waktu malam?
Pegawai	Di sini ada bar dan disko. Setiap minggu ada band dengan penyanyi undangan yang popular.
Tom	Di England, saya sudah biasa pergi ke bar pada setiap minggu.
Serena	Saya boléh agak, kamu tidak sabar nak ke sana.
Tom	*(laughing)* Macam mana dengan makanannya? Saya dah lapar ni.
Pegawai	Malam ini ada bufét masakan Melayu. Buka dari pukul 8 malam.
Tom	Terima kasih.
Pegawai	Ini kunci dan kupon sarapan pagi untuk ésok. Selamat istirehat.

 Quick vocab

daftar masuk	*to register, to check in*
di atas nama	*under the name(s) of*
tempah	*to book, to reserve*
semak	*to check*

bilik standard	*standard room*
pusat kesihatan	*fitness centre*
kesihatan (sihat *a.*)	*health*
biasanya	*usually*
bersenam	*to work out, to exercise*
sauna	*sauna*
mandi wap	*steam bath*
bersarapan pagi	*to have breakfast*
rancangan	*plan*
pada waktu malam	*in the evening, at night time*
penyanyi (nyanyi *v.*)	*singer*
undangan	*invitation*
penyanyi undangan	*guest singer*
agak	*to guess, to form an observation*
tidak sabar	*to be impatient to, can't wait to*
sabar	*patient*
macam mana dengan?	*what about?*
lapar	*hungry*

Translation

Tom	Good afternoon, we would like to check in under the names Tom Black and Serena Danker who booked yesterday.
Employee	Just a moment. I will check on the computer. That's right, two standard rooms under the names Tom Black and Serena Danker.
Serena	Thank you. Is there a fitness centre here? I usually work out every afternoon.
Employee	There is, there is also a swimming pool, sauna and steam bath.
Tom	Very interesting. I usually get up at eight o'clock. Then we can swim, have a sauna and have breakfast.
Serena	That's a good plan. What can we do in the evening?
Employee	Here there is a bar and disco. Every Sunday night there is a band with a popular guest singer.
Tom	In England I am used to going to the bar every Sunday.
Serena	I can tell. You can hardly wait to get there.
Tom	(*laughing*) What about the food? I'm really hungry.
Employee	Tonight there is a Malay buffet. It's open from eight o'clock in the evening.
Tom	Thank you.
Employee	Here is the key and these are the breakfast coupons for tomorrow. Have a nice stay.

How the language works 2

1 In this unit you have met **biasanya** which means *usually*. The base word **biasa**, either on its own or as a set expression with **sudah** are both used to mean *used to* or *to be accustomed to*.

Saya biasa berbahasa Malaysia *I am used to speaking Malay*
  dengan teman-teman. *with friends.*
Adik Mary sudah biasa *Mary's little brother is already*
  mengguna komputer. *used to using a computer.*

When **biasa** and **sudah biasa** are used with verbs, as above, they can be used just as they are. When they are used with a noun, **dengan** must be inserted:

Dia belum biasa *dengan* **cuaca** *He is not yet used to the hot*
  panas di Malaysia. *weather in Malaysia.*

 Quick vocab

cuaca *weather*

Remember that where *used to* has a different meaning, pertaining to something that was happening in the past but has now stopped or changed, such as in the sentence *We used to live here*, either the tense marker **dulu** or **dahulu** must be used.

Dahulu kami tinggal di sini. *We used to live here.*

2 The combination of the prefix **ke-** and the suffix **-an**, when applied to an adjective base, produces a certain type of noun:

baik *good*   **ke-baik-an = kebaikan** *goodness*
indah *beautiful* **ke-indah-an = keindahan** *beauty*
sulit *difficult*   **ke-sulit-an = kesulitan** *difficulty*

> ● **INSIGHT**
> This usage creates what is known as an abstract noun, that is, a noun for something that cannot be seen, or which describes a quality.

Exercise 5

Form abstract nouns from the following adjectives with **ke- -an** and in each case state what you think the noun you created means.

  a **sihat** *healthy*
  b **aman** *safe*
  c **bersih** *clean*
  d **mudah** *easy*
  e **buruk** *ugly*
  f **nyaman** *pleasant*
  g **bodoh** *stupid*
  h **senang** *happy*

Ke- prefix combined with **-an** suffix is used to create certain nouns from verbs:

datang *to come*	**kedatangan** *arrival*
pulang *to return home*	**kepulangan** *return*

Ke- -an with a noun base produces a new noun which often extends the meaning of the base noun, but the resulting meaning is not always as easy to deduce as with the adjective bases. They can often refer to places or institutions. Study the following:

hidup *life*	**kehidupan** *way of life*
bangsa *nation*	**kebangsaan** *nationality*
menteri *minister*	**kementerian** *ministry*
duta *ambassador*	**kedutaan** *embassy*

Using Malay

Exercise 6

Use the sentences below to make a question, replacing the words in bold in each case.

   a Meréka akan berangkat ke England **pada hari Selasa**.
   b Yanti pergi **ke panggung wayang** dengan Siti.
   c Pertunjukan Ramayana mula **pukul lapan**.
   d Penerbangan dari Jakarta ke Kuala Lumpur **kira-kira 2 jam**.
   e **Minggu depan** meréka akan pergi bercuti ke Pulau Redang.
   f Orang tuanya sudah datang **dari luar negeri**.
   g Kita boléh pergi **dengan bas** ke pusat bandar.
   h Bas Kuala Lumpur – Johor Bahru ada **2 kali** sehari.

 Quick vocab

pertunjukan (tunjuk *v.***)**	*performance*

Exercise 7

Over to you!

You are booking a room…

 11.03

A	Selamat tengah hari, Encik. Boléh saya bantu?
B	*Yes, I would like to stay here for a couple of days. Are there still vacancies?*
A	Masih ada.
B	*How much for one night?*
A	RM 250.00
B	*Is breakfast included?*
A	Ya. Encik cadang tinggal sehingga bila?

B	*Until 10 December. Can I pay with another currency apart from US dollars?*
A	Boléh. Maaf, boléh saya lihat pasport encik?
B	*Sure. Just a moment.*
A	Sila isikan borang ini dan bubuh tanda tangan di sebelah kanan.
B	*Is there a sauna here?*
A	Ada juga kolam renang di tingkat tiga. Di sebelahnya ada pusat kesihatan.
B	*What time is it open?*
A	Pukul 9.00 pagi sehingga 8.30 malam.
B	*Thank you.*
A	Selamat istiréhat. Ini kunci bilik dan kupon untuk sarapan pagi.

 **Quick vocab**

cadang	*to suggest*
bubuh	*to place, put*

? Test yourself

1 How would you make a polite request in Malay?

2 What does **menghadap ke** mean?

3 How do you work out the correct position of a question word within a sentence?

4 Which question word do you need to be particularly careful with in order to avoid ambiguity?

5 What suffix do Malays often add to sentences to make questions?

6 How would you express *to be accustomed to* in Malay?

7 What do you need to add to **biasa** when a noun follows it?

8 What effect do the prefix **ke-** and suffix **-an** have on adjectives?

9 What effect does **ke- -an** have on certain verbs?

10 What effect does **ke- -an** have when applied to a noun?

Bargain hunting

In this unit you will learn how to:
▶ *go shopping for clothes*
▶ *talk about sizes, colours and what things are made of*
▶ *barter with a street seller*

PART ONE

Dialogue

Sue-Ann is shopping for clothes with her two children.

 12.01

Puan Sue-Ann	Saya mahu belikan keméja batik untuk suami saya. Apakah ada ukuran paling besar, warna biru?
Pelayan	Sebentar saya cari…Maaf, Puan, warna biru sudah habis dijual. Tinggal warna kelabu dan warna biru ukuran S.
Puan Sue-Ann	Itu terlalu kecil untuk suami saya. Dia tak suka warna kelabu. Ada warna lain?
Pelayan	Ya tetapi kainnya berbéza.
Puan Sue-Ann	Mengapa ini lébih murah daripada yang tadi?
Pelayan	Oh, yang itu batik asli dan ini batik cap.
Puan Sue-Ann	Hmm, saya lébih suka yang itu. Sayang, tidak ada warna biru!
Calvin	Ma…saya suka seluar batik itu. Ia nampak selésa dan coraknya unik.
Puan Sue-Ann	Ia dibuat daripada kain kapas. Apa saizmu?
Calvin	Ma, sebesar itu saja.
Puan Sue-Ann	Seluar itu mémang sesuai untuk kamu. Silvia, kamu mahu apa?
Sylvia	Aku mahu baju berwarna mérah itu.
Puan Sue-Ann	Terlalu séksi untukmu. Pilih yang lain saja!
Pelayan	Ini bilnya. Sila bayar di kasyer.
Puan Sue-Ann	Terima kasih.
Pelayan	Ada diskaun 15 peratus untuk seluar panjang ni. Jumlahnya RM350.00. Ini baki wangnya.

V Quick vocab

belikan (beli *v.***)**	*to buy (something for someone)*
keméja	*shirt*
batik	*batik*
ukuran	*size*
paling besar	*the biggest*
biru	*blue*
habis	*(here) completely*
dijual	*to be sold*
habis dijual	*sold out*
tinggal	*there remains*
kelabu	*grey*
terlalu	*too*
kain	*cloth, material*
berbéza	*different*
lébih murah	*cheaper*
daripada	*(here) than*
tadi	*the last one, the one before*
asli	*original*
cap	*printed*
lébih suka	*prefer*
sayang!	*it's a pity!*
seluar	*trousers*
nampak	*to seem, to look*
corak	*pattern, design*
dibuat daripada	*to be made from*
kapas	*cotton*
saiz	*size*
sesuai	*to suit (someone)*
aku	*I (informal)*
baju	*dress*
baju berwarna mérah	*a red-coloured dress*
séksi	*sexy*
pilih	*to choose*
bil	*bill*
kasyer	*cashier*
diskaun	*discount*
peratus	*per cent*
seluar panjang	*(long) trousers*
baki wangnya	*change*

Translation

Sue-Ann	I want to buy a batik shirt for my husband. Do you have the biggest size in blue?
Shop assistant	Just a moment, I'll look… I'm sorry, madam, the blue ones have all been sold. There are only grey and blue in small left.
Sue-Ann	It is too small for my husband. He doesn't like grey. Are there other colours?
Shop assistant	Yes, but the material is different.
Sue-Ann	Why are these cheaper than the last ones?
Shop assistant	Oh, those are genuine batik and these are printed batik.
Sue-Ann	Hmm, I prefer those. What a shame you don't have them in blue!
Calvin	Mum, I like those batik trousers. They look comfortable and the pattern is great.
Sue-Ann	They are made of cotton. What's your size?
Calvin	Medium, the same size as those (trousers).
Sue-Ann	Those trousers really suit you. Silvia, what do you want?
Silvia	I want that red dress.
Sue-Ann	It's too sexy for you. Choose a different one!
Shop assistant	Here is your bill. Please pay at the cashier.
Sue-Ann	Thank you.
Shop assistant	There is a 15 per cent discount on these trousers. All together that comes to RM350.00. Here is your change.

> **● INSIGHT**
>
> Batik work is Malaysia's most popular traditional craft, even though it originated in Indonesia. The name is derived from the Javanese verb **tik** *to drip*. Malay formal dress for both men and women is made from batik cloth, and out of interest, batik is compulsory dress for entry into Malaysia's only casino!

How the language works 1

1 Terlalu, which you have already met briefly in Unit 11, is one way of saying *too* in Malay. It is used in the same way we use *too* in English.

terlalu besar	*too big*
terlalu kecil	*too small*
terlalu ketat	*too tight*

In addition to **terlalu** certain nouns can also be modified to mean *too* by placing the adjective between the prefix **ke-** and the suffix **-an**. Here are some you may find useful when shopping.

kelonggaran	*too loose*
kemérahan	*too red*
kelembutan	*too soft*
kepéndekan	*too short*
kepanjangan	*too long*

For example:

Pipi Evon nampak kemérahan **di bawah cahaya lampu.**	*Evon's cheeks look too red under the light.*
Kepéndekan **skirt membuat Suzi kelihatan séksi.**	*Too short a skirt makes Suzi look sexy.*
Kepanjangan **tali léhérnya tidak sesudi dengan bajunya.**	*His tie is too long for his shirt.*

 Quick vocab

longgar	*loose*
cahaya	*light*
tali léhér	*tie*
sesudi	*shirt*

Exercise 1

Make *too* expressions using **ke- -an** with these adjectives, then translate them.

- **a** dingin
- **b** panas
- **c** sakit
- **d** pahit
- **e** lapar
- **f** tinggi

 Quick vocab

dingin	*cold*
sakit	*sick*
pahit	*bitter*
lapar	*hungry*

2 Making comparisons. When you wish to compare the qualities of one thing with another, i.e. when you want to say something is *more…than* something else, use **lebih** before the adjective or adverb.

lebih **mahal**	*more expensive*
lebih **murah**	*more cheap (or cheaper)*
Pakaian itu lebih mahal di Amérika.	*These clothes are more expensive in America.*

To express *than* as in *more…than* **daripada** is used:

lebih **mahal** *daripada*	**more** *expensive* **than**
lebih **murah** *daripada*	**more** *cheap* **than** (*or* **cheaper than**)
Batik di Kelantan *lebih* **murah** *daripada* **di Kuala Lumpur.**	*Batik in Kelantan is* **cheaper than** *in Kuala Lumpur.*
Dia datang *lebih* **sering** *daripada* **sebelumnya.**	*He comes* **more often than** *before.*

Exercise 2

Add the missing words to the Malay sentences so that the meaning corresponds to the ones in English.

a Amir goes to the cinema more often than Kamal.

Amir pergi ke panggung wayang _____ kerap _____ Kamal.

b She is more diligent than her brother.

Dia _____ rajin _____ abangnya.

c This house is bigger than that house.

Rumah ini _____ besar _____ rumah itu.

Quick vocab

kerap   *frequent*

One way to express *the most…* or the *…-est*, as in *the biggest*, is formed by placing **paling** before the adjective instead of **lebih**.

Compare:

besar *big*	*lebih* **besar** *bigger*	*paling* **besar** *biggest*
énak *tasty*	*lebih* **énak** *tastier*	*paling* **énak** *tastiest*

Exercise 3

How do you form the following in Malay?

a better
b the cheapest
c the most difficult
d prettier
e more crowded
f spicier
g thirstiest
h hotter
i dirtier
j the smallest

Adding **paling** to an adjective is not the only way to express *the most…* in Malay. The alternative form you need to be aware of is formed with the prefix **ter-** which is applied to the adjective to form exactly the same meaning as **paling**.

baik	*good*	**ter-baik**	**terbaik**	*the best*
besar	*big*	**ter-besar**	**terbesar**	*the biggest*
bodoh	*stupid*	**ter-bodoh**	**terbodoh**	*the most stupid*

3 To say what something is made of, **dibuat daripada** is used in Malay.

Cincin ini dibuat daripada pérak.	*This ring is made of silver.*
Kuih ini dibuat daripada tepung beras.	*This cake is made from rice flour.*
Jakét saya dibuat daripada kulit.	*My jacket is leather.*

 Quick vocab

cincin	*ring*
pérak	*silver*
tepung beras	*rice flour*
kulit	*leather*

Exercise 4

Can you form the following sentences in Malay?

- **a** That statue is made of marble.
- **b** This vase is made of clay.
- **c** This ball is made of rubber.

 Quick vocab

patung	*statue*
batu marmar	*marble*
pasu	*vase*
tanah liat	*clay*
bola	*ball*
getah	*rubber*

The last personal pronoun we shall be looking at in this course is **aku**, an informal word for *I* which Sylvia and Calvin use in the dialogue. It is highly informal and should only be used between family members or with those with whom you are on very familiar terms (i.e. good friends) and with whom you share equal social standing. It would be highly inappropriate to use this when talking to a stranger. In fact, it might be taken as a sign of arrogance or lack of respect for someone if you use it inappropriately. You may hear it used, so you need to know what it means, but the best advice for a foreigner is: if in doubt, use **saya!**

It can also be used as a possessive pronoun whereby it is added to the noun in question as a suffix, like **-mu** in Unit 5. Before it is added to the noun, the **a** drops, leaving you with **-ku** which means *my*.

rumahku   *my house*

keretaku   *my car*

5 There are two ways to express *to wear* in Malay. One way employs the verb **pakai** (or less colloquially *memakai*) which means *to use* as well as *to wear*.

Gadis itu memakai pakaian tradisional.   *That girl is wearing a traditional dress.*

Saya biasa pakai sarung di rumah.   *I'm used to wearing a sarong at home.*

The second way uses the **ber-** prefix to create a verb from the item of clothing being worn. In just the same way as the noun becomes the base for the transport words in Unit 10 (Part Two), the item of clothing becomes the base in this instance:

baju   *dress*

berbaju   *to wear a dress*

kebaya   *kebaya*

berkebaya sutera   *to wear a silk kebaya*

> **● INSIGHT**
>
> A **kebaya** is a long-sleeved Malay traditional outfit for women that is fastened on the front by a set of brooches known as **kerongsang** and worn with a batik or matching cloth (skirt).

Exercise 5

Select words from the clothes vocabulary section below to help you translate the following into Malay.

- **a** to wear a tie
- **b** to wear gloves
- **c** to wear a skirt
- **d** to wear a raincoat
- **e** to wear black trousers
- **f** to wear sunglasses
- **g** to wear a rattan hat

 Quick vocab

tali léhér   *tie*

sarung tangan   *glove(s)*

skirt   *skirt*

baju hujan   *raincoat*

seluar péndek   *short trousers*

topi   *hat*

jakét   *jacket*

blaus	*blouse*
jas	*suit*
sarung kaki, stoking	*sock(s), stocking(s)*
kasut	*shoe(s)*
sepasang	*a pair (of)*
tali pinggang	*belt*
gelang tangan	*bracelet*
kalung	*necklace*

6 Colours

 Quick vocab

mérah	*red*
putih	*white*
hitam	*black*
hijau	*green*
kuning	*yellow*
biru	*blue*
ungu	*purple*
jingga	*orange*
mérah manggis	*maroon*
mérah jambu	*pink*
pérang	*brown*
kelabu	*grey*

Colours can be made light or dark by adding **muda** and **tua** respectively:

biru muda	*light blue*	**hijau muda**	*light green*
pérang tua	*dark brown*	**mérah tua**	*dark red*

> ● **INSIGHT**
> This is a figurative use of **muda** and **tua**, which you already know mean *young* and *old*, respectively.

7 To express *to suit* (someone or something) Malay uses **sesuai untuk**:

Keméja itu sesuai sekali untuk adikmu.   *That shirt really suits your brother.*

Note that the Malay version requires **untuk** *for*. Such words are known as prepositions. Although prepositions are basically location words – *on*, *in*, *around*, etc. – they often occur as an integral part of certain set phrases. In some cases a preposition may be required in one language but not in the other to express a similar concept, as with **sesuai untuk** above, and sometimes the preposition is different in each language. For example, in English we say *we spend money on something*, but the Malay equivalent uses **untuk** **menghabiskan wang untuk**.

Kamu betul-betul menghabiskan   *Did you really spend all your*
  semua wangmu untuk pakaian?   *money on clothes?*

Quick vocab

betul-betul   *really*
menghabiskan (habis *a.***)**   *to spend (money or time)*

The prefix **ter-** used with verbs can sometimes create a form that is similar to a past participle in English. The past participle is the form that you can place after *to be* to indicate that something has happened, for example *I am **lost**.* The emphasis in using the **ter-** verbs in Malay is on the state of completeness of an action. Treat them like adjectives.

terkenal   *famous*
tersedia   *available*
tertarik   *interested*

Some **ter-** prefixed verbs can also imply an accidental occurrence or a misfortune.

terpaksa   *forced (to), obliged (to)*
tersesat   *lost*
terjebak   *stuck*

 Quick vocab

paksa   *force*
jebak   *trap*

Understanding Malay

Exercise 6

Read or listen to the dialogue again and answer the following true/false questions.

   a Sue-Ann ingin membelikan seluar batik untuk suaminya.
   b Sue-Ann mencari ukuran paling besar, warna kelabu.
   c Silvia membeli baju warna mérah yang séksi.
   d Batik asli harganya lebih mahal daripada harga batik cap.
   e Calvin memilih seluar batik yang selésa dan unik.
   f Pelayan memberi diskaun 15 peratus untuk semua belian.

 Quick vocab

membelikan (beli *v.***)**   *to buy (something) for (someone)*
memilih (pilih *v.***)**   *to choose*
memberi (beri *v.***)**   *to give*

Exercise 7

Label the pictures using the clothes vocabulary in Exercise 5.

PART TWO

Dialogue

Serena has taken Tom to a traditional market so he can look for presents to take back to England.

 12.02

Tom	Saya nak cari hadiah untuk teman dan keluarga saya. Rantai léhér ini cantik sekali. Dibuat daripada apa?
Jurujual	Ini daripada pérak.
Tom	Berapa harganya?
Jurujual	RM80.00.
Serena	Kamu boléh tawar. Ini bukan harga tetap.
Tom	Boléh kurangkan harganya? RM60.00?
Jurujual	Tidak boléh, Encik. Saya rugi.
Serena	RM70.00 sajalah kalau boléh.
Jurujual	Baiklah. Rugi sedikit tak apa asalkan Encik datang lagi bila-bila masa. Mahu beli berapa utas?
Tom	Saya nak beli tiga utas.
Serena	Tom, kenapa tak beli yang ini saja? Ia lebih berkilat.
Tom	Tak apalah. Cuma untuk hadiah.

Jurujual	Yang itu lebih mahal kerana ia pérak asli dan buatan tangan.
Tom	Apa ini?
Serena	Itu kain sarung. Kamu boléh pakai di rumah sebagai ganti seluar. Itu biasa di sini.
Tom	Saya nak beli satu.
Jurujual	Saya juga ada kipas batik. Boléh digunakan untuk hiasan dinding.
Tom	Ya, tapi saiznya besar sekali dan berat. Lain kali saja, terima kasih.

 Quick vocab

rantai léhér	*necklace*
dibuat (buat v.**) daripada**	*to be made of*
pérak	*silver*
tawar	*to bargain*
tetap	*invariable*
harga tetap	*fixed price*
kurangkan (kurang a.**)**	*to reduce*
rugi	*loss, lack of profit, to lose out*
asalkan	*as long as, provided that*
bila-bila masa	*anytime*
Berapa utas?	*(here) How many?*
tiga utas	*(here) three (of them)*
berkilat (kilat n.**)**	*to shine, to glimmer*
tak apalah	*it doesn't matter*
buatan tangan	*hand made*
kain sarung	*sarong*
sebagai ganti	*instead of*
biasa	*usual*
kipas	*fan*
digunakan (guna v.**)**	*to be used*
hiasan	*decoration*
dinding	*wall*
lain kali	*another time*

●INSIGHT

Utas has a special meaning that will be discussed in Unit 14. However, if you need to know what it means now, it is a counting word that refers to long, bendable objects.

Translation

Tom	I want to look for some presents for my friends and family. This necklace is very beautiful. What's it made of?
Seller	Silver.
Tom	How much is it?
Seller	RM80.00.
Serena	You can bargain. The price isn't fixed.
Tom	Can you lower the price? RM60.00?
Seller	I can't. I'll make a loss.
Serena	Just RM70.00. If you can.
Seller	OK. I'll make a small loss, as long as you come again sometimes. How many do you want?
Tom	I want three.
Serena	Tom, why did you buy those? This one's more shiny.
Tom	It's OK. (They're) just for presents.
Seller	Those are more expensive because they are made from real silver and they are hand made.
Tom	What's this?
Serena	That's a sarong. You can wear it at home instead of trousers. It's usual here.
Tom	I want to buy one.
Seller	I also have a batik fan. You can use it as a wall decoration.
Tom	Yes, but it's too big and heavy. Another time, maybe, thank you.

How the language works 2

1 Comparisons of equality. Malay has two ways of saying something is *as…as* something else, for example, *She is as rich as her brother*.

▶ Add **se-** to the adjective that describes the quality you are comparing:

kaya rich
Dia sekaya abangnya.
mahal expensive
Kalung ini semahal gelang itu.

se-kaya → sekaya *as rich as*
She is as rich as her brother.
se-mahal → semahal *as expensive as*
This necklace is as expensive as that bracelet.

Exercise 8

Form these comparisons in Malay.

    a as cheap as
    b as heavy as
    c as shy as

▶ Use the construction **sama** + adjective **dengan**:

kaya *rich*	*sama* **kaya** *dengan as rich as*
Dia *sama* **kaya dengan abangnya.**	*She is as rich as her brother.*
mahal *expensive*	*sama* **mahal** *dengan as expensive as*
Kalung ini *sama* **mahal** *dengan* **gelang itu.**	*This necklace is as expensive as that bracelet.*

> ● **INSIGHT**
>
> **Sama dengan** on its own means *the same as*. So you can say, for example: **Rumah dia sama dengan rumah kita**, *His house is the same as our house*.

Exercise 9

Check you can form the following using the construction **sama** + adjective **dengan**:

   a as poor as
   b as bald as
   c as stylish as

 Quick vocab

gelang	*bracelet*
botak	*bald*
bergaya	*stylish*

Sama *dengan* in Malay means *the same as* in English. As you know **dengan** means *with* so Malay speakers think of it as *the same with*. The word **dengan** features in several very common expressions where we use other prepositions, or no preposition, in English. It is worth learning the following list now, noting the difference between the two languages.

sama dengan	*the same as*
berbéza dengan	*different to*
penuh dengan	*full of*
kahwin dengan	*to get married to*
dengan teléfon	*by phone*
dengan keréta	*by car*
dengan bas	*by bus*
berbual dengan	*to chat to*
bercakap dengan	*to talk to*
bertanya dengan	*to ask*
kenal dengan	*to know*
berteman dengan	*to be friends with*

Examples:

Saya akan menghubungi dia dengan teléfon.	*I'm going to contact her by phone.*
Bilik itu penuh dengan asap rokok.	*That room is full of smoke.*

Meskipun harganya sama, kualiti beg
  ini berbéza dengan beg itu.

Although the price is the same, the quality of
  this bag is different to that bag.

 Quick vocab

menghubungi (hubung v.**)**	*to contact*
asap rokok	*(cigarette) smoke*
meskipun	*although*
kualiti	*quality*

2 Me- prefix with **-kan** suffix. Some base words carry the prefix **me-** coupled with the suffix **-kan**. In many cases this combination is simply needed to create a verb from a noun base with no particular distinct meaning.

For example:

me*rencana***kan** *to make plans* (from **rencana**, *plans*)
meng*gambar***kan** *to portray* (from **gambar**, *picture*)

When **me- -kan** is applied to certain adjectives, the result is a verb in Malay that corresponds to an *-ing* adjective in English.

For example:

me*letih***kan** *tiring* (formed from the adjective base **letih** meaning *tired*)

> ● **INSIGHT**
>
> As **me- -kan** often creates a verb that indicates that something has been caused to be in a certain state, the thinking is – it makes me (or someone else) tired, so it is *tiring*.

Exercise 10

Can you work out what the following **me- -kan** verbs are in English, by looking at the base adjectives on the left?

a	**malu** *embarrassed*	**memalukan**
b	**senang** *pleased*	**menyenangkan**
c	**puas** *satisfied*	**memuaskan**
d	**cemas** *worried*	**mencemaskan**
e	**bosan** *bored*	**membosankan**
f	**takut** *frightened*	**menakutkan**

When **me- -kan** is applied to a verb base, a new verb is created that can have one of two basic meanings according to context:

▶ The first is a type of verb that we do not have in English. This type of verb stresses that the action is performed for the benefit of someone or something else, which is why it is known as a benefactive verb. You can see an example of such a verb in the dialogue in Part One – **membelikan** (colloquially **belikan** – remember that the **me-** prefix is often dropped in real speech), *to buy something for someone.*

Saya memberikan dia bunga.   *I gave her a flower.*

As benefactive verbs automatically carry the meaning of doing something for someone, **untuk**, *for*, is not required. However, it is not incorrect to use **untuk** with these verbs, and many Malay speakers do!

Saya mahu membelikan   *I want to buy something for*
  sesuatu untuk teman.   *a friend.*

▶ **me- -kan** creates a new verb from certain verb bases that changes the focus of the action from something that you do yourself into a related verb. You will notice that these base verbs are specifically those which have no receiver of the action. Therefore **me- -kan** creates a related verb that allows you to do that action to something or someone else.

In English, too, we have verbs that perform both functions. You can say *I returned* or you can use the same verb in a different way with a receiver of the action and say *I returned the book to the library.* Although the form of such verbs is often the same in English, Malay needs to create a further verb around the original verb as a base with **me- -kan**.

Take the above example with **kembali**, *return*. You can say:

Saya kembali.   *I returned.*

To make the other form, **me-** and **-kan** are added to the base word **kembali** creating **mengembalikan** (sound change rules will be covered later in the course). The new verb means *to return (something).*

Saya mengembalikan buku   *I returned the book to the public library.*
  itu ke perpustakaan umum.
Dia sudah mengeluarkan sampah.   *She's already put the rubbish (trash) out.*

> **● INSIGHT**
> **Mengeluarkan** *to put something out* comes from the verb **keluar** *to go out.*

 Quick vocab

perpustakaan	*library*
sampah	*rubbish, trash*
umum	*public*

Using Malay

Exercise 11

Answer these questions using the corresponding pictures as a guide.

a Yang mana lebih tinggi, zirafah atau kuda?

b Yang mana lebih laju, kapal terbang atau keréta api?

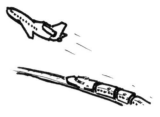

c Siapa yang lebih muda, Ben atau Haris?

d Yang mana lebih luas, Pulau Sumatera atau Pulau Kalimantan?

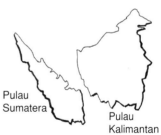

e Negara yang mana lebih panas, Malaysia atau Saudi Arabia?

Quick vocab

zirafah	*giraffe*
luas	*large, broad*

Exercise 12

This exercise takes the form of a short general knowledge quiz to test your geography as well as your Malay! See if you can answer the questions.

    a Negara mana yang paling luas di dunia?

    b Benua mana yang paling besar di dunia?

    c Negara mana yang paling padat penduduknya di dunia?

    d Sungai mana yang paling panjang di dunia?

    e Gunung mana yang paling tinggi di Sabah?

 Quick vocab

benua	*continent*
padat	*dense*
padat penduduknya	*densely populated*
sungai	*river*

Exercise 13

Choose suitable phrases to complete the Malay sentences so that they mean the same as the English ones.

    a Pantai Port Dickson di Negeri Sembilan _____ pelancong setiap hari.
       The Port Dickson beach is full of tourists every day.

    b Minggu depan Ranee akan _____ usahawan muda di Hotél Hilton.
       Next week Ranee will get married to a young businessman at the Hilton Hotel.

    c Saya melihat dia sedang _____ bosnya di pejabat.
       I see her talking to her boss in the office.

    d Gaya jalannya _____ ibunya.
       The way she walks is the same as her mother.

    e Kerana jalannya berbatu, kami harus pergi _____ .
       Because of the stone road we have to go by jeep.

    f Dia _____ saya bagaimana menyediakan nasi lemak.
       She asked me how to make nasi lemak.

    g Apakah kamu _____ jiran baru itu?
       Do you know that new neighbour?

    h Saya _____ nasi goréng untuk sarapan pagi.
       I am used to fried rice for breakfast.

    i Dia suka muzik klasik semenjak _____ Sharifah.
       She likes classical music since she has become friends with Sharifah.

Quick vocab

bos	*boss*
gaya jalannya	*way of walking, gait*
gaya	*style*
berbatu (batu *n.***)**	*stone*
nasi lemak	*coconut milk rice*
jiran	*neighbour*
klasik	*classical*
nasi goréng	*fried rice*
semenjak	*since*

> **● INSIGHT**
>
> **Jiran** refers to a specific neighbour. The phrase **jiran tetangga** refers to neighbours in general, i.e. *the neighbourhood*.

Exercise 14

Look at the pictures. Complete the sentences that refer to each one and answer all the questions in each section.

a Saya mahu membeli …
Dibuat daripada apa …
itu? …

Topi RM50.00

b Saya mahu membeli …
Berapa harganya? …
Apa saiznya? …

Batik, 60–70 cm
(M) RM120.00

c Saya mencari …
Dibuat daripada apa? …

Perak, RM90.00

d Saya mahu mencari …
Berapa harganya?…
Dibuat daripada apa?…

Patung kulit,
RM75.00

Exercise 15

Over to you!

You (**A**) are shopping for a present for your elder brother. You approach the sales assistant (**B**) for help.

 12.03

A	*I want to buy something for my elder brother.*
B	Di sini ada topi, tali léhér dan keméja.
A	*What's this tie made of?*
B	Daripada batik sutera.
A	*How much is it?*
B	80 ringgit.
A	*Is the price fixed?*
B	Ya. Tetapi ada diskaun 10%.
A	*OK. I'll take two which have different designs.*

 Quick vocab

yang coraknya berbéza   *which have different designs*

? Test yourself

1 What are the two ways to say *too* (*big*, etc.) in Malay?

2 How would you express *more…than* in Malay?

3 How would you express *the most…* or *the …-est*?

4 What does **dibuat daripada** mean?

5 What happens to **aku** when added to a noun to show possession?

6 What are the two ways to express *to wear* in Malay?

7 What prefix often expresses an accidental occurrence?

8 In which two ways does Malay form comparisons of equality?

9 What effect do the prefix **me-** and suffix **-kan** have on certain adjectives?

10 What is a benefactive verb, and how do you form one?

13 Eating out

In this unit you will learn how to:

▶ *understand a menu in Malay*
▶ *order food in restaurants and from street vendors*

PART ONE

Dialogue

Stan and his family are having dinner at a restaurant in Putrajaya.

 13.01

Pelayan	Selamat petang, méja untuk berapa orang, Encik?
Stan	Untuk empat orang.
Pelayan	Silakan. Ini menu makanan. Mahu pesan apa?
Puan Sue-Ann	Saya mahu pesan mi goréng, rojak buah, sayur campur, saté kambing, ayam percik.
Stan	Tolong jangan bubuh sos kacang. Saya alergi bila makan kacang.
Pelayan	Baiklah. Rojak buahnya untuk berapa orang?
Puan Sue-Ann	Satu orang saja. Hm…berapa banyak untuk satu orang?
Pelayan	Cukup untuk dimakan dua orang. Ada lagi yang mahu dipesan?
Stan	Apakah hidangan istimewa di sini? Boléh anda cadangkan?
Pelayan	Ya…ikan bakar dengan sos pelam.
Stan	Pedaskah?
Pelayan	Kami boléh sediakan yang tidak pedas. Mahu pesan minuman apa?
Silvia	Saya mahu air kelapa muda sejuk.
Calvin	Apakah ada ais batu campur?
Pelayan	Maaf tak ada, tapi kami ada ais kacang.
Calvin	Saya nak cuba.
Stan	Untuk saya, segelas air suam, dan aiskrim sebagai pencuci mulut.
Puan Sue-Ann	Berapa lama makanan itu akan siap?

Pelayan	Kira-kira 15–20 minit.
Stan	Baiklah. Terima kasih.
...	
Pelayan	Maaf agak terlambat, kami sangat sibuk setiap malam minggu.
Puan Sue-Ann	Mi goréngnya sedap sekali, tapi saténya agak mentah.
Stan	Boléh tambah lagi segelas air. Saya betul-betul haus.
...	
Stan	Boléh berikan bilnya?
Pelayan	Ini bilnya.

 Quick vocab

menu makanan	*menu*
pesan	*to order*
mahu peasan apa?	*what would you like to order?*
mi goréng	*fried noodles*
rojak buah	*fruit salad*
sayur	*vegetables*
campur	*mix*
saté kambing	*goat satay*
kambing	*goat*
ayam	*chicken*
ayam percik	*roast chicken in spicy sauce*
sos	*sauce*
kacang	*peanut*
alergi	*allergic*
dimakan (makan v.)	*to be eaten*
dipesan (pesan v.)	*to be ordered*
cadangkan (cadang v.)	*to recommend, to suggest*
bakar	*to grill, grilled*
sos pelam	*plum sauce*
pedas	*hot, spicy*

> ● **INSIGHT**
>
> Be careful with **pedas**. It means *hot* as in *spicy*, whereas **panas** means *hot to the touch*, and they can easily be confused when talking about food.

 Quick vocab

kelapa	*coconut*
kelapa muda	*young coconut*
air kelapa muda	*young coconut drink (served whole with the top of the coconut sliced off)*

sejuk	*chilled*
ais batu campur	*shaved ice with red beans, jelly cubes, corn and topped with brown and red syrup and condensed milk*
ais	*ice*
batu	*stone*
ais batu	*ice cube*
ais kacang	*red beans with coconut milk and ice*
segelas	*a glass*
suam	*lukewarm*
ais krim	*ice cream*
sebagai	*as*
pencuci mulut	*dessert (literally: something to clean the palate)*
pencuci (cuci *v.***)**	*someone or something that washes*
mulut	*mouth*
siap	*ready*
kira-kira	*about*
sedap	*delicious*
mentah	*raw, undercooked*
tambah lagi	*to order some more*
betul-betul	*really, truly*
haus	*thirsty*
berikan (beri *v.***)**	*to bring (someone) (something)*
bil	*bill, check (US)*

> **● INSIGHT**
>
> **Ais batu campur** is a very popular dessert in Malaysia. Interestingly, you can order it as an **ABC**, pronounced just as we say these letters of the alphabet in English.

Translation

Waiter	Good evening, (a table) for how many, sir?
Stan	(for) Four people.
Waiter	Please. Here's the menu. What would you like to order?
Sue-Ann	I would like (to order) fried noodles, fruit salad, mixed vegetables, goat satay, spicy chicken.
Stan	Please don't put on peanut sauce. I am allergic to peanuts.
Waiter	All right. Fruit salad for how many people?
Sue-Ann	Just one person. Hmm…how much (food) for one person?
Waiter	It's enough for (to be eaten by) two people. What else would you like to order?
Stan	What's the speciality here? Can you suggest (something)?

Waiter	Yes…grilled fish with plum sauce.
Stan	(Is it) spicy?
Waiter	We can make it not spicy (mild) for you. What would you like to drink?
Silvia	I'd like young coconut drink.
Calvin	Do you have *ais batu campur*?
Waiter	Sorry, we don't have (it here), but we do have *ais kacang*.
Calvin	I want to try (it).
Stan	For me, a glass of lukewarm water, and ice cream for dessert.
Sue-Ann	How long before the food is ready?
Waiter	Around 15 to 20 minutes.
Stan	Fine. Thank you.
Waiter	Sorry it took so long, we are very busy every night.
Sue-Ann	The fried noodles are delicious but the satay is a little undercooked.
Stan	Could I have one more glass of water, please? I'm really thirsty.
Stan	Could I have the bill, please?
Waiter	Here you are, sir.

How the language works 1

1 To order food in a restaurant simply use the phrase **Saya mahu pesan…**, *I would like to order…* or **Boléh minta…**, *Could I have…*, or **Boléh pesan…**, *May I order…* followed by the dishes you would like to order. Notice also the phrase **Boléh tambah lagi…**, *Could I have some more…*

Saya mahu pesan sepinggan nasi lemak.   *I'd like a plate of nasi lemak.*

Boléh kami minta rendang daging dan   *Could we have beef rendang and*
** pulut kuning untuk tiga orang.**   *pulut kuning for three.*

Exercise 1

Look at the list of Malaysian foods in 2, choose four things that appeal to you and make sentences using the phrases just seen once each.

2 Malaysian food – understanding the menu

Meats (**daging**):

ayam	*chicken*
babi	*pork*
biri-biri	*lamb*
ikan	*fish*
itik	*duck*
kambing	*goat*
daging lembu	*beef*

Fish (***ikan***) and seafood (***makanan laut***):

ikan keli	*catfish*
ketam	*crab*
tiram	*oysters*
udang	*prawns/shrimp*
udang karang	*lobster*
sotong	*squid*

Cooking styles:

bakar	*roast/grilled*
goréng	*fried*

Some Malaysian specialities (**citarasa istiméwa Malaysia**):

nasi	*(cooked) rice*
nasi ayam	*chicken rice*
nasi campur	*rice with meat and vegetables*
nasi goréng	*fried rice*
nasi briyani	*rice with meat, Indian style*
nasi kerabu	*blue rice with a combination of raw vegetables like beansprouts, herbs and salted fried fish*
nasi lemak	*rice cooked in coconut milk with anchovies, sambal, slices of cucumber, roast groundnuts*
nasi patprik	*rice and beef in a spicy sauce, Thai-style*
nasi pulut	*glutinous rice*
bubur ayam	*rice porridge with chicken*
mi	*noodles*
mi goréng	*fried noodles*
mi kuah	*noodles in soup*
mi rebus	*noodles in spicy gravy*
mi hailam	*noodles in black soy sauce gravy with pieces of squid, prawns and vegetables*
mi laksa	*rice noodles in spicy coconut gravy*
mi kuay teow	*flat rice noodles*
kari	*curry*
dhal kari	*Indian lentil curry*
kari ayam	*chicken curry*
kari kambing	*goat curry, etc.*
ayam masak kurma	*chicken korma*
saté ayam	*chicken meat on skewers dipped in peanut sauce or sweet sauce*
saté kambing	*small pieces of goat on skewers dipped in peanut sauce or sweet sauce*
saté daging	*beef on skewers dipped in peanut sauce or sweet sauce*
rendang ayam	*chicken pieces cooked slowly in thick coconut milk and spices*
rendang daging	*beef cooked slowly in thick coconut milk and spices until tender*

gado-gado	vegetable salad with egg and peanut sauce
murtabak	Indian pancakes with a variety of meat fillings
tempéh	fermented soybean cake
rojak	fruit and vegetable salad with spicy-sweet sauce
roti canai	Indian bread
soto ayam	spicy soup with chicken and an assortment of vegetables
telur téh	eggs cooked in tea
otak-otak	fish fillet mixed with spices, wrapped in banana leaves and cooked
sambal	chilli paste cooked with onions, etc.
keropok	prawn crackers

Sweets (**manisan**):

dodol	a sweet sticky and chewy cake, a Malay delicacy
kuih talam	steamed pudding made from coconut milk
kuih lapis tiga warna	three-coloured layered pudding
puding pulut santan	pudding made from glutinous rice and coconut
puding mangga	mango pudding
ondé-ondé	small green balls made of glutinous flour, stuffed with brown sugar and rolled in freshly grated coconut

Understanding Malay

Exercise 2

Read or listen to the dialogue and say whether the following statements are true or false.

  a Puan Sue-Ann alergi pada kacang.
  b Ikan bakar dengan sos pelam, hidangan istiméwa di restoran.
  c Restoran tidak menyediakan ais batu campur.
  d Stan memesan aiskrim untuk pencuci mulut.
  e Saté yang dipesan terlalu keras.
  f Makanan siap dalam sepuluh minit.

Quick vocab

menyediakan (sedia a.)	to prepare
alergi pada	allergic to
terlalu keras	over-cooked

Exercise 3

13.02

A Malaysian couple, Sam and Rosie, are dining out in a traditional Malay restaurant in the countryside. Familiarize yourself with the menu below and the new vocabulary before you listen to the conversations in the restaurant.

  a First, listen to the dialogue paying attention to what the couple order. Write S next to the items Sam eats or drinks and R next to the items his wife, Rosie, eats or drinks.

Menu Makanan	Makanan Pencuci Mulut
Makanan Utama	ais kacang
sayur campur	ais batu campur
rojak buah	bubur pulut hitam
ayam masak mérah	bubur kacang mérah
rendang	Minuman
gulai ikan	air kelapa muda
nasi goréng	air suam
nasi lemak	bir
pulut kuning	wain mérah
saté ayam	wain putih
saté kambing	
mi goréng	
popiah	
sambal	

b After you have listened enough times to understand the order, listen again and answer the questions.

  i Why does Sam want to sit by the window?

  ii What does Rosie ask the waiter after she has eaten the chicken satay?

  iii How much did the bill come to?

 Quick vocab

méja	table
pemandangan (pandang n.**)**	scenery
tasik	lake
apabila	when
sedia	ready
berseléra (seléra n.**) untuk**	to have an appetite for
seléra	appetite
dengar	to hear
siap	ready
habis	run out of, finished
resipi	recipe
benar-benar	really, truly
tidak mengapa	it doesn't matter
sedap	delicious
set	set
dipesan (pesan v.**)**	to be ordered
berasingan (asing a.**)**	separately
sayang	(here) darling

186

tukar fikiran	*to change one's mind*
fikiran (fikir *v.***)**	*thought*
lazat	*delicious*
terutamanya (utama *a.***)**	*especially*
merasakan (rasa *n.***)**	*to taste*
rahsia	*secret*
chef	*chef*
pencuci mulut	*dessert*
pencuci (cuci *v.***)**	*something that cleans*
mulut	*mouth*
kenyang	*full (of food)*
bubur pulut hitam	*black glutinous rice sweet porridge*
bubur	*porridge*
pulut	*glutinous rice*
mangkuk	*bowl*
jumlah	*total*

PART TWO

Dialogue

Tom and Serena are enjoying the relaxed atmosphere at a side stall.

 13.03

Serena	Saya selalu makan di gerai ini.
Tom	Itu lauk apa?
Jurujual	Namanya otak-otak. Dibuat daripada ikan dan rempah. Masakan istiméwa dari Johor.
Tom	Hm…Baunya sedap sekali, menjamu seléra.
Jurujual	Encik nak pesan apa?
Tom	Itu nasi goréng?
Jurujual	Ya, ada juga mi goréng atau mi rebus.
Tom	Saya mahu pesan nasi goréng saja. Berapa harganya sepinggan?
Jurujual	RM5.00.
Tom	Tolong jangan bubuh stok ayam.
Jurujual	Cik, nak makan apa?
Serena	Seperti biasa, saya mahu mi hailam.
Tom	Mi hailam? Apa masakan itu?
Serena	Itu mi goréng berkicap yang dicampur dengan makanan laut seperti sotong, udang dan sayur-sayuran.
Tom	Ada tambah telur?

Serena	Tidak.
Jurujual	Maaf, mahu pesan minuman apa?
Tom	Coca-cola dengan ais.
(The food comes.)	
Jurujual	Ini pesanannya. Silakan!
Tom	Boléh minta garfu sama sudu?
Serena	O ya, ini agak masin. Boléh berikan kicap manis?
Jurujual	Boléh.
Serena	Terima kasih. Saya mahu pesan satu lagi dibungkus untuk nenek saya. Tolong jangan bubuh cili.

 Quick vocab

gerai	*stall*
lauk	*dish (in a culinary sense)*
jurujual	*vendor*
rempah	*spice*
isteméwa	*speciality*
baunya	*it smells*
bau	*to smell*
menjamu seléra	*to make one's mouth water, entice one to eat*
menjamu (jamu v.**)**	*to invite*
seléra	*appetite*
mi rebus	*noodles cooked in spicy gravy*
pinggan	*dish (the receptacle)*
stok	*stock*
mi hailam	*fried noodles in black soy sauce and prawns, squid and vegetables*
berkicap (kicap n.**)**	*to have soy sauce in it*
kicap	*soy sauce*
dicampur (campur v.**)**	*to be mixed*
makanan laut	*seafood*
sotong	*squid*
udang	*shrimp*
sayur-sayuran	*vegetables*
tambah	*to add*
pesanan (pesan v.**)**	*order*
telur	*egg*
garfu	*fork*
sudu	*spoon*
masin	*salty*
kicap manis	*sweet soy sauce*
manis	*sweet*
dibungkus (bungkus v.**)**	*to be wrapped up (i.e. to take away)*
cili	*chilli*

While it strictly refers to a thick, sweet soy sauce, the word **kicap** has been borrowed into English and now refers to the tomato sauce we all know as ketchup!

Translation

Serena	I always eat at this stall.
Tom	What dish is that?
Vendor	It's called *otak-otak*. It is made with fish and spices. It is a speciality from Johor.
Tom	Hmm… it smells delicious, (it's) making my mouth water.
Vendor	What would you like to order, (sir)?
Tom	Is that *nasi goréng*?
Vendor	Yes, there is also fried noodles or noodles in spicy gravy.
Tom	I just want to order *nasi goréng*. How much is one serving (plate)?
Vendor	Five ringgit.
Tom	Please don't use chicken stock.
Vendor	What would you like to eat?
Serena	As usual, I want *mi hailam*.
Tom	*Mi hailam*? What food is that?
Serena	It's fried noodles in soy sauce mixed with seafood such as squid, shrimp and vegetables.
Tom	Are there eggs in it?
Serena	No.
Vendor	Excuse me, what would you like to drink?
Tom	Coca-cola with ice.
(The food comes.)	
Vendor	Here is your order. Please!
Tom	May I have a fork and a spoon?
Serena	Oh yes, it's rather salty. Could you bring some sweet soy sauce?
Vendor	Sure.
Serena	Thanks. I would like to order one more to take away for my grandma. Please don't put chilli (in it).

How the language works 2

1 In English we are used to talking about *a **packet** of cigarettes, a **bottle** of milk*. These are mostly words that count things or put them into a category based on the type of container the thing comes in. These are some you will find useful:

pinggan	*plate*
mangkuk	*bowl*
botol	*bottle*
gelas	*glass*
cawan	*cup*
kotak	*box*
bungkus	*packet, parcel*
potong	*piece, slice*

When you talk about *one* of something, the counting word, if you are using one, should be prefixed with **se-**, for example:

sepinggan mi	*a plate of noodles*

However, when ordering food, etc., you may also say:

satu pinggan mi	*one plate of noodles* (as opposed to two, three, etc., to make your order clear)

For any number of an item above one, the counting word is used after the number, without the **se-**:

dua mangkuk soup	*two bowls of soup*

Generally speaking, if you are ordering a portion of some type of food, from a street vendor, for instance, you would do so according to what it comes in or on. **Nasi goréng** comes on a plate and **laksa** comes in a bowl, so you would use the appropriate counting word in your order. However, there is an even simpler option. You can use **besar** or **kecil**, which means *large* or *small*, to specify your serving or portion and can be used when you order anything. For example, **semangkuk besar laksa** to mean *a big bowl of **laksa*** or **sepinggan kecil nasi goréng** as in *a small plate of fried rice*.

Boléh saya minta satu pinggan kecil mi goréng?	*Can I have a small serving of fried noodles?*

2 Sometimes the **ke-** prefix **-an** suffix combination occurs with adjectives, nouns and verbs creating an expression that means that something unplanned and usually unfortunate has happened. It is rather like the use of **ter-** mentioned in Unit 12. The following are very common so learn them as set expressions.

ketinggalan	*to miss (e.g. a form of transport)*
keciciran	*to lose something*
kelanggaran	*to collide*
kekenyangan	*to over-eat (to the point of discomfort)*

Using Malay

Exercise 4

Can you translate these dialogues between customers and various street vendors?

a I would like to order *laksa*.
How much for one bowl?
Not too hot.

b I would like to order tea.
How much for one bottle?
Please don't add ice.

c I would like to order *nasi goréng*.
How much for one plate?
Don't use eggs.
To take away, please.

d I would like to order *saté kambing*.
How much for one plate?
Could I have it rare!

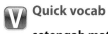
setengah matang   *rare*

Exercise 5

Write a suitable **ke- -an** expression under each of the following pictures. You may need to create expressions from adjectives using what you learnt in Unit 12. The first one has been done for you as an example.

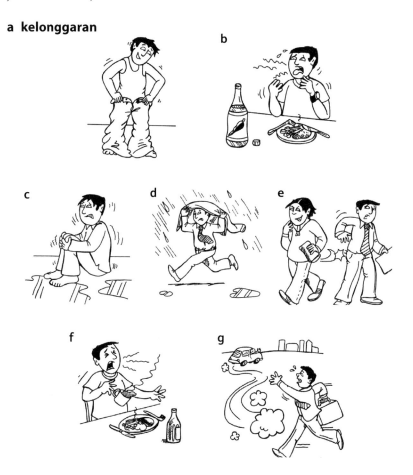

a **kelonggaran**

b

c

d

e

f

g

Exercise 6

Over to you!

You are (**B**), a lady. You have decided to go to a restaurant for dinner. The waiter (**A**) greets you…

13.04

A	Selamat tengah hari, Puan. Untuk berapa orang?
B	*For one person.*
A	Ini menu makanannya. Mahu pesan makanan apa?
B	*I want fried noodles. Is there shrimp (in it)?*
A	Ya, tapi kami boléh sediakan tanpa udang.
B	*Good. I'm allergic to shrimp.*
A	Mahu minum apa?
B	*Is there ais batu campur?*
A	Ya.
B	*I want to order ais batu campur without corn.*
A	Ada apa lagi, Puan?
B	*Oh, that's enough. How long until the food is ready?*
A	Kira-kira 15 minit.
B	*It's no problem. Thank you.*
A	Sila tunggu sebentar.

Quick vocab

jagung	*corn*
sudah cukup	*that's all*

> ● **INSIGHT**
>
> The words **tanpa** *without* and **tambah** *add* are virtual opposites when it comes to ordering food. If you want something without a certain ingredient, be sure to be clear with your pronunciation.

Test yourself

1 What three ways do you know to order food in Malay?

2 What is **ais batu campur** more commonly known as?

3 What expression would you use to order some more of something?

4 If unspecified, what would you expect to receive if you asked for **daging**?

5 What two ways could you use to order a plate of something?

6 How do you know which counting word to use when you order something?

7 What effect can the **ke- -an** combination have on meaning?

8 What other way do you know of to express this?

At the supermarket

In this unit you will learn how to:

▶ *shop for food at a shop or supermarket*
▶ *understand a Malay recipe*

PART ONE

Dialogue

Sue-Ann and her two children, Calvin and Silvia, are shopping at a big supermarket.

 14.01

Calvin	Kita perlu berapa kilo ubi kentang?
Puan Sue-Ann	Kira-kira satu kilo. Kita juga perlu setengah kilo lobak mérah dan beberapa bawang besar.
Calvin	Kita juga kehabisan bawang putih.
Puan Sue-Ann	Ya, kita perlu setengah kilo, juga seikat daun bawang dan daun saderi. Tolong masukkan ke dalam beg plastik untuk ditimbang.
Puan Sue-Ann	Silvia jangan ambil buah orén itu. Ambillah yang di sebelah sana. Berapakah harga seékor ayam?
Jurujual	Harganya RM10.00. Itu beratnya sekilo setengah.
Puan Sue-Ann	Saya juga mahu beli lima keping daging stik. Berapa harganya sekeping?
Jurujual	Satu potong harganya RM12.00.
Puan Sue-Ann	Kenapa mahal sekali?
Penjual daging	Ya kerana dagingnya diimport dari Australia.
Silvia	Aku mahu bahagian minuman. Aku mahu beli beberapa tin coca-cola dan dua tin bir dan satu botol wiski untuk papa.
Calvin	O ya, saya juga mahu beli makanan ringan. Tiga bungkus keropok kentang dan biskut.
Puan Sue-Ann	Pergilah, tapi jangan beli terlalu banyak. Saya dah lupa beli rempah, lada, kunyit, halia, serai dan daun limau purut.

berapa kilo?	*how many kilos?*
kilo	*kilo*
ubi kentang	*potato*
setengah	*half*
lobak mérah	*carrot*
bawang besar	*onion*
kehabisan (habis *v.***)**	*run out of*
bawang putih	*garlic*
seikat	*a bunch of*
daun	*leaf*
daun bawang	*spring onions*
saderi	*celery*
masukkan (masuk *v.***)**	*put in*
plastik	*plastic*
ditimbang (timbang *v.***)**	*to be weighed*
orén	*orange*
ambillah (ambil *v.***)**	*get, take*
seékor ayam	*one chicken*
seékor	*(here) one*
beratnya	*it weighs*
sekilo setengah	*one and a half kilos*
keping	*piece*
daging stik	*beef steak*
stik	*steak*
potong	*cut*
diimport dari	*to be imported from*
import	*to import*
bahagian	*section, part*
tin	*can*
bir	*beer*
botol	*bottle*
wiski	*whisky*
papa	*father, dad*
makanan ringan	*snacks*
keropok kentang	*crisps*
biskut	*biscuit*
pergilah!	*off you go!*
terlalu banyak	*too many*
lada	*pepper*
kunyit	*turmeric*
halia	*ginger*
serai	*lemon grass*
daun limau purut	*kaffir lime leaf*

Translation

Calvin	How many kilos of potatoes do we need?
Sue-Ann	About one kilo. We also need half a kilo of carrots and some onions.
Calvin	We have also run out of garlic.
Sue-Ann	Yes, we need half a kilo, also spring onions and celery. Please put them into a plastic bag to be weighed.
Sue-Ann	Silvia, don't take those oranges. Take the ones over there. How much is one chicken?
Shop assistant	It is 10 ringgit. It weighs a kilo and a half.
Sue-Ann	I would also like five pieces of beef steak. How much is one piece?
Shop assistant	One piece is 12 ringgit.
Sue-Ann	Why is it so expensive?
Butcher	Because the meat is imported from Australia.
Silvia	I want (to go to) the drinks section. I want to buy some cans of cola and two cans of beer and one bottle of whisky for dad.
Calvin	I also want to buy snacks. Three packets of crisps (and) biscuits.
Sue-Ann	Go (and get them), but don't buy too many. I've forgotten the spices – pepper, turmeric, ginger, lemon grass and kaffir lime leaves.

How the language works 1

1 Sedikit means *a little* or *some* but it can only be used with things that you cannot count, such as sugar, knowledge, etc. For things that you can count you cannot use **sedikit**. Instead you must use **beberapa** meaning *a few* or *several*. **Banyak** (*a lot of*), on the other hand, can be used with either.

Exercise 1

Look at the following nouns with **banyak** and the meanings. Write the words out again replacing **banyak** with **sedikit** or **beberapa** as appropriate.

    a **banyak kopi** *a lot of coffee*
    b **banyak nasi goréng** *a lot of fried rice*
    c **banyak resipi** *a lot of recipes*
    d **banyak pengetahuan** *a lot of knowledge*
    e **banyak ikan keli** *a lot of catfish*

 Quick vocab

pengetahuan (tahu *v.***)**   *knowledge*

Note that *how much?* is rendered by **berapa banyak?** in Malay.

2 In Unit 13 you were introduced to counting words that categorize things according to the container they come in, etc. This probably seemed very natural to you, as English categorizes such things in just the same way. In Malay, however, there are more counting words that are used for things you might not expect from an English point of view. In Unit 4 you came across **seorang** which is often used with jobs. This literally means *a person* and it acts like *a/an* in English. There are more such counting words called *classifiers* because they classify different sets of nouns according to certain inherent characteristics:

orang is used for people

ékor is used for animals. **Ékor** means tail, therefore animals are counted in tails. This also includes animals with no tail!

biji is used for fruit

buah is used for large objects such as houses, cars, lorries, ships, refrigerators, computers, etc.

butir is used for small, round objects such as eggs, bullets, pearls, etc.

tangkai is used for objects with stems such as flowers, chillies, mangoes, rambutans

helai is used for flat, soft and thin objects such as paper, cloth, leaf and others

utas is used to refer to long, bendable objects such as necklaces

pucuk is used for fine and thin objects such as for letters, needles and also firearms such as pistols.

It will come as no surprise by now, that to say *one* or *a/an* the classifier must be prefixed by **se-**.

seékor lembu	*a cow*
dua ékor tikus	*two mice*

Exercise 2

Try some counting!

    a eight sheets of paper

    b a papaya

    c a rose

    d four birds

    e three dictionaries

 Quick vocab

betik	*papaya*
bunga mawar/ros	*rose*

● **INSIGHT**

Classifiers are entirely optional. **Sebuah rumah** means *a house*, but so does **rumah** without the classifier! You do need to be aware of classifiers, however, as their usage is very natural for Malay speakers in certain situations, such as when talking about jobs.

Understanding Malay

Exercise 3

Say whether the following questions, based on the dialogue, are true or false.

- **a** Puan Sue-Ann perlukan satu setengah kilo ubi kentang.
- **b** Kentang harus dimasukkan ke dalam beg plastik untuk ditimbang.
- **c** Harga satu ékor ayam dengan berat satu kilo, RM10.00.
- **d** Silvia membeli tiga tin bir dan satu botol wiski untuk Stan.
- **e** Calvin hanya membeli dua bungkus keropok kentang dan biskut.
- **f** Puan Sue-Ann lupa nak beli halia dan serai.

Exercise 4

Read this recipe for beef *rendang* then answer the questions.

Bahan-bahan

1 kg daging lembu

2 biji kelapa untuk diambil santannya

15 tangkai cili (ikut selera)

6 ulas bawang mérah

6 ulas bawang putih

1 sudu ketumbar

halia 4 cm

lengkuas 4 cm

2 batang serai

1 helai daun kunyit

4 helai daun salam

5 helai daun limau purut

Cara membuat

1 Daging dipotong sebesar 5 cm × 4 cm × 1 cm.
2 Kisar semua bahan dengan halus kecuali daun salam, daun limau purut dan daun kunyit.
3 Masukkan daging, santan dan rempah-rempah yang dikisar ke dalam kuali. Masak sehingga daging lembut. Bubuh garam secukupnya, daun limau purut, daun salam serta daun kunyit ke dalam kuali. Tunggu sampai kuahnya menyerap sedikit.
4 Biarkan merénih. Lauk akan siap dihidang dalam masa kira-kira 1 jam.

 Quick vocab

bahan-bahan	*ingredients*
daging	*meat*
daging lembu	*beef*

lembu	*cow*
untuk diambil santannya	*(from which) to obtain the coconut milk*
santan	*coconut milk*
tangkai	*stalk*
ikut selera	*as desired*
ulas	*pip*
bawang mérah	*shallots*
sudu	*spoon*
ketumbar	*coriander*
lengkuas	*galangal*
daun kunyit	*saffron leaves*
daun salam	*bay leaves*
daun limau purut	*kaffir lime leaves*
cara	*manner, way*
cara membuat	*method, directions, instructions*
dipotong (potong *v.***)**	*to be cut into pieces*
sebesar	*as big as, (here) to a size of*
kisar	*to grind*
halus	*delicate, fine*
kecuali	*except*
kuali	*frying pan, wok*
masak	*to cook*
sehingga	*until*
lembut	*soft, (here) tender*
bubuh (bubuh *v.***)**	*to add*
garam	*salt*
secukupnya	*(here) to taste*
serta	*to add*
kuah	*gravy, juice extracted from meat during cooking*
menyerap (serap *a.***)**	*to absorb (of liquid)*
merénih (renih *v.***)**	*to simmer*
dihidang (hiding *v.***)**	*to be served*

- **a** Sebutkan bahan-bahan untuk membuat rendang?
- **b** Berapakah biji kelapa yang diperlukan?
- **c** Berapa kilo daging lembu untuk resipi di atas?
- **d** Apakah daun limau purut harus dikisar?
- **e** Berapa jam diperlukan untuk daging menjadi lembut?

 Quick vocab

diperlukan (untuk)	*needed (for)*
dikisar (kisar *v.***)**	*to be ground up*
sebutkan	*note down*

PART TWO

Dialogue

Serena wants to cook Tom her Malaysian specialty, beef *rendang*, so they go off to the market together to buy what they need.

 14.02

Serena	Berapa harga satu kilo daging?
Jurujual	Satu kilo RM15.00.
Tom	Mahu beli berapa kilo?
Serena	2 kilo cukup.
Tom	Apa lagi yang harus dibeli? Perlu beli kelapa?
Serena	Ya kita perlu dua biji kelapa untuk diperah santannya.
Tom	Apa rempah yang kamu perlukan?
Serena	Saya perlu beli cili dan lengkuas, tiga batang serai, kunyit dan setengah kilo bawang mérah.
Tom	Di mana boléh kita dapatkan semua bahan itu?
Serena	Di bahagian rempah.
Tom	Buah apa itu yang berduri?
Serena	Oh itu buah durian. Kamu bernasib baik sekarang musim buah-buahan. Ada rambutan, buah belimbing, cempedak, jambu. Kamu boléh rasa semuanya.
Tom	Buah durian. Bagaimana rasanya?
Serena	Rasanya manis dan agak pahit, tapi baunya sangat tajam.
Tom	Boléh saya cuba?
Serena	Tentu. Rasanya agak pelik, tapi siapa tahu mungkin kamu suka.
Tom	Boléh saya bawa ke England?
Serena	Saya kurang pasti, mungkin kalau dibungkus dengan baik, sehingga baunya tidak lari.
Serena	Lebih baik kamu cuba dulu.
Tom	Berapa sekilo?
Serena	Kira-kira RM18.00.
Tom	Mari kita beli satu.

Quick vocab

untuk diperah santannya	*to extract the coconut milk*
perah	*to extract, to squeeze*
diperah (perah *v.***)**	*to be squeezed, to be extracted*
perlukan (perlu *a.***)**	*to need to*

berduri (duri *n.*)	to have thorns
bernasib (nasib *n.*)	to be lucky
musim	season
rambutan	rambutan
buah belimbing	star fruit
cempedak	bread fruit
jambu	guava
rasa	taste, to taste
buah durian	durian
pahit	bitter
tajam	sharp (of objects), strong (of smells)
pelik	strange, odd
saya kurang pasti	I'm not sure
pasti	sure
lari	to run, (here) to seep out

Translation

Serena	How much is one kilo of meat?
Vendor	15 ringgit per kilo.
Tom	How many kilos do you want to buy?
Serena	Two kilos are enough.
Tom	What else should we buy? Do (we) need (to buy) coconuts too?
Serena	Yes, we need two coconuts to extract the milk.
Tom	What spices do you need?
Serena	I need chillis and galangal, three stalks of lemon grass, turmeric and half a kilo of red onion.
Tom	Where can we get all those ingredients?
Serena	In the spices section.
Tom	What's the fruit with the thorns?
Serena	Oh those are durians. You are really lucky, now the fruits are in season. There are rambutans, star fruits, bread fruits and guavas. You can try them all.
Tom	Durian. What does it taste like?
Serena	It tastes sweet and a bit bitter but it has a strong smell.
Tom	Can I try it?
Serena	Sure. It tastes a little bit weird but who knows, you may like it.
Tom	Can I take (it) to England?
Serena	I'm not sure, maybe (you can) if it is well wrapped up so the smell does not seep out.

Serena	You'd better try (it) first.
Tom	How much per kilo?
Serena	About 18 ringgit.
Tom	Let's buy one!

> ● **INSIGHT**
>
> The **durian** is a south-east Asian fruit, the size of a coconut, that smells not unlike rotting garbage. The thorny appearance lends the fruit its name. The edible part is yellow and resides in the compartments. In case you're wondering, Tom would not have been able to take a **durian** back to the UK. In fact, in many hotels **durians** are banned from the premises.

How the language works 2

1 Look at the following sentences in English:

A *We boiled the prawns.*

B *The prawns were boiled by us.*

Both sentences have the same meaning but each is expressed in a different way. Sentence (**A**) is known as *active* in that it stresses that someone or something is carrying out an action, but sentence (**B**) is known as *passive* because it stresses that something happened to someone or something not necessarily with the agent of the action (that is, the person or thing that carries out the action) being expressed. We shall concentrate on the passive in this section.

The prefix **di-** indicates a passive.

The passive is mainly formed from verbs beginning with the **me-** prefix. The prefix (**me-, men-**, **mem-** or **meng-**) is removed so you are left with the base verb, and **di-** is added to this base.

to take **mengambil** → **meng-ambil** → **ambil** → *di-***ambil** → *di***ambil** → *to be taken*

to give **memberi** → **mem-beri** → **beri** → *di-***beri** → *di***beri** → *to be given*

> ● **INSIGHT**
>
> Some base verbs are subject to a sound shift when **me-** is added (see Unit 16). The **di-** prefix is added to the original base verb.

Saya diberi wang.   *I was given money.*

Certain other verbs that do not begin with **me-** prefixes can also be made passive such as **minum** and **makan** simply by adding the **di-** prefix to them.

minum *to drink*   **diminum** *to be drunk*

makan *to eat*   **dimakan** *to be eaten*

Kek akan dimakan.   *The cake will be eaten.*

Exercise 5

Write the passive form of these verbs:

a mencari
b memeriksa
c menulis
d mengirim
e menghantar
f menjemput

When you make a passive form in English it is not always necessary to express the agent of the action – you can just say, for instance, *The prawns were boiled*; you do not need to say by whom. You can do the same in Malay. If you do want to express who the action was done by, you can use **oléh** plus a personal pronoun, although the use of **oléh** is optional. Note that the person the action was done by with or without **oléh** must follow the passive verb. Note further that *by him* or *by her* can both be rendered by **oléhnya**.

Dia diperiksa oléh doktor. ⎫ *She was examined by the doctor.*
Dia diperiksa doktor. ⎭

Anda akan dijemput oléh ⎫
  Sarah di lapangan terbang. ⎪ *You will be met at the airport by Sarah.*
Anda akan dijemput ⎪
  Sarah di lapangan terbang. ⎭

Exercise 6

Change these sentences from active into passive ones.

a Kakak sedang mencuci pakaian.
b Meréka membeli sayuran.
c Kami harus minum ubat tiga kali sehari.
d Doktor menyuntik pesakit.

Using Malay

Exercise 7

Look at each of these pictures and write a suitable classifier under each. Use the **se-** form.

a

b

c

d

e

f

Exercise 8

Use the pictures to create a sentence and a question as in the example. Ask how much a kilo of each product costs, except for **d** where you should ask how much a bottle costs.

Example: Saya mahu beli cili. Berapa harga sekilonya?

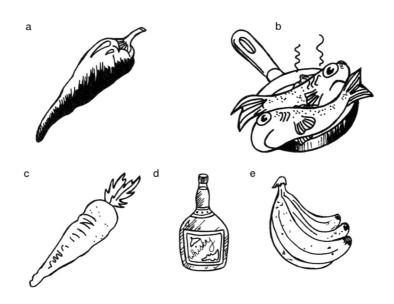

a

b

c

d

e

Exercise 9

Over to you!

Take the part of (**A**) who is shopping for meat.

 14.03

A	*I would like to buy (some) beef.*
B	Berapa kilo, Puan?
A	*Two kilos. How much is that?*
B	RM16.00.
A	*Please cut (it) into pieces.*
B	Baik. Ini dagingnya.
A	*Thank you.*

 Quick vocab

potong sekeping-sekeping   *to cut into pieces*

 Test yourself

1   What is the difference in usage between **sedikit** and **beberapa**?

2   What can you do with **banyak**, that you can't do (grammatically speaking) with **sedikit**?

3   How would you say *how much*? when asking about a quantity of something?

4   How are classifiers used in Malay?

5   What classifier would you use for a Manx cat?

6   What prefix is used to mean one of such and such a classifier?

7   Is the usage of classifiers compulsory?

8   What prefix indicates a passive verb?

9   The passive prefix usually replaces which verbal prefix?

10   How do you express *by* with a passive verb?

Hobbies and leisure

In this unit you will learn how to:
▶ *talk about likes, dislikes and favourites in detail*
▶ *say what your hobbies are and what sports you do*
▶ *say how long something has been happening*

PART ONE

Dialogue

Sue-Ann is catching up with an old friend she has not seen since she moved to the US.

 15.01

Puan Réma	Apa yang kamu lakukan pada masa lapang di Kuala Lumpur?
Puan Sue-Ann	Saya biasanya masak, baca novel, dan tonton filem télevisyen.
Puan Réma	Apakah filem yang kamu paling suka?
Puan Sue-Ann	Filem kegemaran saya adalah drama, komedi dan sejarah. Kamu pun suka menonton télevisyen?
Puan Réma	Ya. Kalau tiada ada rancangan télevisyen yang bagus, kami akan menyéwa video. Saya suka sekali drama dan filem yang penuh aksi, tetapi suami saya pula suka bola sépak, dan filem seram.
Puan Sue-Ann	Saya tidak begitu suka menonton filem seram.
Puan Réma	Selain ini, apa lagi aktiviti harian kamu?
Puan Sue-Ann	Saya hantar anak perempuan saya ke kelas ballét dua kali seminggu, setiap petang Selasa dan Jumaat. Dia ingin menjadi pemain piano dan juga penari ballét.
Puan Réma	Oh, Silvia sibuk sekali.
Puan Sue-Ann	Ya. Apa hobi kamu?
Puan Réma	Dulu semasa belum kahwin, saya suka sekali menyelam, mensnorkel dan mengembara berjalan kaki. Tetapi sekarang semuanya sudah saya tinggalkan. Hanya senaman aérobik dua kali seminggu.
Puan Sue-Ann	Saya kurang suka menyelam dan saya benci berkhémah. Tapi kadang-kadang saya suka aérobik.

Puan Réma	Apa hobi suami kamu?
Puan Sue-Ann	Dia suka komputer dan fotografi. Hampir sepanjang masanya dihabiskan bermain komputer. Dia juga pandai bermain tenis.
Puan Réma	Sama dengan suami saya. Dia paling suka komputer dan menonton bola sépak.

 Quick vocab

masa lapang	*free time*
lapang	*leisure*
novel	*novel*
tonton	*to watch*
filem televisyen	*TV films*
filem	*film*
paling suka	*like the most*
drama	*drama*
komedi	*comedy*
sejarah	*history*
tiada	*not (an alternative to* **tidak***)*
rancangan (rancang *n.***)**	*scheme, schedule*
menyéwa (séwa *v.***)**	*to rent*
video	*video*
filem yang penuh aksi	*action films*
bola sépak	*soccer*
filem seram	*horror movies*
seram	*horror*
selain ini	*apart from this*
aktiviti	*activity*
harian	*daily*
pemain (main *v.***)**	*player*
pemain piano	*piano player*
hobi	*hobby*
semasa (masa *n.***)**	*at the time when, current*
menyelam (selam *v.***)**	*dive*
mensnorkel (snorkel *n.***)**	*to snorkel, snorkelling*
mengembara (kembara *v.***)**	*to go in search of adventure*
mengembara berjalan kaki	*to go hiking*
tinggalkan (tinggal *v.***)**	*to leave, to omit, to neglect*
menyelam (selam *v.***)**	*to go diving*
aérobik	*aerobics*
saya kurang suka	*I don't really like*
benci	*to hate*
berkhémah (khemah *v.***)**	*camping*
fotografi	*photography*

hampir sepanjang masanya	*almost all his time*
hampir	*almost*
sepanjang	*the length of, throughout*
dihabiskan (habis *v.***)**	*to be spent*
bermain komputer	*to play on the computer*
pandai	*to be good at*

Translation

Rema	What do you do in your free time in Kuala Lumpur?
Sue-Ann	I usually cook, read novels and watch films.
Rema	What films do you like the most?
Sue-Ann	My favourite films are drama, comedy and history. Do you like watching TV films, too?
Rema	Yes, if what's on TV is not good, we like to rent a video. I like drama and action movies the most but my husband likes soccer and horror movies.
Sue-Ann	I don't really like horror movies.
Rema	Apart from that what else do you do during the day?
Sue-Ann	I take my daughter to ballet class twice a week, every Tuesday and Friday afternoon. She wants to be a pianist and also a ballet dancer.
Rema	Oh, Silvia's very busy.
Sue-Ann	Yes. What's your hobby?
Rema	Before I was married I loved diving, snorkelling and hiking. But I have given all that up now. I only do aerobics twice a week.
Sue-Ann	I don't really like diving and I hate camping. But sometimes I like aerobics.
Rema	What's your husband's hobby?
Sue-Ann	He loves computers and photography. Almost all his time is spent on playing (on the) computer. He is good at playing tennis too.
Rema	The same as my husband. He loves computers and watching the football.

How the language works 1

1 From previous units, you already know that to talk about what you like you can use **suka**, and to talk about what you do not like **tidak suka**. **Saya suka mendaki gunung**, *I like climbing mountains*. Another good word for *like* is **gemar**, which is less colloquial and tends to sound more formal than **suka** but will give the listener a good impression of your Malay. It is important to note that **gemar** cannot be used to refer to people or animals.

Saya gemar main kad. *I like playing cards.*

To say that you love doing something in Malay, you can use the expressions **suka sekali**, **sangat suka** or **paling suka**.

> ● **INSIGHT**
>
> However, do note that **paling suka** cannot be used together with **sekali** as in **paling suka sekali** as it would mean *love most most*.
>
> This is a very common error amongst foreign learners of Malay.

Saya suka sekali komedi. *I love comedy.*
Saya sangat suka bermain badminton. *I love playing badminton.*
Saya paling suka makanan yang pedas. *I love spicy (hot) food.*

There are some points to remember when you use **paling** – and **sekali** – in your sentence. The word **paling** is always put before an adjective, as in **paling tinggi** or **paling besar**. The word **sekali**, on the other hand, is placed after the adjective, for example, **berat sekali**, **sedap sekali**.

> ● **INSIGHT**
>
> Just in case you need it (you never know!), if you want to say *I love you* to somebody, you can use **saya cinta kamu**.

To express what you do not like, you can simply use **tidak suka**.
Saya tidak suka tiram. *I don't like oysters.*

In English, we tend to use the word *hate* in a fairly casual way when we talk about our likes and dislikes (*I hate washing up!* etc.) In Malay *hate* is rendered by **benci**.
Saya benci memasak. *I hate cooking.*
Saya benci sekali berenang. *I hate swimming so much.*

However, it is generally much better to express oneself in a less extreme way in Malay when talking about negative things. Therefore, you (and the Malay speakers you speak to) might find the phrase **tidak begitu suka** a far more acceptable alternative! It corresponds to *do not really like* in English.
Saya tidak begitu suka sup ayam. *I don't really like chicken soup.*
Saya tidak begitu suka memasak. *I don't really like cooking.*

A similar and very common expression uses **kurang**.
Saya kurang suka pisang goréng. *I don't really like fried bananas.*

Gemar acts as a root to give us **kegemaran** which means *favourite* or *best liked* and follows what it refers to, like other adjectives.

filem kegemaran saya	*my favourite film*
alat muzik kegemaran saya	*my favourite musical instrument*
hidangan kegemaran saya	*my favourite dish*

 Quick vocab

alat muzik   *musical instrument*

Kegemaran or **kesukaan** can be used to talk about a liking or hobbies and activities that you like doing. As with **gemar**, it cannot be used to talk about people or animals. Instead **kesayangan** is used.

Membaca adalah satu kegemaran saya.	*Reading is one of my hobbies.*
Berkebun adalah kegemaran saya.	*Gardening is my hobby.*
Itu warna kesukaan saya.	*That's my favourite colour.*
Dia pemain bola sépak kesayangan saya.	*He's my favourite football player.*
Ini kucing kesayangan saya.	*This is my favourite cat.*

Yet another word for *favourite* is **favorit** which is of foreign origin and popular amongst young people. The usage of **favorit** is not restricted so it can be used with anything, as in English.

filem favorit saya	*my favourite film*
pemain sépak bola favorit saya	*my favourite football player*

Exercise 1

Use the correct form of **kegemaran** or **kesukaan/ kesayangan** with the following words. Use each one at least once.

- **a** sukan
- **b** bintang film
- **c** guru
- **d** drama
- **e** binatang

 Quick vocab

bintang	*star*
drama	*play (at the theatre)*
binatang	*animal*

Another useful word derived from **gemar** is **penggemar** which expresses *a real fan of…* in Malay. As in English, it does not just refer to sports, but can be used with anything.

Saya penggemar muzik jazz.   *I'm a real fan of jazz music.*

Ayah saya penggemar besbol.   *My dad's a real baseball fan.*

Exercise 2

Translate the following sentences into Malay.

   a My girlfriend is a real fan of Leonardo di Caprio.

   b They are real fans of Chinese food.

   c Jani's sister is a real soap opera fan.

   d You're a real soccer fan, aren't you?

Understanding Malay

Exercise 3

Read or listen to the dialogue again and say whether these statements are true or false.

   a Pada masa lapang Sue-Ann biasanya suka menonton filem seram.

   b Sue-Ann menghantar Silvia ke kelas ballét 2 kali seminggu.

   c Semenjak berkahwin Rika masih suka pergi menyelam.

   d Suami Sue-Ann menghabiskan seluruh masanya dengan bermain komputer.

   e Suami Réma hobinya fotografi.

   f Suami Sue-Ann tidak pandai bermain tenis.

 Quick vocab

drama lipur lara   *soap opera*

Exercise 4

Without referring back to the dialogue, see if you can complete the sentences with the correct information by selecting **a**, **b** or **c** in each case.

 1 **Di Kuala Lumpur, Puan Sue-Ann biasanya**

    a memasak, baca surat khabar dan menonton filem.

    b memasak, membaca novél dan menonton filem.

    c memasak, membaca novél dan menonton drama sentimental.

 2 **Puan Réma dan Puan Sue-Ann gemar menonton filem**

    a drama.

    b penuh aksi.

    c komedi.

 3 **Puan Sue-Ann harus menghantar puterinya ke kelas ballét pada**

    a hari Jumaat dan Selasa.

    b hari Selasa dan Rabu.

    c hari Kamis dan Selasa.

4 Suami Sue-Ann dan Réma penggemar

 a tenis.

 b bola sépak.

 c komputer.

PART TWO

Dialogue

Tom and Serena are talking about what they do in their free time.

 15.02

Tom	Serena, Apa kamu buat pada masa lapang?
Serena	Saya suka pergi berjalan-jalan dan membeli-belah dengan kawan-kawan. Kadang-kadang saya berenang. Dan kamu?
Tom	Saya suka membaca buku, memasak dan mendengar muzik.
Serena	Oh, ya saya juga suka muzik. Tiada hari yang berlalu tanpa muzik. Muzik memberi saya semangat dan inspirasi. Muzik apa yang kamu paling suka?
Tom	Saya suka semua muzik, terutama sekali muzik klasik.
Serena	Saya suka jazz, pop, dan dangdut.
Tom	Apa itu dangdut?
Serena	Dangdut, muzik tradisional yang digabung dengan tarian. Seperti muzik India.
Tom	Apa lagi hobi kamu?
Serena	Saya suka menyanyi dan menari. Kalau mahu, kita boléh pergi ke karaoké ésok.
Tom	Saya tidak boléh menyanyi. Saya pemalu!
Serena	Saya tidak percaya.
Tom	Oh, ya, sukan apa yang kamu paling suka?
Serena	Saya suka bola tampar, dan ping pong. Kamu?
Tom	Karaté. Semasa di England, saya pergi berlatih setiap minggu.
Serena	Wah! Berapa lama kamu sudah belajar karaté?
Tom	Sudah tiga tahun. Saya tertarik dengan karaté sejak saya ke Jepun lima tahun yang lalu.
Serena	Tadi kamu kata, suka memasak. Masakan apa yang paling kamu suka?
Tom	Masakan India, terutama kari. Saya tidak pernah jelak makan kari setiap hari.
Serena	Saya pula tidak suka memasak, tetapi saya suka makan.

Quick vocab

berjalan-jalan	*to go for a leisurely walk, (here) to hang around*
mendengar muzik	*to listen to music*
tiada hari yang berlalu tanpa muzik	*there's no day without music*
tiada	*not, to not exist*
berlalu	*to pass*
semangat	*motivation*
inspirasi	*inspiration*
terutama	*especially*
klasik	*classical*
dangdut	*traditional Malay and Indonesian music*
digabung (gabung *n.***)**	*to be combined*
tarian (tari *v.***)**	*dancing*
menyanyi (nyanyi *v.***)**	*to sing*
menari (tari *v.***)**	*to dance*
pemalu (malu *a.***)**	*a shy person*
percaya	*to believe*
bola tampar	*volleyball*
ping pong	*table-tennis*
karaté	*karate*
berlatih (latih *v.***)**	*to train*
tertarik (tarik *v.***) dengan**	*to be interested in*
sejak	*since*
tadi	*just now*
kata	*to say*
jelak	*fed up, bored*

Translation

Tom	Serena, what do you do in your spare time?
Serena	I like hanging around with my friends and shopping. Sometimes I go swimming. And you?
Tom	I like reading books, cooking and listening to music.
Serena	Oh yes, I like music too. There's not a day that passes without music. Music gives me motivation and inspiration. What kind of music do you like the most?
Tom	I like all music, especially classical music.
Serena	I like jazz, pop and *dangdut*.
Tom	What's *dangdut*?
Serena	*Dangdut* is traditional music which is combined with dancing. It is like Indian music.
Tom	What other hobbies do you have?

Serena	I like singing and dancing. If you want, we can go to karaoke tomorrow.
Tom	But I can't sing. I'm a shy person.
Serena	I don't believe (it).
Tom	By the way, what sports do you like the most?
Serena	I like volleyball and table-tennis. You?
Tom	Karate. In England I go to practise every week.
Serena	Wow. How long have you been studying karate?
Tom	For three years. I've been interested in karate since I went to Japan five years ago.
Serena	Just now (you) said (you) like cooking. What food do you like the most?
Tom	Indian food, especially curry. I never get fed up of eating curry every day.
Serena	I don't like cooking, but I like eating.

How the language works 2

1 When we talk about sports in English, we use a variety of verbs to express them. We say, for example, *I play tennis*, but *I go skiing*. In Malay, you will be glad to hear, one verb – **main** – is used for all.

main tenis	*to play tennis*
main ski	*to go skiing*

Main is also used to talk about playing musical instruments (**alat musik**):

main trombone	*to play the trombone*
main piano	*to play the piano*

 Quick vocab

trompet	*trumpet*
biola, violin	*violin*
selo	*cello*
klarinet	*clarinet*
seruling, flut	*flute*
gitar	*guitar*
gendang	*drums*

2 Berapa lama kamu (sudah)…?, *How long have you been…?* To say how long you have been doing something **selama** translates *for* in the Malay version:

Dia berminat main ping pong selama dua tahun.	*She's been interested in table-tennis for two years.*
Saya sudah main piano selama enam tahun.	*I've already been playing the piano for six years.*

You could also say that you have been doing something *since…* In this case **sejak** is used:

Saya berminat dalam wayang kulit　*I have been interested in shadow puppets since*
  sejak melihat pertunjukan di Kelantan.　*I saw a performance in Kelantan.*
Adik Marie mencari pekerjaan　*Marie's brother has been looking for a job*
  sejak dia pulang dari América.　*since he came back from America.*
Meréka belajar silat sejak kecil　*They've been studying silat since they were*
  lagi.　*children. (literally: since they were small)*

 Quick vocab

berminat (minat *n.***)**	*interested in*
wayang kulit	*leather shadow puppets*
silat	*a Malay martial art*

Exercise 5

Can you form these sentences?

  a I have been studying **silat** for three weeks.
  b He has been interested in karate since he went to Japan.

The prefix **pe-** indicates nouns that refer to a person who performs an action. Thus, **pe-** nouns are often connected with jobs and sports. Many, but not all, are derived directly from **ber-** and **me-** prefixed verbs, with the **pe-** replacing the **ber-** or the **me-**.

penari *dancer*	*(from **menari**, to dance)*
perenang *swimmer*	*(from **berenang**, to swim)*
pemain *player*	*(from **main**, to play)*

Exercise 6

See if you can work out the meanings of these performer nouns using some of the verbs you have met already in the course. Remember to think of them in their prefixed form.

  a penulis
  b pembantu
  c pembeli
  d penjual
  e penjaga
  f pengajar
  g pekerja
  h pelari

 Quick vocab

berlari (lari *v.***)**	*to run*

Using Malay

Exercise 7

Match the words to the pictures by writing in the letter of each picture. Choose, and indicate with the symbols shown in brackets, two activities that you love doing (✔✔), two activities that you like doing (✔) and two that you do not like doing (✘). Make six sentences based on this information.

1 … bersenam

2 … berkebun

3 … main bola keranjang

4 … main ski

5 … berjemur

6 … menonton

7 … mendengar muzik

8 … memasak

9 … menari

10 … bersiar-siar

11 … melukis

12 … menyanyi

13 … membaca

14 … berenang

15 … fotografi

16 … makan di restoran

17 … menonton di panggung wayang

 Quick vocab

bola keranjang	*basketball*
mainski	*skiing*
berjemur (jemur *v.***)**	*sunbathing*
bersenam (senam *v.***)**	*exercise, workout*
bersiar-siar	*travelling*
berkebun (kebun *n.***)**	*gardening*

Exercise 8

Over to you!

You (**B**) are having a conversation with your Malay friend (**A**) about your likes, dislikes and hobbies.

 15.03

A	Apa hobi kamu?
B	*I like reading and travelling most.*
A	Buku apa yang paling kamu suka?
B	*Psychology, culture and history books.*
A	Kamu suka baca novel?
B	*Not really, but I like the novels of the author Agatha Christie a lot.*
A	Kamu kata tadi kamu suka pergi bersiar-siar. Negara mana yang kamu sering kunjungi?
B	*Countries in Asia especially Malaysia, Singapore, Brunei Darussalam, Indonesia, Japan, China and so on.*

A	Sukan apa yang kamu gemar?
B	*Hmm, I don't really like (them) (use* **gemar***).*
A	Bagaimana dengan berenang?
B	*I don't like (it) either.*

 Quick vocab

psikologi	*psychology*
budaya	*culture*
tidak sangat	*not really*
karya	*author*
terutamanya	*especially*
dan lain-lain	*and so on*
tidak begitu	*not really*

Test yourself

1. What are the two ways to say *like* in Malay?
2. What restriction is placed on the usage of **gemar**?
3. How would you express *to hate* in Malay when talking about likes and dislikes? (*Be careful!*)
4. How do you express *favourite* in Malay?
5. How do you express *favourite* when talking about animals?
6. What does **favorit** mean, and is its usage restricted?
7. How do you say *a real fan of* in Malay?
8. What verb is used with all sports in Malay?
9. How do you express *for* and *since* with time expressions?
10. What does the prefix **pe**- indicate?

At the doctor's

In this unit you will learn how to:

▶ *talk about your body*

▶ *say how you feel*

▶ *talk about various common ailments*

▶ *deal with a visit to the doctor*

▶ *talk about the weather*

▶ *interact on the telephone*

PART ONE

Dialogue

Stan is not feeling well so he has made an appointment at the private clinic his company uses. He is in the consulting room with a doctor.

 16.01

Doktor	Sakit apa, Encik?
Stan	Asma saya kembali lagi. Saya tidak boléh tidur malam tadi, susah untuk bernafas. Jantung saya berdebar cepat sekali.
Sue-Ann	Tangannya sejuk dan menggigil.
Doktor	Berapa lamakah sudah Encik merasa sakit ini?
Stan	Saya sudah sakit selama dua tahun. Adakalanya sembuh, adakalanya kembali lagi. Saya biasanya selalu berjoging setiap pagi sebelum pergi ke pejabat. Tapi dalam seminggu ini saya sangat sibuk, jadi tidak ada masa.
Doktor	Sudah berapa lama encik berada di Singapura? Mungkin Encik masih belum selésa dengan keadaan cuaca di sini.
Stan	Saya berada di sini kira-kira tiga bulan, lagipun saya dari Florida di US jadi saya sudah biasa dengan keadaan panas. Tapi bagi saya cuaca di Singapura terlalu lembap.
Doktor	Anda ada makan ubat?
Stan	Ya, ini ubat saya.
Doktor	Ada penyakit lain?

Stan	Ya, saya menghidap penyakit darah tinggi.
Doktor	Anda ada merokok atau minum minuman keras?
Stan	Saya tidak merokok, tapi saya minum minuman keras.
Doktor	Mari saya periksa. Saya beri ubat yang boléh dibeli dari farmasi. Jangan lupa untuk terus makan ubat dan banyak beréhat.
Stan	Terima kasih.
Doktor	Mudah-mudahan cepat sembuh.

 Quick vocab

sakit apa?	*in what way are you sick?*
asma	*asthma*
susah	*difficult*
bernafas (nafas *n.***)**	*to breathe*
jantung	*heart*
berdebar (debar *n.***)**	*to throb, to palpitate*
sejuk	*cold*
menggigil (giggil *v.***)**	*to shiver*
merasa (rasa *n.***)**	*to feel*
adakalanya	*sometimes*
sembuh	*to get better* (of illness), *to recover*
berjoging (joging *n.***)**	*to go jogging*
keadaan (ada *v.***)**	*condition*
lagipun	*moreover, besides*
bagi	*for*
lembap	*moist, humid*
makan ubat	*to take medicine*
penyakit (sakit *a.***)**	*illness*
menghidap (hidap *v.***)**	*to suffer from*
darah	*blood*
penyakit darah tinggi	*high blood pressure*
beri	*to give, (here) to prescribe*
terus	*non-stop, to keep on (doing)*
terus makan ubat	*to keep taking the medicine*
beréhat (réhat *v.***)**	*to rest*

Translation

Doctor	What seems to be the trouble?
Stan	My asthma has come back. I couldn't sleep last night (and) found it hard to breathe. My heart was beating very fast.
Sue-Ann	His hand was cold and shivering.
Doctor	How long have you felt like this?

Stan	I have been ill for two years. Sometimes I recover, sometimes it comes back. I always used to go jogging every morning before going to the office. But during this week I have been very busy, so I didn't have time.
Doctor	How long have you been in Singapore? Maybe you are not yet comfortable with the weather conditions here.
Stan	I have been here approximately three months moreover I am from Florida in the US so I am used to hot (weather) conditions. But for me the weather in Singapore is too humid.
Doctor	Are you taking medicine?
Stan	Yes, this is my medicine.
Doctor	Do you have any other illnesses?
Stan	Yes, I suffer from high blood pressure.
Doctor	Do you smoke or drink?
Stan	I don't smoke but I do drink.
Doctor	Let me examine (you). I'll prescribe medicine that can be bought from a pharmacy. Don't forget to keep taking the medicine and get a lot of rest.
Stan	Thank you.
Doctor	With any luck you will get better quickly.

How the language works 1

1 Sakit means *ill* or *sick*. It is also used to express which part of the body feels painful or aching, or ill. The body part follows **sakit**:

Saya sakit perut.   *I have a stomachache.*

> ● **INSIGHT**
> In medical speak **sakit apa**? corresponds to *What seems to be the trouble?*

 Quick vocab

badan	*body*
kepala	*head*
rambut	*hair*
mata	*eye(s)*
bulu kening	*eyebrow(s)*
dahi	*forehead*
telinga	*ear*
hidung	*nose*
pipi	*cheek(s)*

mulut	*mouth*
bibir	*lips*
dagu	*chin*
léhér	*neck*
kerongkong	*throat*
bahu	*shoulder(s)*
dada	*chest*
perut	*stomach*
tangan	*hand(s)*
jari	*finger(s)*
ibu jari	*thumb*
paha	*thigh(s)*
betis	*calf/calves*
kaki	*leg/legs, foot/feet*

● INSIGHT

Malay does not make a distinction between legs and feet! You need to refer to specific parts of the body to distinguish, such as *ankle*, **pergelengan kaki**.

Exercise 1

Translate the following into Malay.

   a He has a headache.
   b Do you have an earache?
   c My hand hurts.

Some other words for ailments you may find useful are:

ketakcernaan	*indigestion*
batuk	*cough*
demam	*feverish*
mabuk	*dizzy*
muntah	*to vomit*

2 In English we always say *to **take*** medicine but in Malay you usually say *to **drink*** medicine, **minum ubat** or, as in the dialogue, you can say **makan ubat**, literally *to **eat*** medicine.

3 This section deals with how to give commands in Malay. There are two types of commands: one tells someone to do something, *positive command* and the other tells someone not to do something, *negative command*.

To give someone a positive command simply state the verb for the action you wish completed:

Makan itu!   *Eat that!*

There are certain factors to take into account regarding the form of the verb when giving commands. This is where an awareness of verb bases comes in useful. If the verb you want to make a command from is a **ber-** or a **me-** verb with a **verb** base, then the **ber-** or **me-** drops leaving just the base to use as the command form. For example:

bermain *to play* **ber**-*main*

Main di sana!   *Play over there!*

mencari *to look for* **men**-*cari*

Cari pekerjaan!   *Look for a job!*

> ● **INSIGHT**
>
> You have been adhering to this rule since you learnt to say *thank you* in Malay. **Terima kasih** is actually a command. **Terima** means *receive* and **kasih** means *affection* or *love*. When you say *thank you* in Malay you are literally saying *Receive love*.

If you make a command from a verb with prefix **me-** combined with suffix **-kan** then just the **me-** is removed leaving verb base + **-kan** as the command form. You have already met this form in expressions such as:

Tolong, buatkan tempahan   *Please make me a reservation for*
  saya untuk ésok.   *tomorrow.*

> ● **INSIGHT**
>
> This comes from **membuatkan**, *to do something for someone.*

Masukkan orén dalam beg ini!   *Put the oranges in this bag!*

> ● **INSIGHT**
>
> This is from **memasukkan**, *to put (something) into.*

Jangan, which means *don't*, is used to form the negative command to tell someone not to do something. In the negative command, however, the prefixes **me-** and **ber-** should be retained when using **jangan**.

Jangan bermain di dalam rumah!   *Don't play inside the house!*

Jangan memasangkan TV!   *Don't turn on the TV!*

 Quick vocab

memasangkan (pasang *n.***)**   *to turn on*

Exercise 2

Try some commands!

   a Take out the garbage!

   b Run faster!

   c Don't work all day long!

   d Don't buy too much chocolate!

 Quick vocab

sampah	*garbage*
sepanjang hari	*all day long*

In informal spoken style, with both positive and negative commands these rules are broken for the sake of brevity and only the base of the verb (with any suffixes like **-kan**) is very often used.

Jangan pasangkan TV!	*Don't turn on the TV!*
Jangan main di sini!	*Don't play here!*
Jangan rokok di bilik tamu, ya?	*Don't smoke in the living room, OK?*

As in the last example, you can add **ya**? to a command to soften it. Another way to reduce the force of a command is to add **-lah** to the verb. It is added directly to the verb or the adjective as a suffix. You should be aware that without it, your commands will have a distinctly forceful tone to them.

Bacalah!	*Read!*

The suffix **-lah** is especially useful when making positive commands using adjectives. If you want to say *Be happy!*, you will remember that there is no verb *to be* in Malay so you just add **-lah** to the adjective.

Gembiralah!	*Be happy!*

Malay often uses the passive form of the verb when making commands. This is due to a cultural necessity to avoid directness if possible, even when giving an explicit instruction.

Jangan dibuka pintu itu. Sejuk!	*Don't open the door. It's cold!*

4 Talking about the weather.

Bagaimana cuacanya?	*How's the weather?*

> ● **INSIGHT**
>
> In Malay, people often refer to **keadaan cuaca** *weather conditions* when talking about the weather, whereas in English we just say *weather*.

 Quick vocab

berawan	*cloudy*
berkabut	*foggy*
panas	*hot*
cerah	*bright*
beribut	*stormy*
berangin	*windy*
basah	*wet*

mendung	*overcast*
lembap	*damp, humid*
hujan	*raining*
renyai-renyai	*drizzle*
banjir	*flood*
taufan	*typhoon*

Musim is used to refer to *seasons* in Malay:

 Quick vocab

musim bunga	*spring*
musim panas	*summer*
musim luruh	*autumn*
musim sejuk	*winter*

> ● **INSIGHT**
>
> Malay-speaking countries, however, only really have two seasons, dry and hot or wet and hot!
>
> **musim panas** *dry season*
>
> **musim hujan** *rainy season*

Understanding Malay

Exercise 3

Answer the following true/false questions based on the dialogue.

  a Bila asmanya kembali, Stan tidak boléh tidur dan susah bernafas.
  b Stan menghidap penyakit asma selama 3 tahun.
  c Stan ada ubat sendiri yang selalu diminumnya.
  d Stan tidak merokok dan tidak minum minuman keras.
  e Stan masih menghidap penyakit darah tinggi.

Exercise 4

Match the number of the body part below to those indicated in the picture using the letters.

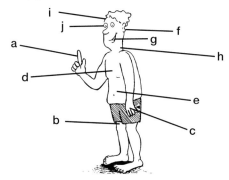

1 perut
2 telinga
3 kepala
4 paha
5 dada
6 jari
7 léhér
8 mata
9 mulut
10 tangan

Exercise 5

16.02

You will hear the week's weather forecast for Kuala Lumpur read by two announcers. As you listen, use the following table to work out which weather forecast goes with which day of the week, using the times and descriptions as a a guide. Write the day of the week below, in Malay. One of them is a red herring!

a	**09.00** *WINDY* *and* *SUNNY*	**18.00** *WINDY* *and* *SUNNY*	**b**	**09.00** *WINDY* *and* *SUNNY*	**18.00** *WINDY* *and* *SUNNY*
c	**11.00** *CLEAR* *and* *SUNSHINE*	**20.00** *CLEAR* *SUNSHINE,* *DRIZZLE*	**d**	**09.00** *CLOUDY*	**20.00** *CLOUDY* *and* *SHOWERS*
e	**06.00** *WET* *and* *HUMID*	**15.00** *FAIR*	**f**	**08.00** *WINDY*	**18.00** *CLEAR* *SKIES*
g	**06.00** *HEAVY* *RAIN*	**14.00** *BRIGHT* *and* *SUNNY*	**h**	**09.00** *HOT* *and* *BRIGHT*	**17.00** *HOT* *and* *BRIGHT*

 Quick vocab

nampaknya	*it seems like, it looks like*
layang-layang	*kites*
bermain layang-layang	*to fly kites*
sinaran	*ray*

PART TWO

Dialogue

Tom is not feeling well.

 16.03

Serena	Tom, kamu kelihatan pucat. Ada apa? Apa kamu sakit?
Tom	Ya…saya sakit perut dan rasa mual.
Serena	Badan kamu panas, kamu demam. Mari kita ke doktor di klinik 24 jam.
Tom	Tidak usah.
Serena	Apa kamu salah makan?
Tom	Saya rasa bukan.
Serena	Kita harus ke sana. Kalau kamu sakit, kita tidak boléh pergi ésok.
Tom	Terpulang pada kamu. Saya ikut nasihatmu saja tapi saya rasa mabuk, tidak boléh berjalan.
Serena	Saya akan teléfon kawan saya, Nasha kalau dia boléh menghantar kita ke klinik.
(On the phone.)	
Serena	Helo, boléh saya bercakap dengan Nasha?
Orang 1	Nasha? Maaf, anda salah nombor.
Serena	Oh, minta maaf.
(Serena tries again.)	
Serena	Helo! Boléh saya bercakap dengan Nasha?
Orang 2	Maaf. Dia dah keluar. Ini ibunya. Siapa yang bercakap ni?
Serena	Ini Serena, kawan Nasha.
Orang 2	Anda nak tinggalkan pesanan?
Serena	Tidak mengapa, terima kasih. Saya akan teléfon lagi lain kali.
Orang 2	OK, Saya akan beritahu dia yang anda teléfon. Selamat tinggal.

Serena	OK. Baik kita naik teksi saja. Saya akan teléfon untuk teksi.
(The taxi arrives and takes Tom to the doctor's. Tom enters the doctor's surgery.)	
Doktor	Selamat malam! Sakit apa?
Tom	Perut saya sakit dan saya muntah-muntah terus.
Doktor	Apa yang kamu makan atau minum.
Tom	Saya cuma makan udang bercili dan minum air téh.
Doktor	Hm…mungkin lauk cili itu terlalu pedas untuk anda. Sudah berapa lama rasa begini?
Tom	Sejak 3 jam yang lalu.
Doktor	Apa lagi yang anda rasa?
Tom	Saya kerap buang air. Saya rasa lemah.
Doktor	Mari saya periksa. Maaf. Anda ada sebarang alergi pada ubat?
Tom	Ya saya alergi pada Augmentin.
Doktor	Baik, saya akan ganti dengan ubat yang lain. Minum 3 kali sehari. Mudah-mudahan lekas sembuh dan jangan makan makanan pedas.

 Quick vocab

pucat	*pale*
ada apa?	*what's wrong? what's up?*
mual	*nauseous*
demam	*feverish*
tidak usah	*there's no need*
saya rasa bukan	*I don't think so*
terpulang pada kamu	*it's up to you, it's your decision*
nasihat	*advice*
salah nombor	*the wrong number*
tinggalkan (tinggal *v.***)**	*to leave (something)*
pesanan	*message*
muntah-muntah	*to vomit*
terus	*to keep on (doing something)*
kerap	*frequent*
buang air	*to urinate*
lemah	*feeble*
sebarang	*any*
alergi (pada)	*allergy (to)*
ganti	*to change*

Translation

Serena	Tom, you look pale. What's up? Are you ill?
Tom	Yes…I have a stomachache and I feel sick.
Serena	Your body is cold, you're feverish. Let's go to the 24-hour doctor's clinic.
Tom	There's no need.
Serena	Have you eaten something that disagreed with you?
Tom	I don't think so.
Serena	We should go (there). If you are sick we can't go tomorrow.
Tom	It's up to you. I'll just follow your advice, but I feel drunk. I can't walk.
Serena	I'll phone my friend, Nasha (and see) if she can take us to the clinic.
(On the phone.)	
Serena	Hello, may I speak to Nasha?
Person 1	Sorry, you've got the wrong number.
Serena	Oh, sorry.
(Serena tries again.)	
Serena	Hello! May I speak to Nasha?
Person 2	Sorry. She's already gone out. This is her mother. Who's speaking?
Serena	This is Serena, a friend of Nasha's.
Person 2	Do you want to leave a message?
Serena	It's OK, thanks. I'll phone again another time.
Person 2	OK. I'll tell her that you called. Bye.
Serena	Bye. OK. Right we'll just take a taxi. I'll phone for a taxi.
(The taxi arrives and takes Tom to the doctor's. Tom enters the doctor's surgery.)	
Doctor	Good evening. What seems to be the trouble?
Tom	I have a stomachache and I keep on vomiting.
Doctor	What have you been eating or drinking?
Tom	I only ate chilli prawns and drank tea.
Doctor	Hmm…maybe that chilli dish was too spicy for you. How long have you been feeling like this?
Tom	For three hours.
Doctor	What else do you feel?
Tom	I am urinating frequently. I feel weak.
Doctor	Let me examine (you). Excuse me. Are you allergic to any medicines?

| Tom | Yes, I am allergic to Augmentin. |
| **Doctor** | Fine, I will change the medicine to another one. Take it three times a day. With a bit of luck you will recover quickly and don't eat spicy foods. |

How the language works 2

1 Throughout the course you will have noticed that there are many expressions where a word is doubled, sometimes with a prefix added and sometimes with a vowel change in the second word. This is technically known as *reduplication*. So far, the only usage we have looked at gave you the information that the doubling of a noun is sometimes required to create a plural form (refer back to Unit 5).

Although there is no particular reason why reduplication occurs in certain expressions, such as **kupu-kupu**, *butterfly* there are three broad categories of (added) meaning that reduplicated expressions fall into:

▶ expressions of time

pagi-pagi *early in the morning*

malam-malam *late at night*

kadang-kadang *sometimes*

sekejap-kejap *now and again*

sekali-sekala *once in a while*

tiba-tiba *suddenly*

▶ doing something in a leisurely way or with no particular goal in mind

duduk-duduk *to sit about (relaxing)*

jalan-jalan *to go out for a stroll, to 'hang around'*

lihat-lihat *to browse*

cakap-cakap *to chat* (this also means *by the way* in certain contexts)

▶ emphasis

kuat-kuat *loudly*

lekas-lekas *hurry up*

tergesa-gesa *to be in a hurry*

terburu-buru *to be in a hurry*

bermacam-macam *different kinds of*

bersama-sama *together*

cepat-cepat *very quickly*

satu-satu *one by one*

dua-dua *two by two, etc.*

2 Prefix/suffix **pe -an** and **per – an**. In some cases **pe- -an** (**per- -an**) nouns that are created from verb bases correspond to what are known as *verbal* nouns in English. That is, they end in *-ing* but are not expressing a continuous tense.

baca *to read*	**pembacaan** *reading*
jual *to sell*	**penjualan** *selling*
beli *to buy*	**pembelian** *buying*

Formed from a concrete noun, the **pe- -an** (**per- -an**) combination often creates a new noun that extends or augments the meaning of the original noun, which now becomes the base. Look at the following examples, noting the meanings of the original noun and the corresponding modified nouns.

gunung *mountain*	**pergunungan** *mountain range*
sahabat *friend*	**persahabatan** *friendship*
bandar *city*	**perbandaran** *urbanized area*
pustaka *book*	**perpustakaan** *library*

> ● **INSIGHT**
>
> **Pustaka** is an archaic word for *book* and **perpustakaan** is *a collection of books*, i.e. *library*. The modern word for *book* is **buku**.

Some of the nouns created by **pe- -an** (**per- -an**) carry meanings that can be a little difficult to relate directly to the original base verb. When the meaning of both the base verb and the created noun are known, however, the link is easy to see, even if it sometimes requires a little lateral thinking as to how the meaning evolved:

menginap *to spend the night (somewhere)*	**rumah penginapan** *inn*
membangun *to build*	**pembangunan** *construction*
terbit *to appear*	**penerbitan** *publishing house*
main *to play*	**permainan** *game*

Penginapan derives its meaning from *a place to spend the night i.e. an inn*.

In Unit 8 we met a few verbs that have different meanings when the prefix **me-** is attached, one of which was **bangun** which, when the prefix is added, means to *build*. The meaning of **pembangunan** is the noun derived from the prefixed verb **membangun**.

> ● **INSIGHT**
>
> If you think of **penerbitan** as a place which makes things appear, i.e. be published, then the link between the verb and the noun becomes clear.

Exercise 6

Using what you know about **pe- -an** (**per- -an**) type nouns from the information given above, see if you can work out the meaning of the nouns in the right-hand column created from the noun (**a–d**) and verb (**e–i**) bases in the left-hand column.

a sekolah *school*   persekolahan
b kampung *village*   perkampungan
c rumah *house*   perumahan
d kebun *garden*   perkebunan
e cakap *to chat*   percakapan
f periksa *to examine*   pemeriksaan
g umum *to announce*   pengumuman
h lawan *to fight*   perlawanan
i cuba *to try*   percubaan

3 Sound changes. You will have noticed that, when you encounter words with the **me-** or **pe-** prefixes, the base words these words are derived from sometimes look different from the base words themselves. This is because some base words undergo changes when they have the **me-** or **pe-** prefixes attached to them.

The rules are as follows:

▶ When **me-** or **pe-** are used as prefixes before **c**, **d** and **j** they become **men-** and **pen-** respectively:

cuci → mencuci   *to wash*
jemput → menjemput   *to pick up, to invite*
jual → penjual   *seller*
daki → pendaki   *climber*

▶ These prefixes also become **men-** and **pen-** before bases beginning with **t** but in this case, the **t** disappears:

terima → menerima   *to receive*
tangis → menangis   *to cry*
tarik → penarikan   *pull*
tari → penari   *dancer*

▶ **me-** and **pe-** become **mem-** and **pem-** before **b**:

buang → membuang   *to throw*
bungkus → membungkus   *to wrap up*
bantu → pembantu   *helper*
beritahu → pemberitahuan   *announcement*

▶ They also become **mem-** and **pem-** before **p** but the **p** disappears:

pinjam → meminjam   *to borrow*
pijak → memijak   *to step*
pilih → pemilihan   *election*
pandu → pemandu   *guide*

- **me-** becomes **meng-** and **pe-** becomes **peng-** before **g** or **h**:

ganti → mengganti	*to replace*
hidup → menghidupkan	*to turn on (an appliance)*
ganggu → pengganguan	*annoying*
habis → penghabisan	*conclusion*

- **meng-** and **peng-** are also used before **k** which disappears:

kira → mengira	*to count*
kirim → mengirim	*to send*
kenal → pengenalan	*identification*
kelas → pengelasan	*classification*

- **me-** and **pe-** become **meng-** and **peng-** before a vowel:

isi → mengisi	*to fill in*
ambil → mengambil	*to take*
urus → pengurus	*manager*
alam → pengalaman	*experience*

- **me-** becomes **meny-** and **pe-** becomes **peny-** before bases beginning with **s** but note that the **s** disappears:

sorok → menyorokkan	*to hide*
sebut → menyebut	*to mention*
seberang → penyeberang	*crossing*
sewa → penyewaan	*renting out*

Exercise 7

How do you think these words will appear when the prefix shown in the left-hand column is added? (For some of the words a suffix has already been added to create a useful word, the meaning of which is given in the right-hand column. The root appears in bold.)

a	me-	**terjemah** kan	*to translate*
b	me-	**usik**	*to tease*
c	me-	**sikat**	*to comb*
d	me-	**bantah**	*to argue*
e	pe-	**bangun**an	*construction*
f	pe-	**serang**	*attacker*
g	pe-	**segar**	*stimulating*
h	pe-	**importan**	*importation*

Using Malay

Exercise 8

Look at the pictures and write the word(s) for each illness.

Exercise 9

Over to you!

You (**B**) have gone to see a doctor (**A**) because you are having trouble with your eyes.

 16.04

A	Silakan duduk, Encik. Apa sakit dan apa masalah Encik?
B	*My eyes are itching and pricking.*
A	Sudah berapa lama?
B	*For two days, since Sunday.*
A	Kenapa boléh begini?
B	*I'm allergic to dust, Doctor. At first my eyes were red, but after that (they became) swollen.*
A	Mari saya periksa. Baiklah, tidak terlalu serius tetapi, saya beri anda dua jenis ubat, satunya ubat titis mata. Dititis tiga kali sehari. Mudah-mudahan anda cepat sembuh.
B	*Thank you, Doctor.*

Quick vocab

gatal	*itching*
perit	*pricking*
mulanya	*at first*
selepas itu	*after that*
bengkak	*swollen*
serius	*serious*
jenis	*type*
ubat titis	*drops*
dititis (titis)	*to be taken* (lit. *to be dropped*)

Test yourself

1 How do you say *sick*, *ill* or *it hurts* in Malay?

2 What verbs are possible in Malay, where we use *to take* (of medicine) in English?

3 When making a positive command, what must be removed from the verb?

4 What happens to the suffix **-kan** when making a positive command?

5 How do you form a negative command?

6 What does the suffix **-lah** do to a command?

7 What three broad meanings does reduplication create?

8 What kind of noun do **per- -an** and **pe- -an** create in Malay?

9 Under what circumstances do **me-** and **pe-** become **men-** and **pen-**?

10 Under what circumstances do **me-** and **pe-** become **meng-** and **peng-**?

Taking it further

Materials and opportunities for studying Malay are rather scarce in comparison to other world languages, but there are a few intermediate to advanced materials out there, if you know where to look for them. Here are a few suggestions to get you started:

▶ Times Editions of Singapore (Times Centre, 1 New Industrial Road, Singapore 536196, Tel: (65) 6213 9288, http://www.timespublishing.sg, E-mail: te@tpl.com.sg) carries a selection of good Malay and Indonesian textbooks at beginner and more advanced levels. The only major drawback is that none of the books has any audio component.

▶ EPB Publishers also of Singapore (EPB Publishers Pte Ltd, 162 Bukit Merah Central #04-3545, Singapore 150162) publish several courses by Malcolm W Mintz for students of Malay and Indonesian, beginner to advanced level. They contain audio components where applicable. You may find Listening Comprehension: Selections from Malaysian and Indonesian History and later Advanced Writings for Students of Malay and Indonesian useful as learning materials after *Complete Malay*.

▶ An excellent dual-text book that focuses on reading comprehension and vocabulary development, and that would be a useful follow-on, is Learning Bahasa Malaysia through its History and Culture 2002, Golden Books Centre Sdn. Bhd., WISMA ILBS, No 10 Jalan 8/5G. Perdana Business Centre, Bandar Damansara Perdana, 47820 Petaling Jaya, Selangor Darul Ehsan. Tel: 03-77273890, http://www.goldenbookscentre.com, E-mail: gbc@pc.jaring.my).

▶ Kamus Dwibahasa Oxford-Fajar: Inggeris-Melayu, Melayu Inggeris by Joyce M. Hawkins (Penerbit Fajar Bakti Sdn.Bhd. (008974-T) 4 Jalan Pemaju U1/15, Seksyen U1, Hicom-Glenmarie Industrial Park, 40150 Shah Alam, Selangor Darul Ehsan), although not ideal, is the most useable dictionary I have found so far.

Internet Resources

ONLINE NEWSPAPERS

http://www.bharian.com.my/

http://www.harakahdaily.net/

http://www.utusan.com.my/

Web radio on a variety of topics, mostly aimed at younger listeners

http://www.radio1.com.my/

http://www.rtmjb.net.my/

http://radio.mmu.edu.my/

http://www.languagelearningsecrets.com/

http://languagelearning.ws/

Internet contacts

It can really help to establish contacts with Malay speakers as soon as possible, both to practise your Malay, and to seek out answers to questions you may have about the language.

The following websites are free to join, and exist expressly to put language learners in contact with native speakers of other languages for mutual language practice. If you are new to the Internet, please note that it is wise to exercise a certain level of caution when joining discussion fora or friendship sites, especially in the early stages. It is best to withhold personal details (except those you need to sign up for the service) until you are very sure the person you are talking to is genuine.

http://www.polyglot-learn-language.com/

http://www.mylanguageexchange.com/

http://www.language-buddy.com/main.asp

All the above web addresses are correct at the time of writing. Neither the authors nor the publishers are responsible for their content.

If you know of, or come across any other useful Malay resources on your linguistic travels, or if you just wish to send me any comments, I would be delighted to hear from you.

Visit http://www.bahasamalaysia.co.uk for contact information. Further resources are also available from this site.

Key to the exercises

(Note: The accent on é is intended as a pronunciation guide only. Written answers missing accents are still correct.)

Pronunciation guide

Down 1 sekolah 3 tempat 6 enam 9 baru 11 nama 13 tidak 15 kedai 18 istiméwa Across 2 empat 4 enak 5 meréka 7 sila 8 hebat 10 makanan 12 satu 14 suka 16 dua 17 tiga 19 lima 20 bilik 21 warna 22 pertama.

Unit 1

1 a Saya John. Saya (berasal) dari England. **b** Saya Kylie. Saya (berasal) dari Australia. **c** Saya Fatimah. Saya (berasal) dari Malaysia. **2 1** Kamal – Singapura – mahasiswa **2** Huzaini – Sumatera – usahawan **3** Farah – Melaka – penari **4** Safia – Brunei Darussalam – pelancong **3 a** T **b** F **c** T **d** T **4 a** Ini kamus. **b** Dia usahawan. **c** Itu kopi. **d** Ini kedai. **e** Dia guru. **f** Ini air. **5 a** Adakah ini kamus? **b** Adakah dia usahawan? **c** Adakah itu kopi? **d** Adakah ini kedai? **e** Adakah dia guru? **f** Adakah ini air? **6** Maaf… Adakah saudara ini Encik Salléh dari Malaysia? Ya, betul. Selamat datang ke England. Nama saya Robert Davies. Adakah anda dari syarikat perniagaan Singapore Seas Imports? Ya saya. Selamat berkenalan. Saya gembira dapat berkenalan dengan anda juga. Excuse me… Are you Mr Salleh from Malaysia? Yes, that's correct. Welcome to England. My name is Robert Davies. Are you from the Singapore Seas Exports Company? Yes, I am. Nice to meet you. I'm pleased to meet you too. **7** Maaf. Adakah saudari ini Puan Fauziah? Saya dari syarikat ABC Exports Business Company. Selamat datang ke England. Nama saya Mark Spencer. Begitu juga dengan saya. **Test yourself 1** Selamat tengah hari **2** Selamat pagi **3** Nama saya ____ (or just Saya ____) **4** Saya dari Singapura or Saya berasal dari Singapura **5** Selamat datang ke England **6 Saudara** is used for males, and **saudari** for females **7** Kita **8** Perkenalkan, ini Puan Walters **9** Adakah **10** Gembira dapat bertemu dengan anda juga (*alternatively*, Saya juga begitu or Begitu juga dengan saya).

Unit 2

1 a foto dia **b** hadiah meréka **c** jam tangan saya **d** gambar kita (*or* kami) **2 a** Biar saya tunggu di sini. **b** Biar saya ambil beg itu. **c** Mari kita bercakap bahasa Melayu! **d** Mari kita pergi ke Ipoh! **3 a** F **b** T **c** F **d** F **4** Dia sudah **menulis** surat. *He has written a letter*. Meréka sedang **membaca** akhbar. *They are reading a newspaper*. Dia **mengajar** bahasa Melayu. *She teaches Malay*. Saya sedang **minum** téh. *I am drinking tea*. Kami sedang **menonton** télevisyen. *We are watching TV*. **5 a** Apakah ini semua bagasi anda? **b** Apakah meréka sedang menunggu di luar? **c** Apakah dia tersangkut dalam kesesakan lalu-lintas? **d** Apakah kami terlewat? **6 1** b **2** a **3** a **4** a **7** Maaf. Saya sedang sibuk. Ya. Bagus kalau begitu. **Test yourself 1** Terima kasih banyak **2 Saya guru** means I am a teacher; **guru saya** means my teacher **3 Bahasa kami** refers to one's native language, but not that of the persons to whom you are speaking; **bahasa kita** is inclusive, and refers to the language you share with the person you are speaking to **4** Biar **5** Because the form remains the same no matter what the time-frame referred to **6** Maaf **7** Apakah **8** Say the statement with a rising intonation **9** Bahasa Melayu, *or officially*, Bahasa Malaysia **10** An accidental occurrence.

Unit 3

1 a orang Sepanyol **b** bahasa Cina **c** orang Scotland **d** orang Indonesia **e** bahasa Belanda **f** orang Amérika **g** orang New Zealand **h** bahasa Melayu **i** orang Singapura **j** bahasa Jepun **2 a** bagasi berat **b** pakaian sukan **c** bilik tidur **d** teman guru bahasa Malaysia saya **e** guru bahasa Malaysia teman saya **3 a** F **b** T **c** T **d** T **4 a** Indonesian **b** fluently **c** English **d** It's too fast **5 a** Dia **tidak** sopan. **b** Meréka **tidak** buta. **c** Kami **tidak** tinggal di Johor Bahru. **d** Itu **bukan** keréta saya. **e** Dia **tidak** gembira. **6 a** bukan **b** tidak **c** tidak **d** tidak **7 a Dari mana** dia masuk? **b Di mana** dia belajar? **c Ke mana** meréka membawa bagasi itu? **d Dari mana** kami datang? **8 a Berapa lama** penerbangan dari London ke Singapura? **b Berapa kali** anda makan nasi? **c Berapa lama** kita menunggu? **d Berapa lama** dia tinggal di Malaysia? **e Berapa kali** dia teléfon? **9 a** Saya tidak pernah melihat film itu. **b** (Apakah/Adakah) kamu pernah (pergi) ke Melaka? **c** Kami pernah makan durian. **d** Dia pernah tinggal di Amérika. **10 a** Meréka tidak tiba semalam. **b** Ini bukan penerbangan ke Kota Kinabalu. **c** Saya tidak bercakap bahasa Arab. **d** Isteri saya bukan orang Singapura. **e** Itu bukan orang utan. **f** Eman tidak keras kepala. **11 a** Dia tidak orang Brazil. X Dia **bukan** orang Brazil. **b** Dia bukan pemain bola sépak. **c** Kami tidak bahagia. **d** Saya bukan bodoh. X Saya **tidak** bodoh. **e** Kelmarin meréka bukan datang. X Kelmarin meréka **tidak** datang. **12 a** Apa khabar? **b** Bagaimana dengan penerbangan anda/saudara? **c** Apa anda (kamu, Encik, etc.) masih bujang? **d** Siapa nama anda/saudara? **e** (Apakah/Adakah) anda/saudara pernah ke Miami? **f** Berapa lama meréka mahu tinggal di Miri? **g** (Apakah/Adakah) anda/saudara orang Malaysia/Singapura/Indonesia etc.)? **13** Apakah anda orang Malaysia? Apa khabar? Maaf. Siapa nama anda? Nama saya Stuart. Anda boléh panggil saya Stu. Jangan bimbang. Saya pernah belajar bahasa Malaysia di sekolah. Di mana anda tinggal? Bagaimana dengan Australia? Berapa lama anda tinggal di Canberra? Selamat bercuti! **Test yourself 1** Apa khabar? **2** A French person **3** Bahasa Inggeris **4** dalam **5** can, to be able to **6** Saya tidak faham (*may occur with* **Maaf**) **7** You use **siapa** (*who*) not **apa** (*what*) **8 Bukan** is used with nouns and pronouns; **tidak** is used with verbs and adjectives **9** after **10 Selamat tinggal** is said by the person leaving; **selamat jalan** by the person staying.

Unit 4

1 a Sila(kan) menyany! *Please sing!* **b** Sila(kan) bercakap bahasa Melayu! *Please speak Malay!* **c** Sila(kan) minum! *Please drink!* **d** Sila(kan) menari *Please dance!* **e** Sila(kan) masuk! *Please enter/come in!* **2 a** Sila(kan) memandu dengan berhati-hati! **b** Sila(kan) menulis dengan tepat! **c** Sila(kan) membaca dengan perlahan-lahan! **3 a** T **b** F **c** F **d** T **e** F **4** David Teng is the best choice. He can use a computer, can speak English and has the longest time in sales and marketing. **5 a** kameramu **b** cermin matamu **c** kuncimu **d** pasportmu **6 a** tahun (yang) lalu **b** bulan depan (hadapan/akan datang) **c** dua tahun yang lalu **d** minggu (yang) lalu **e** tadi petang / petang ini **7 a** Dia sudah/Telah menulis **b** Meréka sedang menaip **c** Saya sedang bercakap/berbual **d** Dia sudah/Telah membaca **e** Kamu sedang belajar? / Apa / Apakah /

Adakah kamu sedang belajar? **8 a** iii **b** i **c** ii **d** iv **9 a** doktor, jururawat **b** suri rumah tangga **c** tukang masak **d** arkitek **e** wartawan **10** Saya guru bahasa. Saya ada banyak pengalaman mengajar bahasa Inggeris dan saya fasih dalam tiga bahasa. Di Institusi Bahasa Antarabangsa. Dua ribu dolar, jika boléh. Bulan depan. **Test yourself 1** Sila, *or even more politely*, silakan **2** *can* and *may* **3** mampu **4** use **dengan** + adjective **5** seorang **6** bulan depan, bulan hadapan, bulan akan datang **7** ésok pagi *or* bésok pagi **8** use the tense marker **sedang** **9** sudah *and* telah **10** when the time frame is obvious from the context.

Unit 5

1 a Dia sedang tidur, bukan? *He's sleeping, isn't he?* or *She's sleeping, isn't she?* **b** Itu salah, bukan? *That's wrong, isn't it?* **c** Meréka bukan askar, bukan? *They aren't soldiers, are they?* **2 a** sangat gelap, gelap sekali **b** sangat luas, luas sekali **c** sangat bagus, bagus sekali **d** sangat kuat, kuat sekali **e** sangat penat, penat sekali **3 a** cucu perempuan **b** mertua lelaki **c** anak saudara lelaki **d** kakak perempuan **4 a** pukul tangannya **b** sekolah rendahnya **c** kebunnya **d** alat CDnya **e** Anak saudara perempuannya comel sekali. **5 a** Kita / Kami (sedang) menunggu meréka. **b** Dia (sudah) meneléfon saya. **c** Meréka (sudah) mengganggu dia. **d** Dia mencintainya. **e** Kita/Kami (sudah) pergi dengan meréka. **6 a** Umur kembar saya empat tahun. **b** Angie berumur sembilan tahun. **c** Umur yang sulong tiga tahun. **d** Adik lelakinya berumur lima tahun. **7 a** T **b** F **c** T **d** F **e** F **f** T **g** T **8 1** a; **2** e; **3** b; **4** c; **5** d. **9 a Anak-anak** *children* (without a double plural this would mean *'child'*) **b** saudara perempuan **c** buku **d filem-filem** *films* (without a double plural this would mean *'film'*) **e beg-beg** *bags* (without a double plural it would mean *'bag'*) **10 a** Dengan siapa **b** Daripada siapa **c** Untuk siapa **d** Kepada siapa **11 a** Amir **b** Evon **c** Sue **d** Amir **e** Dev **f** Sue **12 a** dapur **b** bilik tidur **c** bilik keluarga **d** bilik makan **13 a** di belakang **b** di antara **c** di sebelah kanan **d** di depan **e** di sebelah kiri **14** Terima kasih. Tak payah susah-susah. Ya, betul. Saya ada dua anak. Yang pertama tujuh tahun dan yang kedua empat tahun. Di mana dapur? Terima kasih. Bilik siapa itu? **Test yourself 1** bukan **2** sangat **3** add **ke-** to the cardinal **4** yang **5** ada *and* mempunyai **6 –nya** means *his, her* or *their* and it is attached to the noun or adjective **7** nama saya, saya bernama; umur saya, saya berumur **8** use **dulu** or **dahulu 9** by doubling the noun **10** when the context is clear doubling the noun is unnecessary.

Unit 6

1 a Ada kedai cenderamata. **b** Ada restoran-restoran tradisional. **c** Apa(kah) ada kuih-kuih yang lain di kedai ini? **d** Tidak ada hotél. **e** Apa(kah) ada keterangan/maklumat? **f** Apa(kah) ada pusat sukan? **g** Tidak ada balai seni. **2 a** filem yang panjang dan bosan **b** anak yang bersemangat dan pandai **c** perjalanan yang panjang dan meletihkan **d** tempat peranginan yang meriah, ramai dan mahal **e** bilik yang besar, nyaman dan moden **3 a** lima puluh empat **b** tujuh puluh lapan **c** lapan puluh satu **d** sembilan puluh sembilan **4 a** Pukul tujuh. **b** Pukul empat setengah. **c** Pukul sembilan empat puluh lima minit. **d** Pukul sepuluh suku. **e** Pukul satu dua suku. **5 a** Hari ini hari Jumaat. **b** Ésok hari Khamis. **c** Lusa hari Jumaat. **d** Ésok hari Khamis. **6 a** rumah yang dia bina **b** bandar yang kami lawat **c** gadis yang dulu bekerja di sini **7 a** F **b** T **c** T **d** F **e** F **8 a** Pukul empat setengah (4.30) **b** Pukul tiga empat suku (3.45) **c** Pukul tujuh lima puluh lima minit (7.55) **d** Pukul satu dua puluh minit (1.20) **e** Pukul enam lima minit (6.05) **f** Pukul dua belas setengah (12.30) **g** Pukul sembilan empat puluh lima minit (9.45) **h** Pukul tiga suku (3.15) **9 a** Bunga apa ini? **b** Program apa itu? **c** Bahasa apa ini? **10 a** Apa anda / saudara / kamu mahu lagi? **b** Saya harus / mesti mandi lagi. **11 a** Dia bukan penari lagi. **b** Dia tidak kaya lagi. **12 a** Kami hendak pergi ke Kelantan pada hari Ahad. **b** Di Poring ada banyak kemudahan seperti air panas, kolam renang dan restoran. **c** Dari pusat kota ke sana memakan masa dua jam. **13 a** Pukul sebelas. **b** Pukul dua empat puluh minit (tengah hari). **c** Pukul dua belas sepuluh minit. **d** Hari Khamis. **e** Pukul lapan setengah. **14** Ya, saya ingin beberapa maklumat tentang Kuala Lumpur. Apa yang boléh saya lihat di sana? Ada hiburan malam yang sangat baik? Naik pesawat apa ke sana? Adakah termasuk makanan? Berapa harganya? Terima kasih atas maklumat anda. **Test yourself 1** ada **2** use **belas 3** use **puluh 4** pukul **5** by using the numbers 15 or 30, or by using **suku** and **setengah** respectively **6 pada hari Rabu** (or just **hari Rabu** in spoken Malay) **7** use them when what you say can be replaced by *what is it that* and *who is it that* respectively **8** Hari apa? **9** in positive sentences it means *further*, *more* and *again*, and in negative sentences it means *not…any* and *not…any longer* **10** atas.

Unit 7

1 a Kami **sekelas** ada ujian. **b** Dia **seumur** dengan saya. **2 a** Sampaikan salam saya kepada dia. **b** Sampaikan salam kami kepada Sue. **c** Sampaikan salam kami kepada meréka. **d** Sampaikan salam saya sekeluarga kepada meréka. **3 a** T **b** F **c** F **d** T **e** F **f** T **g** F **4** 1 c **2** d **3** f **4** e **5** a **6** b **5 a** Meréka (sudah) pergi berdua. **b** Kami bertiga bersahabat dengan baik. **c** Kami bersepuluh (sudah) mendaki Gunung Kinabalu. **6 a** drink **b** reply **c** toy **d** choice **e** purchase **f** entertainment **g** work **h** thought **7 a** No. 9 Jalan Melati – pukul 4 petang – Riana dan Ramona **b** Déwan Suria – 7 haribulan Jun – pukul 7 malam **c** Universiti Sains Antarabangsa – 9 haribulan Jun – pukul 10 pagi **d** 31 Disember – Khamis – pukul 8 malam **8** Terima kasih. Bilakah? Boléh. Saya tidak ada pekerjaan ésok. Maaf kami tidak biasa. Terima kasih. Sehingga kita berjumpa lagi. **Test yourself 1** the same **2 mengapa?** or **kenapa?**, the latter being more conversational **3** –lah **4** a prefix is added to the beginning of a word, a suffix is added to the end **5** berlima **6** bersama dengan **7** pada bulan Ogos, *or just* bulan Ogos **8** nouns, verbs and adjectives **9** it extends the meaning of the base noun **10** it reflects the quality of the adjective base.

Unit 8

1 a (Maaf, tumpang tanya), bagaimana menuju ke hotél Mandarin Pacific? **b** (Maaf, tumpang tanya), Bagaimana boléh saya pergi ke KLIA? **c** (Maaf, tumpang tanya), bagaimana menuju ke Menara Genesis? **2 a** T **b** F **c** F **d** T **e** F **f** T **3 a** Taman Orkid **b** Tugu Negara **c** LRT Universiti **d** Zoo Negara **e** Hotél Milah **4 a** lurus, bélok, menyeberang, antara **b** keluar, bélok, terus, menyeberang, belakang **c** keluar, bélok, lurus, sudut **5** Saya tersesat. Saya mahu pergi ke pejabat pos. Itu dekat stésen LRT? Boléh saudara tunjukkan di peta ini? Kita di mana sekarang? Terima kasih banyak-banyak. **Test yourself 1** di mana? di manakah? bagaimana menuju ke? bagaimana boléh saya ke? **2** tumpang Tanya **3** false **4** as complete vocabulary items **5** the **r** drops **6** me- **7** no **8 melepas** means *to let go*; **berlepas** means *to depart* **9 membuat** means *to make*; **berbuat** means *to do* **10** di samping kanan.

Unit 9

1 a sembilan belas ribu empat ratus tiga puluh dua **b** dua juta lapan ratus enam puluh lima ribu tujuh ratus empat belas **c** tiga ribu seratus sembilan puluh tujuh **d** lapan juta enam ratus ribu seratus sebelas e dua puluh lima juta seratus lima puluh lima ribu enam ratus tiga belas **2 a** T **b** T **c** T **d** F **e** T **f** T **3** 1st Xiao Ling, 2nd Michael, 3rd Ravin (unless you win!) **4 a** Beratnya 56 kilo. **b** Tingginya 45 sentimeter. **c** Lebarnya 100 meter. **d** Dalamnya 2 meter. **e** Lamanya 7 jam. **5 a** to fast **b** to move **c** to have a family / to be married **6 a** to slice **b** to paddle **c** to tax **7 a** dua puluh lima juta **b** empat ribu seratus **c** sembilan belas lima puluh tujuh **d** dua juta **e** tiga belas **f** lima belas sebelas **g** sembilan belas sembilan puluh lapan **h** empat ratus lima puluh dua **i** dua ribu **j** tiga ratus enam puluh sembilan **k** sembilan puluh sembilan **l** seratus tiga puluh satu ribu lapan ratus lima **m** lima ratus enam puluh tujuh **8** Selamat tengah hari. Boléh saya tukar dolar kepada ringgit? Tidak, dolar Singapura. Berapakah kadar pertukaran? 1.000 dolar. Tolong beri saya beberapa wang kecil. **Test yourself 1** by using **ratus 2** by using **ribu 3** by using **juta 4** se- **5** add the numbers after **tahun 6** it creates expressions such as *hundreds* and *millions* **7** it can express *the*, and it is also used with prices, fares, weights and measures **8** in expressions where the subject is already established, and with prices, fares, weights and measures **9** it creates a verb meaning to do what is implicit in the noun base **10** it creates a verb meaning to do what is implicit in the noun base.

Unit 10

1 a Berapa tambang(nya) ke Penang? **b** Berapa tambang(nya) dari Bangsar ke Klia? **2 a** tujuh bulan lagi **b** lima puluh lima minit lagi **c** tiga minggu lagi **3 a** dua kali setahun **b** tiga kali sehari **c** satu kali seabad **4 a** F **b** T **c** F **d** F **e** T **f** F **5 a** ii **b** i **c** vi **d** v **e** iii **f** vii **g** viii **h** iv **6 a** beg yang mana **b** idea yang mana **7** (possible answers) **a** nombor berapa **b** Boléh kami dapat **c** Tolong buat **d** Tolong hantarkan **e** Berapa **f** Berapa lama **g** tertinggal **h** Naik apa **8** Saya mahu beli tikét ke Melbourne. Kelas ekonomi. Minggu depan pada 15 September. Berapa tambangnya? Berapa lama penerbangan ke Melbourne dari Kuala Lumpur? Baik. Tolong buat tempahan atas nama Daniel Johnson. Boléh dapatkan saya tempat duduk dekat tingkap? **Test yourself 1** tambang **2** boléh saya dapatkan…? **3** you should not do whatever follows **Dilarang 4** in **5 lagi** means *in*, as in after a certain amount of time has passed, whereas **dalam masa** refers to the time it takes to do something **6** *once*, as in *once a day* **7 semasa** or **ketika** are used to express the past; **kalau** or **jika** refer to the future **8** naik **9** ber- **10** which one?

Unit 11

1 Bila lalu Rosa bercuti dengan sepupunya di Genting Highlands? Tahun lalu siapa bercuti dengan sepupunya di Genting Highlands? Tahun lalu Rosa bercuti dengan siapa di Genting Highlands? Tahun lalu Rosa bercuti dengan sepupunya di mana? **2 a i** Does he eat? **ii** What does he eat? **b i** Do you want to order? **ii** What do you want to order? **c i** Do you read? **ii** What do you read? **3 a** T **b** F **c** F **d** T **e** F **f** F **4** Answers will vary. **5 a** kesihatan *health* **b** keamanan *safety* **c** kebersihan *cleanliness* **d** kemudahan *ease* **e** keburukan *ugliness* **f** kenyamanan *pleasantness* **g** kebodohan *stupidity* **h** kesenangan *happiness* **6 a** Meréka akan berangkat ke England pada hari apa? **b** Yanti pergi ke mana dengan Siti. **c** Pertunjukan Ramayana mula pukul berapa? **d** Penerbangan dari Jakarta ke Kuala Lumpur berapa lama? **e** Bila meréka akan pergi bercuti ke Pulau Redang? **f** Orang tuanya sudah datang dari mana? **g** Kita boléh pergi dengan apa ke pusat bandar? **h** Bas Kuala Lumpur – Johor Bahru ada berapa kali sehari? **7** Ya. Saya ingin tinggal di sini untuk beberapa hari. Apakah masih ada bilik yang kosong? Berapa harganya satu malam? Apakah sudah termasuk sarapan pagi? Sehingga 10 hari bulan Disember. Boléh saya bayar dengan mata wang selain dolar Amérika? Boléh, sebentar. Apakah di sini ada sauna? Ia buka pada pukul berapa? Terima kasih. **Test yourself 1** Apa boléh dapatkan? *or* Apa boléh beri? **2** to look out onto (*or* with a view of) **3** it should replace the thing asked about in the corresponding statement **4** apa? **5** -kah **6** biasa **7** dengan **8** they form a noun that refers to the quality referred to in the adjective **9** they create nouns **10** they form another noun, sometimes referring to institutions.

Unit 12

1 a kedinginan *too cold* **b kepanasan** *too hot* **c kesakitan** *too sick* **d kepahitan** *too bitter* **e kelaparan** *too hungry* **f ketinggian** *too tall* **2 a** lebih daripada **b** lebih daripada **c** lebih daripada **3 a** lebih baik **b** paling murah **c** paling sulit **d** lebih cantik **e** lebih ramai **f** lebih pedas **g** paling lapar **h** lebih panas **i** lebih kotor **j** paling kecil **4 a** Patung itu dibuat daripada batu marmar. **b** Pasu ini dibuat daripada tanah liat. **c** Bola ini dibuat daripada getah. **5 a** bertali léhér **b** bersarung tangan **c** berskirt **d** berbaju hujan **e** berseluar hitam **f** berkaca mata gelap **g** bertopi rotan **6 a** F **b** F **c** F **d** T **e** T **f** F **7 a** keméja **b** tali léhér **c** jaket **d** seluar (panjang) **e** sarung kaki **f** kasut **g** blaus **h** skirt **i** kalung **8 a** semurah **b** seberat **c** semalu **9 a** sama miskinnya dengan **b** sama botaknya dengan **c** sama bergayanya dengan **10 a** embarrassing **b** pleasing **c** satisfying **d** worrying **e** boring **f** frightening **11 a** zirafah **b** kapal terbang **c** Ben **d** Pulau Sumatera **e** Saudi Arabia **12 a** Rusia **b** Asia **c** China **d** Amazon **e** Gunung Kinabalu **13 a** penuh dengan **b** kahwin dengan **c** bercakap dengan **d** sama dengan **e** dengan jip **f** bertanya dengan **g** kenal dengan **h** biasa dengan **i** berteman dengan **14 a** topi-topi bambu **b** seluar batik RM50.00 24 **c** cincin pérak **d** wayang RM75.00 kayu **15** Saya mahu membeli sesuatu untuk abang saya. Tali léhér ini dibuat daripada kain apa? Berapa harganya? Apakah itu harga yang tetap? Baiklah, saya nak dua dengan corak yang berlainan. **Test yourself 1 terlalu** and by using **ke- -an 2** lebih…daripada **3** paling **4** made of/from **5** it becomes **-ku 6** the verb **pakai** or the prefix **ber**- added to the clothing item **7** ter- **8** by adding **se**- to the adjective and by using **sama…dengan 9** they create a verb that can often be translated by an *-ing* adjective in English **10** it is a verb used to express an action carried out for someone's benefit, and it is formed with the prefix **me-** in combination with the suffix **-kan**.

Unit 13

1 (possible answers) Saya mahu pesan (sepinggan) nasi goréng. Boléh minta (sepinggan) nasi kerabu. Boléh pesan (sepinggan) mi hailam? Boléh tambah lagi otak-otak? **2 a** F **b** T **c** T **d** T **e** F **f** F **3 a** Rosie: saté ayam, rojak buah, popiah, sambal, bubur pulut hitam, wain putih; Sam: saté ayam, pulut kuning, rendang, sambal, wain mérah. **b i** to view the scenery **ii** if she could have the recipe **iii** 48 ringgit **4 a** Saya mahu pesan laksa. Berapa harganya semangkuk? Jangan terlalu pedas. **b** Saya mahu pesan teh. Berapa harganya sebotol? Tolong jangan bubuh ais. **c** Saya mahu pesan nasi goréng. Berapa harganya sepinggan? Jangan bubuh telur. Tolong dibungkus. **d** Saya mahu pesan saté kambing. Berapa harganya sepinggan? Boléh minta setengah matang. **5 a** kelonggaran **b** kepedasan **c** kesejukan **d** kehujanan **e** kecurian **f** kepanasan **g** ketinggalan **6** Untuk satu orang. Saya mahu pesan mi goréng. Apakah itu mengandung udang? Bagus kalau begitu. Saya alergi kalau makan udang. Apa ada ais campur? Saya mahu pesan ais campur tanpa tape. Cukup itu saja. Berapa lama makanannya siap? Tidak apa-apa. Terima kasih. **Test yourself 1** Saya mahu pesan, Boléh minta *and* Boléh pesan **2** ABC **3** Boléh tambah lagi? **4** beef **5** sepinggan *or* satu pinggan **6** The choice depends on what the item comes in **7** It can indicate something unplanned, usually unfortunate, has happened **8** The prefix **ter-.**

Unit 14

1 a sedikit kopi **b** sedikit nasi goréng **c** beberapa resipi **d** sedikit pengetahuan **e** beberapa ikan keli **2 a** lapan helai kertas **b** sebuah betik **c** setangkai bunga mawar **d** empat ékor burung **e** tiga buah kamus **3 a** F **b** T **c** T **d** F **e** F **f** T **4 a** daging lembu, santan, cili, bawang mérah, bawang putih, halia, ketumbar, lengkuas, serai, daun kunyit, daun salam, daun limau purut **b** 2 **c** 1 **d** ya **e** (kira-kira) 1 jam **5 a** dicari **b** diperiksa **c** ditulis **d** dikirim **e** dihantar **f** dijemput **6 a** Pakaian dicuci (oléh) kakak. **b** Sayuran dibeli (oléh) meréka. **c** Ubat harus diminum tiga kali sehari. **d** Pesakit disuntik (oléh) doktor. **7 a** seékor **b** sebuah **c** sebutir **d** sehelai **e** setangkai **f** sepucuk **8 a** Saya mau beli ikan. Berapa harga sekilonya? **b** Saya mahu beli lobak mérah. Berapa harga sekilonya? **c** Saya mahu beli whiski. Berapa harga sebotolnya? **d** Saya mahu beli pisang. Berapa harga sekilonya? **9 a** Saya mau beli daging lembu. **b** Dua kilo. Berapa harganya? **c** Tolong potong sekeping-sekeping. **d** Terima kasih. **Test yourself 1 sedikit** can only be used for uncountable things, and **beberapa** can only be used with countable ones **2** you can use it for countable or non-countable things **3** berapa banyak? **4** they are used to count objects according to what category they belong to **5** ékor **6** se- **7** no **8** di- **9** me- **10** oléh.

Unit 15

1 a sukan kegemaran **b** bintang filem kesukaan / kesayangan **c** guru kesukaan / kesayangan **d** drama kegemaran **e** binatang kesukaan/kesayangan **2 a** Teman wanita saya penggemar Leonardo di Caprio. **b** Meréka penggemar makanan Cina. **c** Adik (Kakak) perumpuan Jani penggemar drama lipur lara. **d** Anda (Kamu / Saudara) penggemar bola sépak, (bu)kan? **3 a** F **b** T **c** F **d** T **e** F **f** T **4** 1 **b** 2 a **3** a **4** c **5 a** Saya (sudah) belajar silat selama tiga minggu. **b** Dia tertarik dengan karaté sejak dia pergi ke Jepun. **6 a** writer **b** helper **c** buyer **d** seller **e** guard **f** teacher **g** worker **h** runner **7 a** 3 **b** 4 **c** 7 **d** 13 **e** 14 **f** 8 **g** 5 **h** 15 **i** 17 **j** 16 **k** 12 **l** 9 **m** 6 **n** 1 **o** 11 **p** 15 **q** 2 (possible sample sentences) Saya suka sekali membaca. Saya suka sekali berjemur. Saya suka memasak. Saya suka fotografi. Saya tidak suka begitu menonton di panggung wayang. Saya kurang suka menari. **8** Saya paling suka membaca dan pergi bersiar-siar. Buku-buku psikologi, budaya dan sejarah. Tidak sangat, tapi saya suka sekali novel – novel karya Agatha Christie. Negara-negara di Asia terutamanya Malaysia, Singapura, Brunei Darussalam, Indonesia, Jepun, China dan lain lain. Hm. Saya tidak begitu gemar sukan. Saya juga tidak suka. **Test yourself 1 suka** and **gemar 2** it cannot be used to refer to people or animals **3** use **tidak begitu suka** or **kurang**. (Remember the word **benci** is harsher in Malay than *to hate* in English.) **4** Use **kegemaran** or **kesukaan 5** kesayangan **6** it also means *favourite* and its usage is unrestricted **7** penggemar **8** main **9 selama** and **sejak** respectively **10** it indicates the performer of an action.

Unit 16

1 a Dia sakit kepala. **b** Apakah/Adakah/Ada anda/kamu (etc.) sakit telinga? **c** Tangan saya sakit. **2 a** Keluarkan sampah! **b** Lari lebih cepat! **c** Jangan bekerja sepanjang hari! **d** Jangan beli terlalu banyak coklat. **3 a** T **b** F **c** T **d** F **e** T **4 1** e **2** f **3** i **4** b **5** d **6** a **7** h **8** j **9** g **10** c **5 a** Khamis **b** red herring **c** Jumaat **d** Selasa **e** Ahad **f** Sabtu **g** Rabu **h** Isnin **6 a** schooling **b** rural area **c** accommodation **d** plantation **e** conversation **f** examination **g** announcement **h** fight/struggle **i** experiment **7 a** menterjemahkan **b** mengusik **c** menyikat **d** membantah **e** pembangunan **f** penyerang **g** penyegar **h** pengimportan **8 a** sakit gigi **b** batuk **c** demam **d** sakit kerongkong **e** sakit mata **9** Mata saya gatal dan perit. Sudah dua hari, sejak hari Ahad. Saya alergi pada debu, Doktor. Mulanya mata saya mérah, tetapi selepas itu bengkak. Terima kasih, Doktor. **Test yourself 1** sakit **2** minum *or* makan **3** the **me-** prefix **4** it remains **5** use **jangan 6** it softens it **7** time expressions, doing something with no particular goal in mind and for emphasis **8** one that extends or augments the meaning of the base **9** before **c**, **d**, **j** and **t 10** before **g**, **h**, **k** and vowels.

Listening transcripts

Unit 1, Exercise 2

a Nama saya Kamal. Saya berasal dari Singapura. Saya seorang mahasiswa.

b Nama saya Huzaini. Saya berasal dari Sumatera. Saya seorang usahawan.

c Saya Farah. Saya berasal dari Melaka. Saya seorang penari joget.

d Saya Safia. Saya datang dari Brunei Darussalam. Saya seorang pelancong.

Unit 1, Exercise 6

A	Maaf… Adakah saudara ini Encik Salleh dari Malaysia?
B	Ya, betul.
A	Selamat datang ke England. Nama saya Robert Davies.
B	Adakah anda dari syarikat perniagaan Singapore Seas Imports?
A	Ya, saya. Selamat berkenalan.
B	Saya gembira dapat berkenalan dengan anda juga.

Unit 3, Exercise 4

Rani	Siapakah nama anda?
Interviewee	Nama saya Eva, Eva Nyimas.
Rani	Anda berasal dari Malaysia?
Interviewee	Tidak, saya berasal dari Sumatera di Indonesia.
Rani	Anda bertutur dengan lancar dan jelas sekali. Boléhkah anda bertutur dalam bahasa Cina?
Interviewee	Maaf, boléh Puan tolong ulangi sekali lagi. Saya tidak begitu faham. Puan bertutur dengan lancar dan lembut.
Rani	Boléhkah anda bertutur dalam bahasa Cina?
Interviewee	Tidak, saya hanya boléh bertutur dalam bahasa Indonesia, Melayu dan Inggeris saja.

Unit 5, Exercise 8

1 Nama saya Dayang Suhaila belum berkahwin dan berasal daripada keluarga besar. Ibu dan ayah saya pegawai kerajaan. Saya ada tiga adik-beradik, dua adik lelaki dan seorang kakak. Seorang adik saya, pelajar. Adik saya yang bongsu berumur empat tahun dan belum bersekolah.

2 Saya Gerald, duda dengan dua orang anak. Saya sudah bercerai tiga tahun yang lalu. Anak saya Anna tujuh tahun dan Betty sepuluh tahun. Meréka berdua murid di sekolah rendah.

3 Saya bernama Chan, pengurus di syarikat swasta di Singapura. Isteri saya seorang peréka fesyen di syarikat pakaian kanak-kanak. Anak saya dua orang, seorang lelaki dan seorang perempuan. Justin berumur lapan tahun dan May Li berumur enam tahun.

4 Saya Daniel, masih bujang berasal daripada keluarga kecil. Saya menuntut di Universiti Sains Malaysia, Pulau Pinang. Saya anak tunggal. Ibu saya sibuk bekerja di butik dan ayah saya seorang pensyarah.

5 Saya bernama Vera dari Sabah. Saya sudah berkahwin tapi belum mempunyai anak. Saya tinggal dengan mertua saya.. Suami saya mekanik di sebuah bengkel keréta. Saya tukang jahit baju.

Unit 8, Exercise 3

a	A	Maaf Encik, boléh tumpang tanya. Di mana Taman Orkid Kuala Lumpur?
	B	Kira-kira 200 meter dari sini, dekat Taman Burung. Jalan terus sampai ke satu persimpangan, kemudian bélok kanan.
	A	Terima kasih.

b	A	Tumpang tanya, Encik. Di mana Tugu Negara Malaysia?
	B	Oh, Tugu Negara, maksud cik?
	A	Ya. Betul.
	B	Dari sini jalan terus sampai ke lampu isyarat, kemudian bélok kiri. Tugu Negara terletak dekat Bangunan Parlimen.

c	A	Maaf, Encik. Di mana Stésen LRT Bangsar?
	B	Dekat sini tidak ada Stésen LRT Bangsar, yang ada Stésen LRT Universiti di sebelah blok-blok kondominium itu.
	A	Terima kasih, Encik. Stésen LRT Universitilah yang saya maksudkan.

d	A	Boléh tumpang tanya, Encik. Di mana Zoo Negara?
	B	Maaf, saya tidak tahu. Saya bukan dari sini. Cuba tanya di kedai buku di seberang jalan?
	A	Terima kasih.
	A	Maaf, Encik. Di mana Zoo Negara?
	C	Jalan terus sampai ke hujung jalan ini. Ia terletak dekat Akuarium Tunku Abdul Rahman.

<table>
<tr><td>e</td><td>A</td><td>Maaf, Encik. Bagaimana jalannya ke Hotél Vistana?</td></tr>
<tr><td></td><td>B</td><td>Mana? Hotél Vistana?</td></tr>
<tr><td></td><td>A</td><td>Ya, Vistana. Nanti dulu, Encik, saya tersilap. Maksud saya Hotél Milah.</td></tr>
<tr><td></td><td>B</td><td>Hotél Milah? Oh, jalan terus saja ikut jalan ini sampai ke bulatan, kemudian belok kanan. Hotél Milah ada di sebelah Plaza Raya.</td></tr>
</table>

Unit 9, Exercise 3

The numbers called out in the lottery game (in this order) are: 47, 18, 56, 13, 6, 69, 43, 85, 50, 16, 63, 94, 61, 30, 28, 72, 9, 11, 83, 24, 58, 77, 38, 20, 59, 41, 12, 22, 34, 17, 29, 10, 98, 70, 32, 79, 37, 91, 7, 36, 21, 87, 3, 52, 60, 99, 93, 25, 66, 45.

Unit 13, Exercise 3

Pelayan	Selamat malam. Méja untuk dua?
Sam	Ya. Boléh ada méja dekat tingkap? Saya suka pemandangan tasik.
Pelayan	Tentu, Encik. Sila ikut saya. Ini menunya. Satu untuk puan dan ini untuk tuan. Saya akan kembali apabila Tuan dan Puan sudah sedia.
Rosie	Wow! Saya lapar sekali.
Sam	Saya juga. Saya berselera untuk makan.
Rosie	Mudah-mudahan ada saté kambing. Eh, lihat ada ni. Saya dengar saté kambing di sini terkenal.
Pelayan	Apakah puan dan tuan sudah bersedia?
Sam	Kamu ada yang siap dipesan?
Rosie	Ya.
Sam	Boléh saya pesan saté ayam dan pulut kuning? Hm... tunggu sebentar. Boléh saya pesan rendang juga?
Pelayan	Saté ayam, pulut kuning, rendang daging dan untuk puan pula?
Rosie	Hm, saya mahu saté kambing dan e…
Pelayan	Oh maaf, Puan. Saté kambing sudah habis, yang ada hanya saté ayam. Lazat sekali. Ini resipi kami sendiri.
Rosie	Sayang sekali. Saya benar-benar ingin makan saté kambing, tetapi tidak mengapa. Tentu saté ayam juga sedap.
Pelayan	Satu set saté ayam, dan yang lain?
Rosie	Ya, saya mahu rojak buah.
Pelayan	Saté ayam, rojak buah. Itu saja?
Rosie	Um, saya juga mahu popiah.

Pelayan	Baik, jadi saté ayam, rojak buah dan popiah.
Sam	Apakah makanannya diberi sambal?
Pelayan	Maaf, harus dipesan berasingan.
Sam	Tolong beri sambal untuk dua orang.
Pelayan	Baik. Mahu pesan minuman apa?
Sam	Ya, segelas wain merah untuk saya dan bagaimana dengan kamu, sayang?
Rosie	Saya juga, sama.
Pelayan	Baik, jadi dua gelas wain mérah.
Rosie	Tunggu sebentar, saya dah tukar fikiran. Boléh segelas wain putih untuk saya?
Pelayan	Tidak masalah. Satu gelas wain putih.
Pelayan	Bagaimana makanannya, Puan?
Rosie	Lazat sekali, terima kasih, terutamanya saté ayam. Saya belum pernah merasakan saté ayam yang selazat ini. Apakah resipinya?
Pelayan	Maaf, Puan. Itu rahsia chef. Saya tidak boléh beritahu. Nak pesan pencuci mulut?
Sam	Saya sudah kenyang. Kamu nak cuba?
Rosie	Ya. Ada bubur pulut hitam?
Pelayan	Ya, ada. Satu mangkuk bubur pulut hitam?
Rosie	Ya.
Sam	Boléh beri bilnya sekali?
Pelayan	Tentu, Encik. Ini bilnya.
Rosie	Berapa jumlahnya?
Sam	RM48.00.
Rosie	Murah sekali, ya?

Unit 16, Exercise 5

Ini Ramalan cuaca sepanjang minggu ini untuk Kuala Lumpur, Malaysia.

Juruhebah 1 kepada Juruhebah 2	Nampaknya cuaca sepanjang minggu ini adalah panas dan lembap.
Juruhebah 2	Ya, betul kata kamu.
Juruhebah 1	Cuaca pada hari Isnin adalah panas dan cerah sepanjang hari.
Juruhebah 2	Cuaca pada hari Selasa adalah berawan dengan hujan pada lewat tengah hari dan malam.
Juruhebah 1	Hujan lebat dijangka turun pada awal pagi Rabu dan pada masa yang lain cerah dan bermatahari.

Juruhebah 2	Cuaca pada hari Khamis adalah cerah dan berangin. Sesuai sekali untuk bermain layang-layang.
Juruhebah 1	Cuaca pada hari Jumaat, cerah dengan sinaran matahari sepanjang hari dan hujan renyai-renyai pada sebelah malam.
Juruhebah 2	Cuaca pada hari Sabtu adalah berangin dan langit cerah sepanjang hari.
Juruhebah 1	Cuaca pada hari Ahad adalah basah dan lembap pada awal pagi dan pada masa yang lain baik.

Malay–English glossary

You will find only the most important words used in this course listed below.

a. = adjective; n. = noun; v. = verb

abang *older brother/sister*

ada *to have, to be, there is, there are*

Ada apa? *What's wrong?*

Ada gula ada semut. *Where there's sugar there are ants. (proverb)*

Adakah saudara ini…? *Are you…?*

adakalanya *sometimes*

adalah *is, are*

adik *younger brother/sister*

aérobik *aerobics*

agak *rather, somewhat, to guess, to form an observation*

Ahad *Sunday*

ahli *expert*

ahli muzik *musician*

ahli sains *scientist*

air *water, liquid*

air kelapa muda *young coconut drink*

air panas *hot water, hot spring*

ais *ice*

ais batu *ice cube*

ais batu campur *sweet dessert made with shaved ice, syrup and evaporated milk*

ais kacang *red beans with coconut milk and shaved ice*

ais krim *ice cream*

ajak *to invite*

ajar *to teach*

akad nikah *marriage vows*

akademi *academy*

akal *intelligence, mind*

akan *will, shall*

akaun *account*

akhbar *newspaper*

akhir *final*

aksen *accent*

aksi *action*

aktiviti *activity*

aku *I*

alam *experienced*

alam sekitar *environment*

alamat *address*

alat *device, gadget*

alat CD *CD player*

alat muzik *musical instrument*

alergi (pada) *allergic (to)*

alih *to displace*

amal *charity*

aman *safe*

ambil *to take*

ambil bahagian dalam *to take part in*

ambillah (ambil *v.***)** *get, take*

Amérika *America*

anak *child, son, daughter, children*

anak lelaki *son*

anak perempuan *daughter*

anak saudara *niece, nephew*

anak tunggal *only child*

anda *you*

anda sekeluarga *you and your family*

angin *wind*

angkat *to leave*

antara *between*

antarabangsa *international*

antik *antique*

apa *any*

Apa khabar? *How are you?*

Apa? or **Apakah?** *What?*

Apa pekerjaan anda? *What's your job?, What do you do?*

apa saja *anything*

apabila *when*

api *fire*

April *April*

aras laut *sea level*

asalkan *as long as, provided that*

asap rokok *smoke*

asing (a.**)** *foreign*

askar *soldier(s)*

asli *authentic, original, native*

asma *asthma*

atas *above, for*

awan *cloud*

awas *caution*

ayah *father*

ayam *chicken*

ayam masak kurma *chicken korma*

ayam percik *roast chicken in spicy sauce*

babi *pork*

badan *body*

Bagaimana? or **bagaimanakah?** *What kind of…?, How's…?*

Bagaimana cuacanya? *How's the weather?*

Bagaimana nak ke sana? *How do I get there?*

Bagaimana pendapat anda tentang…? *What's your opinion of…?*

Bagaimanakah dengan? *How is…?, How was…?*

bagasi *luggage*

bagi *for*

bagus *good*

bagus kalau begitu *so that's good*

bagus sekali *great*

bahagia *happy*

bahagian *section, part*

bahan *ingredients*

bahasa *language*

bahasa Arab *Arabic*

bahasa Malaysia *Malay (language)*

bahasa Mandarin *Mandarin*

bahu *shoulder(s)*

baik *well, good*

baiklah *all right, OK*

baiklah kalau begitu *that's fine, OK then*

baju *dress, clothes*

baju hujan *raincoat*

bakar *roast, grilled*

baki *remainder*

balai polis *police station*

balai seni *art gallery*

balak *log*

balas *to reciprocate, to reply*

bandar *city*

bangsa *nation*

bangun *to get up*

bangunan (bangun *v.***)** *building*

banjir *flood*

bantu *help, to help*

bantuan (bantu *v.***)** *help*

banyak *a lot of*

barang *goods*

baru *new*

bas *bus*

basah *wet*

batik *batik*

batu *stone*

batu marmar *marble*

batuk *cough*

bau *to smell*

baunya *it smells*

bawa *to bring, to take*

bawah *below*

bawah tanah *underground*

bawang besar *onion*

bawang mérah *shallot*

bawang putih *garlic*

bayar *to pay, to pay for*

beberapa *a few*

beca *trishaw, rickshaw*

beg *bag*

begitu *so, like that*

bekerja (kerja *v.***)** *to work*

belajar (ajar *v.***)** *to study*

belakang *the rear*

Belanda *Holland*

belanja *to spend*

belayar (layar *v.***)** *sail*

beli *to buy*

belian (beli *v.***)** *purchases, items purchased*

belikan (beli *v.***)** *to buy (something for someone)*

bélok *to turn*

bélok kanan *turn right*

bélok kiri *turn left*

belum *not yet*

belum berkahwin *not married*

benar *true, it's true, really*

benci *to hate*

bengkak *swollen*

béngkel *workshop*

benua *continent*

berada (ada *v.***)** *to be (at a place)*

beradik *brothers and sisters*

berakal (akal *n.***)** *to be intelligent*

berakhir (akhir *a.***)** *to finish*

beranak (anak *n.***)** *to have children*

berangin (angin *n.***)** *(to be) windy*

berangkat (angkat *v.***)** *to leave for*

Berapa? *How many?, How much?*

Berapa banyak? *How much?, How many?*

Berapa harganya? *How much is the cost?*

Berapa jam? *How many hours?*

Berapa kali? *How many times?*

Berapa kilo? *How many kilos?*

Berapa lama? *(For) how long (time)?*

Berapa malam? *How many nights?*

Berapa panjang? *How long (distance)?*

Berapa tambangnya? *What's the fare?*

Berapa tinggi? *How tall?*

Berapakah? *How many?*

Berapakah umur? *How old?*

berasingan (asing *a.***)** *separately*

berat *heavy, weight*

beratnya *it weighs*

berawan (awan n.) *to be cloudy*

berbaju (baju n.) *to wear a dress*

berbatu (batu n.) *to be made of stone*

berbelanja (belanja v.) *to spend*

berbéza (béza v.) *different*

berbéza dengan *different from*

berbincang (bincang v.) *to discuss*

berbual dengan *to chat to*

berbuat (buat v.) *to do*

bercakap (cakap v.) *speak, to speak*

bercakap (cakap v.) **dengan** *to talk to*

bercerai (cerai v.) *to be divorced, to get divorced*

bercuti (cuti n.) *to be on holiday*

berdebar (debar n.) *to throb, to palpitate*

berdiri (diri v.) *to stand, to stand up*

berdua *both*

berduri (duri n.) *(to be) spiky*

beréhat (réhat v.) *to rest*

berenang (renang v.) *to swim*

bergaul (gaul v.) *to socialize, to spend time together*

bergaya (gaya n.) *(to be) stylish*

bergerak (gerak n.) *movement*

bergurau (gurau n.) *to joke*

berhati (hati v.) *careful*

berhenti (henti v.) *to stop*

berhubung (hubung n.) *to communicate*

beri *to give*

beribadat (ibadat n.) *to worship*

beribut (ribut n.) *(to be) stormy*

berikan (beri v.) *to bring, to give (someone) (something)*

beristeri *to have a wife (i.e. to be married)*

berita *news*

beritahu (tahu v.) *to inform, to tell*

berjalan (jalan n.) *to walk*

berjalan kaki *go on foot*

berjaya (jaya n.) *to succeed*

berjemur (jemur v.) *sunbathing*

berjenaka (jenaka n.) *to joke around*

berjoging (joging n.) *to go jogging*

berkabut (kabut n.) *foggy*

berkahwin (kahwin v.) *married*

berkebaya (kebaya n.) **sutera** *to wear a silk kebaya*

berkebun (kebun n.) *gardening*

berkeluarga (keluarga n.) *to have a family/ to be married*

berkhémah (khémah v.) *camping*

berkicap (kicap n.) *to have soy sauce in it*

berkilat (kilat n.) *to shine, to glimmer*

berkumpul (kumpul v.) *to gather, to hang out*

berlainan (lain a.) **dengan** *different from*

berlalu (lalu v.) *to pass*

berlari (lari v.) *to run*

berlatih (latih v.) *to train*

berlepas *to take off*

berlepas (lepas v.) *departure, to depart*

bermacam *different kinds of*

bermain (main v.) *to play*

bermain bola sépak *to play football (soccer)*

bermain komputer *to play on the computer*

bermain laying *to fly kites*

berminat (minat n.) *to be interested in*

bermula (mula v.) *to begin*

bernafas (nafas n.) *to breathe*

bernama (nama n.) *to be called*

bernasib (nasib n.**)** to be lucky

berpakaian (pakai v.**)** to dress, to get dressed

berpakaian kemas to dress well

berpendapat (pendapat n.**)** to be of the opinion

berpuasa (puasa n.**)** to fast

bersahabat (sahabat n.**)** to be friends

bersahabat dengan baik to be good friends

bersama together

bersara to retire, retired

bersarapan (sarapan n.**) pagi** to have breakfast

bersedia (sedia a.**)** to be ready to, to be willing to

bersejarah (sejarah n.**)** historical

bersekolah (sekolah n.**)** to go to school

berseléra (seléra n.**) untuk** to have an appetite for

bersemangat (semangat n.**)** enthusiastic, keen

bersiar travelling

bersiar-siar travelling

bersih clean

bersukan (sukan n.**)** to play sport

bertanya (tanya v.**)** to ask

bertanya dengan to ask

berteman (teman n.**)** to be with a friend (i.e. to have a friend)

berteman dengan to be friends with

bertemu (temu v.**)** to meet

bertiga three of us

bertolak (tolak v.**)** to depart

bertukar (tukar v.**)** to change

bertutur (tutur n.**)** to speak

berwarna (warna n.**)** to be coloured

besar big

besbol baseball

bésok tomorrow

betik papaya

betis calf, calves

betul really

betul sekali quite right

béza to differ

biar let, allow

Biar saya bantu. Let me help.

biasa to be used to, usual

biasanya usually

bibir lips

bidang field (i.e. of expertise, etc.)

biji classifier for fruit

bil bill, check

Bila? or **Bilakah?** When?

bila masa anytime

bilik room

bilik guru staff room

bilik kosong vacancies

bilik mandi bathroom

bilik penghubung connecting rooms

bilik standard standard room

bilik tamu guest room

bimbang to be anxious, worry

bina to construct, build

binatang animal

bincang to discuss

biola violin

biologi biology

bir beer

biri lamb

biro pengiklanan advertising bureau

biru blue

biskut biscuit

bisnes *business*

blaus *blouse*

bodoh *stupid*

bola *ball*

bola keranjang *basketball*

bola sépak *football (soccer)*

bola tampar *volleyball*

boléh *can, be allowed to*

Boléh beri saya…? *Could you give me…?*

Boléh saya dapatkan…? *Could I have…? Could you give me…?*

Boléh saya dapatkan…? *May I have…?*

Boléh saya minta…? *May I request…?*

Boléh saya tahu? *Could you let me know?*

Boléhkah anda bercakap dengan lebih kuat? *Could you speak more loudly, please?*

Boléhkah anda bercakap dengan lebih perlahan? *Could you speak more slowly, please?*

Boléhkah anda tolong éjakan? *Could you spell it, please?*

Boléhkah anda tolong tuliskan? *Could you write it down, please?*

Boléhkah anda ulangi sekali lagi? *Could you repeat that, please?*

bongsu *youngest*

borang *form, document*

bos *boss*

bosan *bored*

botak *bald*

botol *bottle*

brosur *brochure*

buah *counter used for large objects such as houses, cars, lorries, ships, refrigerators, computers, etc.*

buah belimbing *star fruit*

buah durian *durian fruit*

buang *to discard, to throw*

buang air *to urinate*

buat *to do, to make*

buatan tangan *hand-made*

buatlah *make*

buatlah seperti rumah sendiri *make yourself at home*

bubuh *to put, to place, to add*

bubuh garam secukup rasa *add salt to taste*

bubur *porridge*

bubur ayam *rice porridge with chicken*

bubur pulut hitam *black glutinous rice sweet porridge*

budak *child*

budaya *culture*

bufét *buffet*

bujang *single*

bukan *no*

bukit *hill*

buku *book*

bulan *month*

bulatan (bulat *a.***)** *roundabout*

bulu kening *eyebrow*

bunga *flower*

bunga mawar *rose*

bungkus *to wrap up*

bungkusan (bungkus *v.***)** *present, parcel*

buruk *ugly*

burung *bird*

buta *blind*

butik *boutique*

butir *counter for small, round objects*

butir peribadi *curriculum vitae, personal details*

cadang *to suggest*

cadangkan (cadang *v.***)** *to recommend, to suggest (to someone)*

cakap *to chat*

campur *mix*

cantik *beautiful*

cap *printed*

cara *way, method*

cara berjalan *gait*

cara membuat *method, directions, instructions*

cari *to look for*

cawan *cup*

cemas *worried*

cempedak *bread fruit*

cenderamata *souvenir*

cepat *quickly*

cerah *bright*

cerai *to divorce*

cerita *story*

ceritakan (cerita *n.***)** *to tell*

cermin mata *spectacles*

chef *chef*

China *China*

cicir *to spill*

cili *chilli*

cinta *love*

comel *cute*

corak *pattern, design*

cuaca *weather*

cuba *to try*

cuci *to wash*

cucu *grandchild, grandson, granddaughter*

cukai *tax*

cukup *enough*

cuma *only*

cuti *holiday, leave*

dada *chest*

daftar *list*

daftar masuk *check-in*

daging *eat, meat*

daging lembu *beef*

dagu *chin*

dah *already (short for* **sudah***)*

dahi *forehead*

dahulu *before, formerly, previous*

daki *to climb*

dalam *in*

dalam masa 30 minit lagi *in another 30 minutes*

dalam transit *in transit, stop over*

damai *peaceful*

dan *and*

Dan anda pula bagaimana? *And how about you?*

dan lain *and so on*

dangdut *traditional Malay and Indonesian music*

dapat *to be able*

dapatkan (dapat *v.***)** *to get*

dapur *kitchen*

darah *blood*

dari *from*

Dari mana…? *Where from…?*

daripada *from, than (in comparisons)*

datang *to come*

datang ke *to come over (to a place)*

datanglah *please come, come over*

datuk *grandfather*

daun *leaf*

daun bawang *spring onions*

daun kunyit *saffron leaf*

daun limau purut *kaffir lime leaf*

daun purut *kaffir lime leaf*

daun salam *bay leaf*

dayung *paddle*

debar *palpitation*

dekat *close, near*

demam *feverish*

dengan *with*

dengan baik *well*

dengan baik sekali *very well*

dengan bas *by bus*

dengan fasih *fluently*

dengan keréta *by car*

dengan lebih perlahan *more slowly*

dengan pantas *quickly*

dengan secepat mungkin *as soon as possible*

dengan teléfon *by phone*

dengar *to hear*

depan *in front of*

desa *village*

destinasi *destination*

dewan *hall*

dewan sekolah *school hall*

dhal kari *Indian lentil curry*

di atas nama *under the name(s) of*

Di jalan mana? *On what street?*

di luar *outside*

di luar negeri *abroad*

di mana *where*

di samping kiri *on the left-hand side*

di sebelah *next to*

di sebelahnya *next to it*

di seberang jalan *across the road*

di sini *here*

dia *he/she*

dibina (bina *v.***)** *to be built*

dibuat (buat *v.***) daripada** *to be made of*

dibuka (buka *v.***)** *to be opened*

dibungkus (bungkus *v.***)** *to be wrapped up (i.e. to take away)*

dicampur (campur *v.***)** *to be mixed*

dicari (cari *v.***)** *to be looked for*

didik *to educate*

digabung (gabung *n.***)** *to be combined*

digunakan (guna *v.***)** *to be used*

dihabiskan (habis *v.***)** *to be spent*

dihidang (hidang *v.***)** *to be served*

dihidangkan (hidang *v.***)** *served*

diimport dari *to be imported from*

dijual *sold out*

dikenali (kenal *v.***) sebagai** *known as*

dilarang (larang *v.***)** *it is forbidden, not allowed*

dilarang merokok *no smoking*

dimakan (makan *v.***)** *to be eaten*

dinding *wall*

dingin *cold*

dipakai (pakai *v.***)** *to be used*

diperlukan (perlu *v.***) untuk** *needed for*

dipesan (pesan *v.***)** *to be ordered*

diri *to stand*

Disember *December*

diskaun *discount*

disko *disco*

ditelan (telan *v.***)** *to be swallowed*

ditimbang (timbang *v.***)** *to be weighed*

dititis (titis *n.***)** *to be taken*

dodol *a sticky, chewy sweet*

doktor *doctor*

doktor gigi *dentist*

dolar *dollar*

drama *drama, play*

drama lipur lara *soap opera*

dua *two*

dua dua *two by two*

dua hari yang akan datang *the day after tomorrow*

dua hari yang lalu *the day before yesterday*

dua minggu *two weeks*

dua puluh *twenty*

dua ribu *two thousand*

duda *widower*

duduk *to sit about (relaxing), seat*

duduk dekat tingkap *window seat*

dulu *before, formerly*

dunia *world*

duri *spike, thorn*

durian (duri *n.)* *a thorny kind of fruit*

duta *ambassador*

ekonomi *economy*

ékor *tail*

e-mel *e-mail*

empat *four*

empat puluh *forty*

enam *six*

Encik *Mr*

ésok *tomorrow*

faham *understanding, to understand*

fasih *fluent*

Februari *February*

feri *ferry*

fesyen *fashion*

fikir *to think*

fikiran (fikir *v.)* *thought*

filem *film*

filem seram *horror movie*

filem télevisyen *TV film*

filem yang penuh aksi *action film*

foto *photo*

fotografi *photography*

gabung *to join*

gado *vegetable salad with peanut sauce*

gagal *fail*

gaji *salary*

gambar *picture*

gambaran *description*

ganggu *to bother, disturb*

ganti *to change*

garam *salt*

garang *lurid*

garfu *fork*

gatal *itching*

gaul *to mix*

gaya *style*

gayung *scoop*

gelang *bracelet*

gelang tangan *bracelet*

gelap *dark*

gelas *glass*

gemar *to be fond of*

gembira *happy*

Gembira bertemu dengan saudara. *Glad to meet you.*

Gembira dapat bertemu dengan…
Pleased to meet…?

gendang *drum*

geografi *geography*

gerai *stall*

gerak *movement*

getah *rubber*

gigil *to shiver*

gitar *guitar*

goréng *fried*

gula *sugar*

guna *to use*

gunting *scissors*

gunung *mountain*

gurau *joke*

guru *teacher*

guru besar *head teacher, senior lecturer*

habis *run out of, finished, to finish*

hadap *to face*

hadiah *gift, present*

hadir *to attend*

halia *ginger*

halus *delicate, fine*

hampir *almost*

hampir sepanjang masanya *almost all the time*

hantarkan (hantar *v.***) saya ke…** *take me to…*

hanya *only*

harap *hopefully*

harap kamu berjaya *I wish you luck, I hope you succeed*

harapkan (harap *v.***)** *to hope, to expect*

harga *price, cost*

harga tetap *fixed price*

hari *day*

hari ini *today*

haribulan *date*

hari jadi *birthday*

harian *daily*

harus *should*

haus *thirsty*

helai *counter for flat objects*

hélo *hello*

hendak *to want, to desire to*

henti *to stop*

hiasan *decoration*

hibur *to entertain*

hiburan (hibur *v.***)** *entertainment*

hidang *to serve*

hidangan (hidang *v.***)** *dish, i.e. food*

hidangan istimewa *(culinary) specialities*

hidap *to suffer from*

hidung *nose*

hidup *life, alive*

hijau *green*

hingga sampai *until you reach*

hitam *black*

hitung *count*

hobi *hobby*

hospital *hospital*

hotél *hotel*

hubung *joint, connection*

hubungan (hubung *n.***)** *connection*

hubungan masyarakat *human relationship*

hubungi (hubung *v.***)** *to contact*

hujan *raining*

hujung *end*

ia *it*

iaitu *namely, that is to say*

ibadat *religious worship*

ibu *mother*

ibu jari *thumb*

ijazah *degree, diploma, permission*

ikan *fish*

ikan keli *catfish*

ikat *cord, bunch*

iklan *advertisement*

ikut *to follow*

import *to import*

inap *to spend the night*

indah *beautiful*

ingat *to remember*

ingin *to want*

ini *this/this is*

inilah sifat lelaki! *typical man!*

inspirasi *inspiration*

Institusi Pengajian Tinggi *Institute of Higher Education*

ipar *brother/sister-in law*

isi *content, to fill in*

isikan (isi *n.***)** *to fill in*

Isnin *Monday*

isteri *wife*

istiméwa *special*

isyarat *signal*

Itali *Italy*

itik *duck*

itu *that*

jadi *to be, to become, so*

jaga *to awake*

jagung *maize*

jakét *jacket*

jala *net*

jalan *to go out for a stroll, to 'hang around', street*

jalan kaki *to go on foot*

jalan raya *main road*

jalan terus *keep walking*

jam tangan *watch*

jambu *guava*

jamu *to give a feast to*

janda *widow*

jangan *don't*

jangan bimbang *don't worry*

jangan lupa *don't forget*

jangan lupa untuk… *don't forget to…*

jangan malu, malu *don't be shy*

jangan risau *don't worry*

jantina *sex*

jantung *heart*

Januari *January*

jari *finger*

jari kaki *toe*

jas *suit*

jauh *far*

jauh dari sini *far from here*

jawab *to reply*

jawapan (jawab *v.***)** *answer*

jaya *victory, success*

jelak *fed up, bored*

jelas *clear*

jemput *to pick up, fetch, invite*

jemputan (jemput *v.***)** *guests, invitation*

jemur *to sunbathe*

jenaka *banter*

jenis *type*

Jepun *Japan*

Jerman *Germany*

jika *if, when*

jika boléh *if possible*

jingga *orange*

Joget *a traditional dance*

joging *jogging*

Jomlah! *(slang) Let's go!*

jual *to sell*

jualan *sales*

juang *to fight*

juga *too, as well*

Julai *July*

Jumaat *Friday*

jumlah *amount, total*

jumpa janji *to go dating*

Jun *June*

jurubahasa *interpreter*

jurufoto *photographer*

jurugambar *photographer*

jurujual *vendor*

jurulatih *(sports) coach*

jururawat *nurse*

jurutera *engineer*

kabut *fog*

kacang *peanut*

kad kredit *credit card*

kad nama *business card*

kadang-kadang *sometimes*

kadar pertukaran *exchange rate*

kahwin *to marry, married*

kahwin dengan *to get married to*

kain *cloth, material*

kain sarung *sarong*

kakak *older brother/sister*

kaki *leg, foot*

kalau *if, when*

kalau begitu *in that case*

kalau saya tidak silap *if I'm not mistaken*

kalau suka *if you want*

kalung *necklace*

kambing *goat*

kamera *camera*

kami *we*

kampung *village*

kampus *campus*

kamu *you*

kamus *dictionary*

Kanada *Canada*

kanan *right*

kapal *ship*

kapal terbang *plane*

kapas *cotton*

karaté *karate*

kari *curry*

kari ayam *chicken curry*

kari kambing *goat curry*

karya *author*

kasét *tape, cassette*

kasih *love, affection*

kasut *shoe*

kasyer *cashier*

kata *to say, word*

katil *bed*

katil saiz queen *queen-sized bed, double bed*

katil twin *twin bed*

kawasan *area*

kaya *rich*

Kayalah saya! *I'm rich!*

kayu balak *timber*

ke *to*

ke hotél mana *to which hotel*

ke mana *where to*

keadaan (ada *v.***)** *condition*

kebaikan *goodness*

kebangsaan *nationality*

kebaya *kebaya*

kebetulan *by coincidence, by accident*

kebun *garden*

keciciran (cicir *v.***)** *to lose something*

kecuali *except*

kedai *shop*

kedai buku *book shop*

kedai cenderamata *souvenir shop*

kedatangan (datang *v.***)** *arrival*

kedua *second*

kedutaan (duta *n.***)** *embassy*

kehabisan (habis *v.***)** *run out of*

kehidupan (hidup *n.***)** *way of life*

keindahan (indah *a.***)** *beauty*

kejuruteraan (jurutera *n.***)** *engineering*

kekenyangan *to overeat*

kelabu *grey*

kelanggaran (langgar *v.***)** *to collide*

kelapa *coconut*

kelapa muda *young coconut*

kelas *class*

kelihatan (lihat *v.***)** *to seem, to look like*

keliling *around*

keliru *confused*

kelmarin *the day before yesterday*

keluarga *family*

keluarkan (luar) *to get (something) out*

kemahiran (mahir *n.***)** *skill*

kemalangan (malang *a.***)** *accident*

kemas *neat, tidy*

kemasyarakatan (masyarakat *n.***)** *humanities*

kembali *to come back*

kembar *twin*

kembara *travelling*

keméja *shirt*

kementerian (menteri *n.***)** *ministry*

kemerdékaan (merdéka *a.***)** *independence*

kemudahan (mudah *a.***)** *amenity*

kemudian *then*

kenal (dengan) *to know*

kental *thick, strong*

kenyang *satiated*

kepada *to*

kepala *head*

keping *piece*

kepingan *piece*

kepulangan (pulang *v.***)** *return*

keputusan (putus *v.***)** *decision*

kerajaan (raja *n.***)** *government*

kerana *because (of)*

kerap *frequent*

keras kepala *stubborn*

keréta *car*

keréta api *train*

kerja *to work*

kerongkong *throat*

keropok *prawn crackers*

keropok kentang *crisps (US chips)*

kesesakan (sesak *a.***)** *congestion*

kesesakan lalu lintas *traffic jam*

kesetiausahawan (setiausaha n.**)** secretarial

kesihatan (sihat a.**)** health

kesulitan (sulit a.**)** difficulty

ketakcernaan indigestion

ketam crab

ketawa (tawa n.**)** to laugh

keterangan (terang a.**)** explanation, information

keterangan yang lebih lanjut further information

ketiga third

ketinggalan (tinggal v.**)** to miss (a form of transport)

ketumbar coriander

kewangan finance

kewarnanegaraan nationality

khabar baik I'm fine

Khamis Thursday

khas special

kicap soy sauce

kicap manis sweet soy sauce

kilo kilo

kimia chemistry

kini these days, nowadays

kipas fan

kira about, approximately, to calculate

kiri left

kirim to consign, to send

kisar to grind, to mill

kita we

klarinet clarinet

klasik classical

kolam renang swimming pool

koléj college

komedi comedy

komputer computer

kondominium condominium

kopi coffee

kosong vacant, empty

kota fort

kotak box

kotor dirty

kotoran (kotor a.**)** dirt, rubbish, trash

kuah gravy, stock

kuali frying pan, wok

kualiti quality

kuat loudly, strongly

kubu fort

kucing cat

kuih lapis tiga warna three-coloured pudding

kuih talam coconut milk pudding

kulit leather

kumpul to gather

kumpulan (kumpul v.**)** group

kunci key

kuning yellow

kunyit turmeric

kupon coupon

kurang less

kurangkan (kurang) to reduce

lada pepper

lagi more, still

lagipun moreover, besides

lain other

lain kali another time

lakukan to do

lalu lintas traffic

lama *long*

lampu isyarat *traffic signal*

lancong *to go sightseeing, tour*

langgar *to collide*

langsing *slim*

lanjut *continuously, to continue*

lapan *eight*

lapang *leisure, of leisure*

lapar *hungry*

larang *to prohibit*

lari *to run*

latar *background*

latihan *exercise*

lauk *food, dish*

laut *sea*

lautan (laut n.**)** *ocean, seas*

lawat *to visit*

lawatan (lawat v.**)** *visit*

layan *to attend*

lazat *delicious*

lebar *wide*

lebih *more*

lebih bagus *better*

lebih mahal *more expensive*

lebih murah *cheaper*

lebih suka *prefer*

lega *free from anxiety, relieved*

léhér *neck*

Lekas lekas! *Hurry up!*

lelah *tired*

lelaki *male, boy, man*

lemah *feeble*

lembap *moist, damp, humid*

lembu *cow*

lembut *soft, tender*

lengkuas *galangal*

lepas *to let go, depart*

lésén *licence*

lésén memandu *driving licence*

letak *place*

letak keréta *to park a car*

léwat *late*

lihat *to see*

lihat lihat *to browse*

lima *five*

lima tahun yang lalu *five years ago*

liput *covering*

lobak mérah *carrot*

lorong *aisle*

luar *outside*

luar negeri *abroad*

luas *large, broad*

lupa *forget*

lupa *to forget*

lusa *the day after tomorrow*

maaf *excuse me, I am sorry*

Maaf, saya tidak faham. *I'm sorry, I don't understand.*

maafkan *to forgive*

maafkan saya *I'm sorry*

mabuk *dizzy, drunk*

Mac *March*

macam *like*

macam macam *various, different sorts of*

macam mana dengan *what about*

mahal *expensive*

mahasiswa *student (at college or university)*

mahir *adept, skilled person*

mahir dalam *adept in*

mahu *to want, to desire to*

mahu ke mana *where to*

main *to play*

mainan (main *v.***)** *toy*

majlis *ceremony*

makan *to eat*

makan malam *dinner*

makan ubat *to take medicine*

makanan (makan *v.***)** *food*

makanan laut *seafood*

makanan ringan *snacks*

makcik *aunt*

maklumat *information*

makmal *lab*

maksud *to mean*

maksudkan (maksud *v.***)** *to mean*

malam malam *late at night*

malam nanti *tonight*

malam tadi *yesterday evening*

malang *unlucky*

malu *embarrassed, shy*

Malu bertanya nanti sesat di jalan. *If you're too shy to ask you will get lost in the street. (proverb)*

mampu *to have the ability to, can*

mandi *to take a bath*

mandi wap *steam bath*

mangkuk *bowl*

manis *sweet*

manisan (manis *a.***)** *sweets*

manja *spoilt, pampered*

manusia *human being*

marah *angry*

maraton *marathon*

mari ikut saya *(please) follow me*

mari saya bantu *let me help*

masa *time, occasion*

masa lapang *free time*

masak *to cook*

masakan (masak *v.***)** *cookery, cuisine*

masalah *problem*

masih *still*

masin *salty*

masuk *to enter*

masukkan (masuk *v.***)** *put in*

masyarakat *society*

mata *eye*

matematik *mathematics*

Mau pesan apa? *What would you like to order?*

Mau saya tunggu? *Do you want me to wait?*

Méi *May*

méja *table*

mekanik *mechanic*

melancong *to go sightseeing*

melawat *to visit*

melawat keluarga *visiting relatives*

melepas *to let go*

meletak (letak *n.***)** *to park*

meletihkan (letih *a.***)** *tiring*

melihat (lihat *v.***)** *to see*

meliputi (liput *n.***)** *to cover, to include*

memahami (faham *v.***)** *to understand*

memakan masa *take time*

memalukan (malu *a.***)** *embarrassing*

memanaskan (panas *a.***)** *to heat up*

memandu (pandu *n.***)** *to drive*

mémang *indeed, actually*

memasak (masak *v.***)** *to cook*

membaca *to read*

membalas (balas *v.***) surat** *to answer a letter*

membangun (bangun *v.***)** *to build*

membantu (bantu *v.***)** *to help, helps*

membawa (bawa *v.***)** *to bring, take*

membeli (beli *v.***)** *to buy*

membeli belah *to go shopping*

membelikan (beli *v.***)** *to buy (something) for (someone)*

memberi (beri *v.***)** *to give*

membosankan (bosan *a.***)** *boring*

membuang (buang *v.***)** *to throw*

membuat *to make*

membungkus (bungkus *v.***)** *to wrap up*

memeriksa (periksa *v.***)** *to examine*

memijak (pijak *n.***)** *to step*

memilih (pilih *v.***)** *to choose*

meminjam (pinjam *v.***)** *to borrow*

meminta (minta *v.***)** *to ask for, to request*

memotong (potong *v.***)** *to cut*

memotong (potong *v.***)** *to overtake*

memperoléh (oléh *n.***)** *to gain*

memuaskan (puas *a.***)** *to satisfy*

menaiki (naik *v.***)** *to climb, to take transport, to travel on/by*

menaip (taip *n.***)** *to type*

menakutkan (takut *a.***)** *frightening*

menangis (tangis *v.***)** *to cry*

menangkap (tangkap *v.***)** *to catch*

menari (tari *n.***)** *to dance*

menarik (tarik *v.***)** *interesting, to attract*

mencari (cari *v.***)** *to look for*

mencemaskan (cemas *a.***)** *worrying*

mencintai (cinta *n.***)** *to love*

mencuci (cuci *v.***)** *to wash*

mencukai (cukai *n.***)** *to tax*

mendahului (dahulu) *to overtake*

mendaki (daki *v.***)** *to climb*

mendapat (dapat *v.***)** *to get*

mendayung (dayung *n.***)** *to paddle*

mendekati (dekat *a.***)** *to draw close to*

mendengar (dengar *v.***)** *to hear*

mendengar muzik *to listen to music*

mendung *overcast*

meneléfon (teléfon *v.***)** *to telephone*

menerima (terima *v.***)** *to accept*

mengajar (ajar *v.***)** *to teach*

mengambil (ambil *v.***)** *to take*

mengarang (garang *a.***)** *to write, compose*

mengawasi (awas *n.***)** *to keep an eye on*

mengembara (kembara *a.***)** *to go in search of adventure*

mengembara berjalan kaki *to go hiking*

mengesahkan (sah *a.***)** *to authenticate*

mengetahui (tahu *v.***)** *to comprehend*

menggambarkan *to portray*

mengganggu (ganggu *v.***)** *to disturb*

mengganti (ganti *v.***)** *to replace*

menggigil (gigil *v.***)** *to shiver*

mengguna (guna *v.***)** *to use*

menggunting (gunting *n.***)** *to cut with scissors*

menghabiskan (habis *a.***)** *to spend*

menghadap (hadap *v.***) ke** *to look out onto*

menghadiri (hadir *v.***)** *to attend*

menghantar (hantar *v.***)** *to take, convey*

menghidap (hidap *v.***)** *to suffer from*

menghidupkan (hidup *a.***)** *to turn on (an appliance)*

menghubungi (hubung *v.***)** *to contact*

menginap (inap v.**)** to spend the night (somewhere)

mengira (kira v.**)** to count

mengirim (kirim v.**)** to send

mengisi (isi n.**)** to fill in

mengurangi (kurang) to reduce

mengurus (urus v.**)** to look after

menguruskan (urus v.**)** to deal with, to handle

meninggal (tinggal v.**)** to die

meninggal dunia pass away, died

menjadi (jadi v.**)** to become

menjaga (jaga v.**)** to look after

menjala (jala n.**)** to net

menjamu (jamu v.**)** to invite

menjamu selera to make one's mouth water

menjemput (jemput v.**)** to pick up, fetch, invite

menjual (jual v.**)** to sell

menonton to watch

mensnorkel (snorkel n.**)** to snorkel, snorkelling

mentah raw, undercooked

mentéga butter

menteri minister

menu makanan menu

menulis (tulis v.**)** to write

menunggu (tunggu v.**)** to expect

menuntut (tuntut v.**)** to claim, assert

menyanyi (nyanyi v.**)** to sing

menyebut (sebut v.**)** to mention

menyediakan (sedia a.**)** to prepare

menyelam (selam v.**)** to go diving

menyelesaikan (selesai v.**)** to finish

menyenangkan (senang a.**)** pleasing

ményerang (sérang v.**)** to attack

ményerap (serap a.**)** to absorb

ményewa (séwa n.**)** to rent

menyombongkan (sombong a.**)** to be proud

menyuntik (suntik v.**)** to inject

mérah red

mérah jambu pink

mérah manggis maroon

meraikan (raya v.**)** to celebrate

merancang (rancang v.**)** to plan, design

merasa (rasa v.**)** to feel

merasakan (rasa v.**)** to taste

merdeka free, independent

meréka they

merencanakan (rencana n.**)** to make plans

merenih (renih v.**)** to reduce, simmer

meriah lively

merokok (rokok n.**)** to smoke

mertua father/mother-in-law

mesin ATM ATM machine

mesin faks fax machine

meskipun although

mesti must

mesyuarat meeting

meter metre

mi noodles

mi goréng fried noodles

mi hailam noodles, black soy sauce, squid and vegetables

mi kuah noodles in soup

mi kuay teow flat rice noodles

mi laksa rice noodles in spicy coconut gravy

mi rebus noodles in spicy gravy

milik to own

minat enthusiasm

minggu week

minggu depan next week

minta to ask

minum to drink

minuman (minum v.**)** drink

minuman tanpa beralkohol alcohol-free drinks

miskin poor

moden stylish

mohon to apply

motorsikal motorbike

mual nauseous

muda young

mudah convenient, easy, simple, hopefully

mudahan hopefully

muka surat page

mula to begin, to start

mulanya at first

mulut mouth

mungkin maybe

muntah to vomit

murah cheap

murid (primary school) pupil

murtabak Indian pancakes with meat fillings

musim season

musim bunga spring

musim hujan rainy season

musim luruh autumn

musim panas dry season, summer

musim sejuk winter

muzik music

muzium museum

naik to ascend, to go up

naik ke atas to go upstairs

nak to want to, need

nama name

Nama saya… My name is…

nampak to seem, to look

nampaknya it seems like, it looks like

nanti later

nasi (cooked) rice

nasi ayam chicken rice

nasi briyani Indian-style rice with meat

nasi campur rice with meat and vegetables

nasi goréng fried rice

nasi kerabu blue rice with raw vegetables and salted fish

nasi lemak coconut rice with various condiments

nasi patprik Thai-style rice and beef

nasi pulut glutinous rice

nasib chance, fate, destiny

nasihat advice

negara country

negeri state, country

nénék grandmother

niaga trade

nombor number

novél novel

November November

nyaman pleasant

nyanyi to sing

Ogos August

Oktober October

oléh by, to obtain

ondé-ondé a green sweet from coconut, flour and brown sugar

orang *person*

orang anak *child, children*

orang Brazil *Brazilian*

orén *orange*

otak-otak *fish cooked in banana leaves*

pada bulan hadapan *next month*

pada waktu malam *in the evening, at night-time*

padat *dense*

padat penduduknya *densely populated*

pagi pagi *early in the morning*

pagi tadi *this morning*

paha *thigh(s)*

pahit *bitter*

pahitan *bitterness*

pakai *to wear, to use, by way of*

pakaian (pakai *v.***)** *clothes*

pakaian kanak *children's clothes*

pakcik *uncle*

pakej percutian *package holiday*

paksa *to force to*

paling besar *the biggest*

paling suka *to like the most*

panas *hot*

pancutan *fountain*

pandai *clever, to be good at*

pandang *to look, examine*

pandu *chauffeur, to chauffeur*

panggil *to call*

panggil saya… *call me…*

panggung wayang *cinema*

panjang *long*

Panjangnya…sentimeter. *It is… centimetres long.*

pantas *brisk, quick*

papa *father*

pasar *market*

pasport *passport*

pasti *sure*

pasu *vase*

patah *broken*

patung *statue*

patutlah *that's the reason, that's why*

pedas *hot (spicy)*

pegawai *employee*

pegawai kerajaan *civil servant*

peguam *lawyer*

pejabat *office*

pejabat pentadbiran *administration office*

pejabat pelancongan *travel agency*

pejalan (jalan *n.***) kaki** *pedestrian*

pekedai (kedai *n.***)** *shopkeeper*

pekerja (kerja *n.***)** *employee*

pekerjaan (kerja *n.***)** *job*

pelajar (ajar *v.***)** *student*

pelajaran (ajar *v.***)** *lesson*

pelancong (lancong *n.***)** *tourist*

pelancongan (lancong *n.***)** *tourism*

pelayan (layan *v.***)** *waiter*

pelayaran persiaran *cruise*

pelik *strange, odd*

pemain (main *v.***)** *player*

pemain piano *piano player*

pemain sépak bola *football player*

pemalu (malu *a.***)** *shy person*

pemandangan (pandang *v.***)** *scenery*

pemandu (pandu *n.***)** *guide*

pemandu teksi *taxi driver*

pemasaran (pasar *n.***)** *marketing*

pembacaan (baca v.) reading

pembangunan (bangun v.) construction

pembantu (bantu v.) helper

pembantu rumah maid

pembelian (beli v.) buying

pemberitahuan (beritahu v.)
    announcement

pemilihan (pilih v.) election

pemilik (milik v.) owner

penari (tari n.) dancer

penat tired

pencuci (cuci v.) cleaner (agent and person)

pencuci mulut dessert

pendaki (daki v.) climber

pendapat opinion

péndek short

pendidikan (didik v.) education

penduduk (duduk v.) population

penerbangan flight

penerbitan (terbit v.) publishing house

pengajar (ajar v.) instructor

pengalaman (alam a.)
    experience

pengalaman kerja work experience

pengaturcara komputer computer
    programmer

pengelasan (kelas n.) classification

pengenalan (kenal v.) identification

pengetahuan (tahu v.)
    knowledge

pengganguan (ganggu v.) annoying

penghabisan (habis n.) conclusion

penghubung (hubung v.) link

penginapan (inap v.) inn

pengumuman (umum a.) announcement

pengurup wang bureau de change

pengurus (urus v.) manager

pengurusan (urus v.) management

pengurusan (urus v.) perniagaan (niaga
    n.) business management

penjual (jual v.) seller

penjualan (jual v.) selling

pensél pencil

pensyarah (syarah n.) lecturer

pentadbiran (tadbir n.) administration

penuh full

penuh dengan full of

penulis (tulis v.) writer

penyakit (sakit a.) illness

penyakit darah tinggi high blood pressure

penyanyi (nyanyi v.) singer

penyanyi undangan guest singer

penyeberang (seberang v.) crossing

penyéwaan (séwa n.) renting out

per jam per hour

perah to extract

pérak silver

perakaunan (akaun n.) accounting

peramah friendly

Perancis France

perang brown

peraturan (atur v.) restriction, regulation

peratus percent

perbandaran (bandar n.) urbanized area

perbankan (bank n.) banking

percaya to believe

peréka (réka v.) designer, inventor

peréka fesyen fashion designer

perempuan girl

perenang (renang n.) swimmer

pergi *to go*

pergi berjalan (jalan *v.***)** *to go for a walk*

pergunungan (gunung *n.***)** *mountain range*

perguruan (guru *n.***)** *teaching*

perhentian (henti *v.***)** *stop*

peribadi *personal*

perigi *well, shaft*

periksa *to check, to examine*

perit *pricking*

perjalan kaki *pedestrian, passer-by*

perjalanan (jalan *n.***)** *journey*

perkahwinan (kahwin *v.***)** *marriage, wedding*

perkampungan (kampung *n.***)** *settlement*

perkantoran *office complex*

perkataan (kata *n.***)** *words*

perkenalkan (kenal *v.***)** *to introduce*

Perkenalkan, ini… *Let me introduce…*

perlahan *slow*

perlahan-lahan *slowly*

perlu *to need, it's necessary*

perlukan (perlu *v.***)** *need*

permainan (main *v.***)** *game*

permohonan (mohon *v.***)** *application*

pernah *ever, never*

perniagaan (niaga *n.***)** *business*

perpustakaan (pustaka *n.***)** *library*

persahabatan (sahabat *n.***)** *friendship*

persegi *square*

persembahan (sembah *n.***)** *show*

persimpangan (simpang *n.***)** *crossroads*

pertama *first*

pertanian (tani *n.***)** *agriculture*

pertimbangkan (timbang *v.***)** *to consider*

pertunjukan (tunjuk *v.***)** *performance*

perubatan (ubat *n.***)** *medicine*

perut *stomach*

pesan *to order*

pesanan (pesan *v.***)** *message, order*

pesawat *aircraft*

pésta *festival*

peta *map*

petang nanti *this afternoon*

pijak *pedal*

pilih *to choose, to select*

pilihan (pilih *v.***)** *choice*

pinggan *dish (receptacle)*

pinjam *to borrow*

pinjamkan (pinjam *v.***)** *to lend*

pintu keluar *exit*

pipi *cheek*

plastik *plastic*

polis *police*

popular *popular*

potong *piece, slice, to cut*

potong sekeping *to cut into pieces*

presidén *president*

produk *product*

psikologi *psychology*

puas *satisfied*

puasa *fast (as in a religious fast)*

pucat *pale*

pucuk *counter for thin objects*

puding mangga *mango pudding*

puding pulut santan *glutinous rice and coconut pudding*

pukul… *at… (o'clock)*

pukul berapa *what time*

pula *likewise*

pulang to return home

Pulau Pinang Penang

pulut glutinous rice

pun also, yet, still

pusat kesihatan fitness centre

pusat sukan sports centre

pustaka book (archaic)

putih white

putus to break

putus hubungan to break up

Rabu Wednesday

rahasia secret

raja king

rakan friend

rakan sekelas classmate

ramai crowded

rambut hair

rambutan a hairy fruit

rancang to plan, to think deeply

rancangan (rancang v.**)** plan

rantai léhér necklace

rasa to feel, think, taste

réhat to rest

réka to invent

rempah spice

renang to swim

rencana article

rendah low

rendang ayam chicken in coconut milk

rendang daging beef in coconut milk

renih to simmer

rentak rhythm

rentak lagu types of songs

renyai-renyai drizzle

resépsi reception

resipi recipe

restoran restaurant

ribut storm

ringan light (of weight)

risau anxious, worry, apprehensive

rojak fruit salad with spicy sauce

rojak buah fruit salad

ros rose

rosak broke down

roti canai Indian bread

rugi loss, lack of profit, to lose out

rumah house

rumah beribadat house of worship

rumah urut massage parlour

sabar patient

Sabtu Saturday

saderi celery

sah authentic

sahabat friend

sahaja just, only

saintis scientist

saiz size

saja only, just

sakit sick

Sakit apa? How are you sick?

salah wrong

salah nombor the wrong number

sama ada either

sama dengan equal to, the same as

sambal chilli paste cooked with onions

sambil while

Sambil menyelam minum air. To kill two birds with one stone.

sambilan *part time*

sampah *rubbish, trash*

sampai *to reach, arrive*

sampaikan salam saya kepada meréka *give them my regards*

sampan *small boat*

sangat *very*

sangkut *to hang*

santan *coconut milk*

sarapan pagi *breakfast*

sarjana *master's degree*

sarung kaki *sock*

sarung tangan *glove*

saté ayam *chicken on skewers in peanut sauce*

saté daging *beef on skewers in peanut sauce*

saté kambing *goat meat on skewers in peanut sauce*

satu *one, a*

satu satu *one by one*

saudari *you*

sauna *sauna*

sawah padi *rice field*

saya *I, I am*

saya ada *I have*

Saya berasal dari… *I am from…*

Saya dah tidak sabar lagi. *I can hardly wait.*

Saya dari… *I am from…*

Saya juga begitu. *I am (pleased to meet you) too.*

Saya juga begitu. *Me too.*

Saya kurang pasti. *I'm not sure.*

Saya kurang suka *I don't really like*

Saya rasa bukan. *I don't think so.*

Saya suka sekali… *I love…*

Saya tidak tahu. *I don't know.*

sayang *darling*

sayang sekali *unfortunately*

sayang! *it's a pity!*

sayur *vegetable*

sayur campur *mixed vegetables*

sayuran (sayur *n.*) *vegetables*

sayur-sayuran *vegetables*

sebagai *as*

sebagai ganti *instead of*

sebanyak *as much as, to the amount of*

sebarang *any*

sebelah *side*

sebelum *before*

sebentar-sebentar *now and again*

seberang *crossing*

sebilik *for one room, per room*

sebuah *a*

sebuah bengkel keréta *car repair garage*

sebut *to mention*

secukupnya *sufficient*

sedang *now*

sedang belajar *studying*

sedang menunggu *am waiting (for)*

sedap *delicious*

sedia *ready*

sediakan (sedia *a.*) *to prepare*

sedih *sad*

seékor *one, a (counter for animals)*

segala *all*

segelas *glass*

sehingga *until*

Sehingga berjumpa lagi. *See you.*

Sehingga kita berjumpa lagi. *See you again.*

seikat *a (tied) bunch of*

sejak *since*

sejarah *history*

sejuk *chilled, cold*

sekali *once, very*

sekali sekala *once in a while*

sekarang *now*

sekejap *moment*

sekejap-kejab *now and again*

sekeluarga *one family*

sekilo setengah *one and a half kilos*

sekolah *school*

sekolah rendah *primary school*

seksi *sexy*

selain ini *apart from this*

selain itu *apart from that*

selalu *always*

selam *to dive*

selama *for (with time)*

Selamat bekerja. *Enjoy your work.*

Selamat belajar. *Enjoy your studies.*

Selamat berangkat. *Have a good trip.*

Selamat datang. *Welcome.*

Selamat datang ke… *Welcome to…*

Selamat hari jadi. *Happy birthday.*

Selamat Hari Raya. *Happy Eid.*

Selamat jalan. *Goodbye.*

Selamat makan. *Enjoy your food.*

Selamat malam. *Good evening. Good night.*

Selamat Menyambut Hari Krismas. *Merry Christmas.*

Selamat pagi! *Good morning!*

Selamat petang! *Good evening!*

Selamat Tahun Baru. *Happy New Year.*

Selamat tengah hari! *Good afternoon!*

Selamat tinggal. *Goodbye.*

Selasa *Tuesday*

selepas itu *after that*

selera *appetite*

selesa *comfortable*

selesai *completed, to finish, to complete*

selo *cello*

seluar *trousers*

seluar panjang *long trousers*

seluar péndek *short trousers*

seluas *as wide as*

seluruh *the whole (of)*

semak *to check*

semalam *yesterday*

semangat *motivation, spirit*

semasa (masa *n.***)** *at the time when, current*

sembah *respectful greetings*

sembilan *nine*

sembuh *to recover, to get better (of illness)*

semenanjung *peninsula*

semenjak *since*

seminggu *week*

semua *all*

semua (ini) *all (this)*

semuanya *all of them, all of it*

semula *again*

semut *ant*

senam *to work out, to exercise*

senang *easy, happy, pleased*

seni *art*

seni bina *architecture*

sentimeter *centimetre*

seorang *a, alone*

sepanjang *length, throughout, through the time of*

sepanjang hari *all day long*

Sepanyol *Spain*

sepasang *a pair of*

sepenuh masa *full time*

seperti *like, similar to*

seperti orang asli *like a native*

September *September*

sepuluh *ten*

sepupu *cousin*

sepupu-sepupunya *the cousins*

serai *lemon grass*

seram *horror*

serang *to attack*

serap *absorbent*

serbulan *per month*

sering *often*

serius *serious*

seronok *enjoy*

serta *along with, to add*

seruling, flut *flute*

sesak *congested*

sesat *astray/lost*

seseorang *someone*

sesuai *to suit (someone)*

set *set*

setelah *after*

setengah *half*

setengah matang *rare*

setiap *every*

setiausaha *secretary*

séwa *rent*

siap *ready*

siap dihidang *ready to be served up*

Siapa? *Who?*

Siapakah? *Who?*

Siapkan (siap *a.***)** *to prepare*

sibuk *busy*

sifat *nature*

sihat *healthy*

Sila duduk. *Please sit down.*

silap *mistaken*

silat *a Malaysian/Indonesian martial art*

simpan *to keep*

sinar *to illuminate*

sinaran (sinar *v.***)** *ray*

Singapura *Singapore*

ski *ski*

skirt *skirt*

sombong *conceited, proud*

sopan *polite*

sos kacang *peanut sauce*

sos pelam *plum sauce*

soto ayam *chicken soup with vegetables*

sotong *squid*

stésen *station*

stik *steak*

stok *stock*

stokin *stocking*

suam *lukewarm*

suami *husband*

suatu *a*

suatu hari *one of these days*

suatu masa dahulu *a long time ago*

sudah *already*

sudah cukup *that's all*

sudah lupa *already forgotten*

sudah tentu *sure*

sudu *spoon, spoonful*

suka *to like*

sukan *sport*

sukar *difficult*

sulit *difficult*

sulong *eldest, first born*

sumbang *to contribute*

sumber *source*

sumber manusia *human resources*

sungai *river*

sungguh *really*

supaya *so that*

surat *letter*

surat khabar *newspaper*

surat-menyurat *correspondence*

susah *difficult*

swasta *private*

syarah *lecture*

syarikat *company*

syarikat swasta *private company*

tadbir *administration*

tadi *just now*

tahu *to know*

tahun *year*

tahun baru *new year*

taip *typewriter*

tajam *sharp, strong (of smells)*

tak *no, not*

Tak apalah. *It doesn't matter.*

Tak payah susah, susah. *Don't go to any trouble.*

takut *frightened*

tali *string*

tali léhér *tie*

tali pinggang *belt*

taman *garden*

tamat pengajian *to graduate*

tambah *to add*

tambah lagi *to order some more*

tambang *fare*

tamu *guest*

tanah liat *clay*

tanda *sign*

tanda tangan *signature*

tangan *hand*

tangis *to cry*

tangkai *stalk, counter for objects with stems*

tangkap *to catch*

tani *farmer*

tanpa *without*

tape *fermented soya beans*

taraf perkahwinan *marital status*

tari *dance*

tarian (tari *v.***)** *dancing*

tarik *to pull*

tarikh *date*

tarikh lahir *date of birth*

tasik *lake*

taufan *typhoon*

tawa *laugh*

tawar *to bargain*

tawaran (tawar *v.***)** *bargain*

tebal *thick*

téh *tea*

teksi *taxi*

telan *to swallow*

teléfon *telephone, to telephone*

teléfon mudah alih *mobile phone*

télevisyen *television*

telinga *ear*

telur *egg*

telur téh *eggs cooked in tea*

teman *friend*

teman lelaki *boyfriend*

tempah *to book, to reserve*

tempahan (tempah *v.***)** *reservation, booking*

tempat duduk (di sebelah tingkap) *(window) seat*

tempat lahir *place of birth*

tempat peranginan *holiday resort*

tempat tinggal *place where someone lives*

tempéh *fermented soybean cake*

tempoh tinggal *length of stay*

temu *to meet*

temu janji *appointment*

tengok *to take a look at*

tentang *about*

tentu *of course*

tentu boléh *of course I can*

tepat *accurate*

tepat sekali *that's right*

tepi pantai *seaside*

tepung beras *rice flour*

terakhir (akhir *a.***)** *the last*

terang *bright, bold (of colours)*

terbaik (baik *a.***)** *excellent*

terbang *to fly*

terbit *to appear, to publish*

terburu-buru *to be in a hurry*

terdiri daripada *to consist of*

tergesa-gesa *to be in a hurry*

terima *to receive*

terima kasih *thank you*

Terima kasih atas… *Thank you for…*

Terima kasih banyak-banyak. *Thanks a million.*

terjebak *stuck*

terkenal *famous, well-known*

terkenal dengan *known as*

terlalu banyak *too many*

terlalu kecil *too small*

terlalu keras *over cooked*

terlambat (lambat *a.***)** *late*

terletak (letak *n.***)** *to be situated*

terléwat (lewat *a.***)** *late*

terlupa (lupa *v.***)** *to forget*

termasuk (masuk *v.***)** *to include, to be included*

terowong *tunnel*

terpaksa (paksa *v.***)** *forced (to), obliged (to)*

terpelajar (ajar *v.***)** *educated*

terpulang (pulang *v.***)** *persistent*

tersangkut (sangkut *v.***)** *to be stuck*

tersedia (sedia *a.***)** *available*

tersesat (sesat *a.***)** *to be lost*

tersilap (silap *a.***)** *to be mistaken*

tertarik *interested*

tertarik (tarik *v.***) dengan** *to be interested in*

tertinggal (tinggal *v.***)** *to miss*

terus *straight on, direct, non-stop, to keep on doing*

terutama (utama *a.***)** *especially*

terutamanya (utama *a.***)** *especially*

tetamu *guest*

tetamu jemputan *the person invited*

tetanga *neighbour*

tetap *invariable*

tetapi *but*

Thai *Thai*

tiada *no, not*

Tiada hari yang berlalu tanpa musik. *There's no day without music.*

tiap *every*

tiba *to arrive*

tiba-tiba *suddenly*

tidak ada masalah *(it's) no problem*

tidak begitu *not really*

tidak boléh kembalikan wang
   unrefundable

tidak jelas *unclear*

tidak mengapa *it doesn't matter, it's OK*

tidak sabar *to be impatient to, can't wait to*

tidak sangat *not really*

tidak termasuk makanan *food is not*
   included

Tidak, terima kasih. *No, thank you.*

tidak usah *there's no need*

tidur *to sleep*

tiga *three*

tiga hari *three days*

tiga puluh *thirty*

tikét *ticket*

tikét pulang balik *return ticket*

tikét satu jalan *one way ticket*

tikus *mouse*

tikus besar *big rat*

timbang *to deliberate, to weigh*

tin *can*

tinggal *to stay, live*

tinggalkan (tinggal *v.***)** *to leave,*
   to omit, to neglect

tinggi *high, tall*

tingkap *window*

tingkat *floor, storey*

tingkat atas *upstairs*

tingkat bawah *downstairs*

tiram *oysters*

titis *to let fall, to drop*

tonton *to watch*

topi *hat*

tradisional *traditional*

trompet *trumpet*

tu *this*

tugu *monument*

tujuan lawatan *reason for visit*

tujuh *seven*

tukang jahit baju *tailor*

tukang masak *chef*

tukar *to change*

tukar fikiran *to change one's mind*

Tumpang tanya…? *Do you mind if I ask*
   you…?

tunai *cash, ready money*

tunggal *only, single*

tunggu *to expect, to wait*

tunjukkan (tunjuk *v.***)** *to show*

tuntut *to claim, assert*

turun *to get off or out of a vehicle*

tutup *to close*

tutur *utterance*

ubat *medicine*

ubat titis *drops*

ubi kentang *potato*

udang *shrimp, prawn*

udang karang *lobster*

uji *to test*

ujian (uji *v.***)** *test*

ukur *measure*

ukuran (ukur *n.***)** *size*

ulas *pip*

umum *public, to announce*

umur *age*

undangan (undang *v.***)** *invitation*

undang-undang *law*

ungu *purple*

unik *unique*

universiti *university*

untuk *for, (in order) to*

untuk berapa orang *for how many persons*

untuk diperah santannya *to extract the coconut milk*

untung *luck*

untung sekali! *what luck!*

upacara *ceremony*

upacara ijazah *graduation ceremony*

urus *to manage*

uruskan (urus *v.***)** *to deal with, to sort out*

urut *massage*

usahawan (usaha *n.***)** *businessman*

utas *counter for long, bendable objects*

video *video*

violin *violin*

wain *wine*

walaupun *although*

wang *money*

wang bakinya *change*

wang besar *big money*

wang kecil *small money*

wang kertas *bank note*

wang tunai *cash*

wanita *female*

warganegara *nationality*

warna *colour*

wartawan *journalist*

wayang kulit *leather shadow puppet*

wiski *whiskey*

ya *yes*

ya, betul *sure, of course*

Yakah? *Really?*

yang coraknya berbéza *which have different designs*

yang depan itu *the one in front of that*

yang lain *other*

zirafah *giraffe*

zoo negara *national zoo*

English–Malay glossary

a **sebuah, suatu**

able (to be) **dapat**

about **tentang**

above **atas**

abroad **di luar negeri, luar negeri**

absorb (to) **menyerap (serap** *a.***)**

absorbent **serap**

academy **akademi**

accent **aksen**

accept (to) **menerima (terima** *v.***)**

accident **kemalangan (malang** *a.***)**

accident: by ~ **kebetulan**

account **akaun**

accounting **perakaunan (akaun** *n.***)**

accurate **tepat**

across the road **di seberang jalan**

action **aksi**

action film **filem yang penuh aksi**

activity **aktiviti**

actually **memang**

add (to) **serta, tambah**

address **alamat**

adept in **mahir dalam**

administration **pentadbiran
    (tadbir** *n.***), tadbir**

administration office **pejabat pentadbiran**

advertisement **iklan**

advertising bureau **biro pengiklanan**

advice **nasihat**

aerobics **aérobik**

after **setelah**

after that **selepas itu**

afternoon: this ~ **petang nanti**

again **semula**

age **umur**

ago: five years ~ **lima tahun yang lalu**

agriculture **pertanian (tani** n.**)**

aircraft **pesawat**

aisle **lorong**

alcohol-free drinks **minuman tanpa
    beralkohol**

alive **hidup**

all **segala, semua**

all (this) **semua (ini)**

all of them/it **semuanya**

allergic (to) **alergi (pada)**

allow **biar**

almost **hampir**

almost all the time **hampir sepanjang
    masanya**

alone **seorang**

along with **serta**

already **sudah, dah**

also **pun**

although **meskipun, walaupun**

always **selalu**

ambassador **duta**

amenity **kemudahan (mudah** *a.***)**

America **Amérika**

amount, total **jumlah**

and **dan**

angry **marah**

animal **binatang**

announce (to) **umum**

announcement **pemberitahuan (beritahu** *v.*)**, pengumuman (umum** *a.*)

annoying **pengganguan (ganggu** *v.*)

answer **jawapan (jawab** *v.*)

answer a letter (to) **membalas (balas** *v.*) **surat**

ant **semut**

antique **antik**

anxious **risau**

anxious (to be) **bimbang**

any **sebarang, apa**

anything **apa saja**

anytime **bila masa**

apart from that **selain itu**

apart from this **selain ini**

appear (to) **terbit**

appetite **selera**

application **permohonan (mohon** *v.*)

apply (to) **mohon**

appointment **temu janji**

apprehensive **risau**

approximately **kira**

April **April**

Arabic **bahasa Arab**

architecture **seni bina**

Are you…? **Adakah saudara ini…?**

area **kawasan**

around **keliling**

arrival **kedatangan (datang** *v.*)

arrive (to) **tiba**

art **seni**

art gallery **balai seni**

article **rencana**

as **sebagai**

as long as **asalkan**

as much as **sebanyak**

as soon as possible **dengan secepat mungkin**

as wide as **seluas**

ascend (to) **naik**

ask (to) **bertanya (tanya** *n.*)**, bertanya dengan, minta**

ask for (to) **meminta (minta** *v.*)

asthma **asma**

astray **sesat**

at first **mulanya**

at the time when **semasa (masa** *n.*)

at… (o'clock) **pukul…**

ATM machine **mesin ATM**

attack (to) **menyerang (serang** *v.*)

attend (to) **hadir, layan, menghadiri (hadir** *v.*)

attract (to) **menarik (tarik** *v.*)

August **Ogos**

aunt **makcik**

authentic **sah, asli**

authenticate (to) **mengesahkan (sah** *a.*)

author **karya**

autumn **musim luruh**

available **tersedia (sedia** *a.*)

awake (to) **jaga**

background **latar**

bag **beg**

bald **botak**

ball **bola**

bank note **wang kertas**

banking **perbankan (bank** *n.*)

banter **jenaka**

bargain **tawaran (tawar** *v.*)

bargain (to) **tawar**

basketball **bola keranjang**

bathroom **bilik mandi**

batik **batik**

bay leaf **daun salam**

be (at a place) (to) **berada (ada** *v.*)

be (to) **jadi**

beautiful **cantik, indah**

beauty **keindahan (indah** *a.*)

because (of) **kerana**

become (to) **jadi, menjadi (jadi** *v.*)

bed **katil**

beef **daging lembu**

beef in coconut milk **rendang daging**

beef on skewers in peanut sauce **saté daging**

beer **bir**

before **sebelum, dahulu, dulu**

begin (to) **bermula (mula** *v.*)

believe (to) **percaya**

below **bawah**

belt **tali pinggang**

better **lebih bagus**

biggest: the ~ **paling besar**

bill **bil**

biology **biologi**

bird **burung**

biscuit **biskut**

bitter **pahit**

bitterness **pahitan**

black **hitam**

blind **buta**

blood **darah**

blouse **blaus**

blue **biru**

boat: small ~ **sampan**

body **badan**

bold (of colours) **terang**

book **buku**

book (archaic) **pustaka**

book (to) **tempah**

book shop **kedai buku**

booking **tempahan (tempah** *v.*)

bored **bosan, jelak**

boring **membosankan (bosan** *a.*)

borrow (to) **meminjam (pinjam** *v.*)

boss **bos**

both **berdua**

bother (to) **ganggu**

bottle **botol**

boutique **butik**

bowl **mangkuk**

box **kotak**

boy **lelaki**

boyfriend **teman lelaki**

bracelet **gelang, gelang tangan**

Brazilian **orang Brazil**

bread fruit **cempedak**

break (to) **putus**

break up (to) **putus hubungan**

breakfast **sarapan pagi**

breathe (to) **bernafas (nafas** *n.*)

bright **cerah**

bright (of colours) **terang**

bring (to) **bawa**

brisk, quick **pantas**

broad **luas**

brochure **brosur**

broke down **rosak**

broken **patah**

brother-in-law **ipar**

brothers and sisters **beradik**

brown **perang**

browse (to) **lihat lihat**

buffet **bufét**

build (to) **bina, embangun (bangun** v.**)**

building **bangunan (bangun** v.**)**

built (to be) **dibina (bina** v.**)**

bureau de change **pengurup wang**

bus **bas**

bus: by ~ **dengan bas**

business **bisnes, perniagaan (niaga** n.**)**

business card **kad nama**

business management **pengurusan (urus** v.**) perniagaan (niaga** n.**)**

businessman **usahawan (usaha** n.**)**

busy **sibuk**

but **tetapi**

butter **mentéga**

buy (to) **membeli (beli** v.**)**

buy something for someone (to) **membelikan (beli** v.**)**

buying **pembelian (beli** v.**)**

by **oléh**

calculate (to) **kira**

calf/calves **betis**

call (to) **panggil**

call me... **panggil saya...**

called (to be) **bernama (nama** n.**)**

camera **kamera**

camping **berkhémah (khemah** v.**)**

campus **kampus**

can **tin**

can (be allowed/able to) **boléh**

Canada **Kanada**

car **keréta**

car repair garage **sebuah béngkel keréta**

car: by ~ **dengan keréta**

careful **berhati (hati** v.**)**

carrot **lobak mérah**

case: in that ~ **kalau begitu**

cash **wang tunai**

cashier **kasyer**

cassette **kasét**

cat **kucing**

catch (to) **menangkap (tangkap** v.**)**

catfish **ikan keli**

caution **awas**

CD player **alat CD**

celebrate (to) **meraikan (raya** v.**)**

celery **saderi**

cello **selo**

centimetre **sentimeter**

ceremony **majlis, upacara**

change **wang bakinya**

change (to) **bertukar (tukar** v.**), ganti**

change one's mind (to) **tukar fikiran**

charity **amal**

chat (to) **cakap**

chat to (to) **berbual dengan**

chauffeur **pandu**

chauffeur (to) **pandu**

cheap **murah**

cheaper **lebih murah**

check (to) **periksa, semak**

check-in **daftar masuk**

cheek **pipi**

chef **chef, tukang masak**

chemistry **kimia**

chest **dada**

chicken **ayam**

chicken curry **kari ayam**

chicken in coconut milk **rendang ayam**

chicken korma **ayam masak kurma**

chicken on skewers in peanut sauce
saté ayam

chicken rice **nasi ayam**

chicken soup with vegetables **soto ayam**

child **budak, anak**

child, children **anak, anak-anak**

child: only ~ **anak tunggal**

children's clothes **pakaian kanak-kanat**

chilled, cold **sejuk**

chilli **cili**

chilli paste cooked with onions **sambal**

chin **dagu**

China **China**

choice **pilihan (pilih** v.**)**

choose (to) **memilih (pilih** v.**)**

cinema **panggung wayang**

city **bandar**

civil servant **pegawai kerajaan**

claim, assert (to) **menuntut (tuntut** v.**)**

clarinet **klarinet**

class **kelas**

classical **klasik**

classification **pengelasan (kelas** n.**)**

classmate **rakan sekelas**

clay **tanah liat**

clean **bersih**

cleaner (agent and person) **pencuci (cuci** v.**)**

clear **jelas**

clever (to be good at) **pandai**

climb (to) **mendaki (daki** v.**)**

climber **pendaki (daki** v.**)**

close **dekat**

close (to) **tutup**

cloth **kain**

clothes **pakaian (pakai** v.**), baju**

cloud **awan**

cloudy (to be) **berawan (awan** n.**)**

coconut **kelapa**

coconut milk **santan**

coconut milk pudding **kuih talam**

coconut rice with various condiments
nasi lemak

coffee **kopi**

coincidence: by ~ **kebetulan**

cold **sejuk, dingin**

college **kolej**

collide (to) **kelanggaran (langgar** v.**)**

colour **warna**

coloured (to be) **berwarna (warna** n.**)**

combined (to be) **digabung (gabung** n.**)**

come (to) **datang**

come back (to) **kembali**

come over (to a place) (to) **datang ke**

comedy **komedi**

comfortable **selésa**

communicate (to) **berhubung (hubung** n.**)**

company **syarikat**

complete (to) **selesai**

completed **selesai**

compose (to) **mengarang (garang** a.**)**

comprehend (to) **mengetahui (tahu** v.**)**

computer **komputer**

computer programmer **pengaturcara komputer**

conceited **sombong**

conclusion **penghabisan (habis** n.**)**

condition **keadaan (ada** v.**)**

condominium **kondominium**

confused **keliru**

congested **sesak**

congestion **kesesakan (sesak** a.**)**

connect (to) **hubung**

connecting rooms **bilik penghubung**

connection **hubungan (hubung** n.**)**

consider (to) **pertimbangkan
(timbang** v.**)**

consign (to) **kirim**

consist of (to) **terdiri daripada**

construct, build (to) **bina**

construction **pembangunan
(bangun** v.**)**

contact (to) **menghubungi (hubung** v.**)**

content **isi**

continent **benua**

continue (to) **lanjut**

continuously **lanjut**

convenient **mudah**

convey (to) **menghantar (hantar** v.**)**

cook (to) **memasak (masak** v.**)**

cookery **masakan (masak** v.**)**

coriander **ketumbar**

correspondence **surat-menyurat**

cost **harga**

cotton **kapas**

cough **batuk**

Could I have…? **Boléh saya dapatkan…?**

Could you give me…? **Boléh beri saya…?**

Could you let me know? **Boléh saya tahu?**

Could you repeat that, please? **Boléhkah
anda ulangi sekali lagi?**

Could you speak more loudly, please?
**Boléhkah anda bercakap dengan
lebih kuat?**

Could you speak more slowly, please?
**Boléhkah anda bercakap dengan
lebih perlahan?**

Could you spell it, please? **Boléhkah anda
tolong éjakan?**

Could you write it down, please? **Boléhkah
anda tolong tuliskan?**

count **hitung**

count (to) **mengira (kira** v.**)**

counter for flat objects **helai**

counter for objects with stems **tangkai**

counter for small, round objects **butir**

counter for thin objects **pucuk**

country **negara, negeri**

coupon **kupon**

course: of ~ **tentu**

cousin **sepupu**

cousins: the ~ **sepupu-sepupunya**

cover (to) **meliputi (liput** n.**)**

covering **liput**

cow **lembu**

crab **ketam**

credit card **kad kredit**

crisps (US chips) **keropok kentang**

crossing **penyeberang (seberang** v.**)**

crossroads **persimpangan (simpang** n.**)**

crowded **ramai**

cruise **pelayaran persiaran**

cry (to) **menangis (tangis** v.**)**

cuisine **masakan (masak** v.**)**

culture **budaya**

cup **cawan**

current **semasa (masa** n.**)**

curriculum vitae **butir peribadi**

curry **kari**

cut (to) **memotong (potong** v.)

cut into pieces (to) **potong sekeping**

cut with scissors (to) **menggunting
    (gunting** n.)

cute **comél**

daily **harian**

damp **lembap**

dance **tari**

dance (to) **menari (tari** n.)

dancer **penari (tari** n.)

dancing **tarian (tari** n.)

dark **gelap**

darling **sayang**

date **tarikh, haribulan**

date of birth **tarikh lahir**

daughter **anak perempuan**

day **hari**

day: all ~ long **sepanjang hari**

day: one of these ~s **suatu hari**

day: the ~ after tomorrow **dua hari yang
    akan datang, lusa**

day: the ~ before yesterday **dua hari yang
    lalu, kelmarin**

deal with (to) **menguruskan (urus** v.)

December **Disember**

decision **keputusan (putus** v.)

decoration **hiasan**

degree **ijazah**

deliberate (to) **timbang**

delicate **halus**

delicious **lazat, sedap**

dense **padat**

densely populated **padat penduduknya**

dentist **doktor gigi**

depart (to) **berlepas (lepas** v.), **bertolak
    (tolak** v.)

departure **berlepas (lepas** v.)

description **gambaran**

design **corak**

design (to) **merancang (rancang** v.)

designer **peréka (réka** v.)

desire to (to) **hendak, mahu**

dessert **pencuci mulut**

destination **destinasi**

device **alat**

dictionary **kamus**

die (to) **meninggal (tinggal** v.)

died **meninggal dunia**

differ (to) **beza**

different **berbéza (béza** v.)

different from **berbéza dengan, berlainan
    (lain** a.) **dengan**

different kinds of **bermacam**

difficult **sukar, sulit, susah**

difficulty **kesulitan (sulit** a.)

dinner **makan malam**

diploma, permission **ijazah**

direct **terus**

directions **cara membuat**

dirt **kotoran (kotor** a.)

dirty **kotor**

discard (to) **buang**

disco **disko**

discount **diskaun**

discuss (to) **berbincang (bincang** v.)

dish **lauk**

dish (food) **hidangan (hidang** v.)

dish (receptacle) **pinggan**

displace (to) **alih**

disturb (to) **mengganggu (ganggu** v.**)**

dive (to) **selam**

divorce (to) **cerai**

divorced (to be) **bercerai (cerai** v.**)**

dizzy **mabuk**

do (to) **berbuat (buat** v.**), lakukan**

Do you mind if I ask you...? **Tumpang tanya...?**

Do you want me to wait? **Mahu saya tunggu?**

doctor **doktor**

document **borang**

dollar **dolar**

don't **jangan**

downstairs **tingkat bawah**

drama **drama**

draw close to (to) **mendekati (dekat** a.**)**

dress **baju**

dress well (to) **berpakaian kemas**

dressed (to get) **berpakaian (pakai** v.**)**

drink **minuman (minum** v.**)**

drink (to) **minum**

drive (to) **memandu (pandu** n.**)**

driving licence **lesen memandu**

drizzle **renyai-renyai**

drop **titis**

drop (to) **titis**

drops **ubat titis**

drum **gendang**

drunk **mabuk**

dry season **musim panas**

duck **itik**

durian fruit **buah durian**

ear **telinga**

early in the morning **pagi pagi**

easy **senang, mudah**

eat **daging**

eat (to) **makan**

eaten (to be) **dimakan (makan** v.**)**

economy **ekonomi**

educate (to) **didik**

educated **terpelajar (ajar** v.**)**

education **pendidikan (didik** v.**)**

egg **telur**

eggs cooked in tea **telur téh**

eight **lapan**

either **sama ada**

eldest **sulong**

election **pemilihan (pilih** v.**)**

e-mail **e-mel**

embarrassed **malu**

embarrassing **memalukan (malu** a.**)**

embassy **kedutaan (duta** n.**)**

employee **pegawai, pekerja (kerja** n.**)**

empty **kosong**

end **hujung**

engineer **jurutera**

engineering **kejuruteraan (jurutera** n.**)**

enjoy **seronok**

Enjoy your food. **Selamat makan.**

Enjoy your studies. **Selamat belajar.**

Enjoy your work. **Selamat bekerja.**

enough **cukup**

enter (to) **masuk**

entertain (to) **hibur**

entertainment **hiburan (hibur** v.**)**

enthusiasm **minat**

enthusiastic **bersemangat (semangat** n.**)**

environment **alam sekitar**

equal to **sama dengan**

especially **terutama (utama** a.**),
terutamanya (utama** a.**)**

evening: in the ~ **pada waktu malam**

ever **pernah**

every **setiap, tiap**

examine (to) **memeriksa (periksa** v.**)**

excellent **terbaik (baik** a.**)**

except **kecuali**

exchange rate **kadar pertukaran**

excuse me **maaf!**

exercise **latihan**

exit **pintu keluar**

expect (to) **menunggu (tunggu** v.**)**

expensive **mahal**

experience **pengalaman (alam** a.**)**

experienced **alam**

expert **ahli**

explanation **keterangan (terang** a.**)**

extract (to) **perah**

eye **mata**

eyebrow **bulu kening**

face (to) **hadap**

fail **gagal**

family **keluarga**

famous, well-known **terstanal, terkenal**

fan **kipas**

far **jauh**

far from here **jauh dari sini**

fare **tambang**

farmer **tani**

fashion **fesyen**

fashion designer **peréka fesyen**

fast (as in a religious fast) **puasa**

fast (to) **berpuasa (puasa** n.**)**

father **ayah, papa**

father-in-law **mertua**

fax machine **mesin faks**

February **Februari**

feeble **lemah**

feel (to) **merasa (rasa** v.**)**

female **wanita**

ferry **feri**

fetch (to) **menjemput (jemput** v.**)**

feverish **demam**

few: a ~ **beberapa**

field (i.e. of expertise, etc.) **bidang**

fight (to) **juang**

fill in (to) **isikan (isi** n.**), mengisi**

film **filem**

final **akhir**

finance **kewangan**

fine **halus**

fine: I'm ~ **khabar baik**

fine: that's ~ **baiklah kalau begitu**

finger **jari**

finish (to) **berakhir (akhir** a.**), habis,
menyelesaikan (selesai** v.**)**

finished **habis**

fire **api**

first **pertama**

fish **ikan**

fish cooked in banana leaves **otak otak**

fitness centre **pusat kesihatan**

five **lima**

fixed price **harga tetap**

flight **penerbangan**

flood **banjir**

floor (storey) **tingkat**

flower **bunga**

fluent **fasih**

fluently **dengan fasih**

flute **seruling, flut**

fly (to) **terbang**

fog **kabut**

foggy **berkabut (kabut** n.**)**

follow (to) **ikut**

follow: (Please) ~ me. **Mari ikut saya.**

fond of (to be) **gemar**

food **makanan (makan** v.**), lauk**

foot **kaki**

foot: go on ~ **berjalan kaki**

football (soccer) **bola sépak**

football player **pemain bola sépak**

for **bagi, atas**

for (with time) **selama**

forbidden: it is ~ **dilarang (larang** v.**)**

force to (to) **paksa**

forced (to be) **terpaksa (paksa** v.**)**

forehead **dahi**

foreign **asing**

forget **lupa**

forget (to) **terlupa (lupa** v.**)**

forget: don't ~; don't ~ to… **jangan lupa; jangan lupa untuk…**

forgive (to) **maafkan**

forgotten: already ~ **sudah lupa**

fork **garfu**

form **borang**

formerly **dahulu, dulu**

fort **kubu**

forty **empat puluh**

fountain **pancutan**

four **empat**

France **Perancis**

free **merdeka**

free time **masa lapang**

frequent **kerap**

Friday **Jumaat**

fried **goréng**

fried noodles **mi goréng**

fried rice **nasi goréng**

friend **rakan, sahabat, teman**

friend (to have a) **berteman (teman** n.**)**

friendly **peramah**

friends (to be) **bersahabat (sahabat** n.**)**

friends with (to be) **berteman dengan**

friendship **persahabatan (sahabat** n.**)**

frightened **takut**

frightening **menakutkan (takut** a.**)**

from **dari**

from: I am ~… **Saya berasal dari…, Saya dari…**

front: in ~ of **depan**

fruit salad **rojak buah**

fruit salad with spicy sauce **rojak**

frying pan **kuali**

full **penuh**

full of **penuh dengan**

full time **sepenuh masa**

further information **keterangan yang lebih lanjut**

gadget **alat**

gain (to) **memperoléh (oléh** n.**)**

gait **cara berjalan**

galangal **lengkuas**

game **permainan (main** v.**)**

garden **kebun, taman**

gardening **berkebun (kebun** *n.***)**

garlic **bawang putih**

gather (to) **kumpul**

geography **geografi**

Germany **Jerman**

get **ambillah (ambil** *v.***)**

get (to) **dapatkan (dapat** *v.***), mendapat**

get married to (to) **kahwin dengan**

get off or out of a vehicle (to) **turun**

get something out (to) **keluarkan (luar)**

get up (to) **bangun**

gift **hadiah**

ginger **halia**

giraffe **zirafah**

girl **perempuan**

give (to) **memberi (beri** *v.***)**

give a feast to (to) **jamu**

give someone something (to) **berikan (beri** *v.***)**

Glad to meet you. **Gembira bertemu dengan saudara.**

glass **segelas, gelas**

glove **sarung tangan**

go (to) **pergi**

go dating (to) **jumpa janji**

go diving (to) **menyelam (selam** *v.***)**

go for a walk (to) **pergi berjalan (jalan** *v.***)**

go hiking (to) **mengembara berjalan kaki**

go in search of adventure (to) **mengembara (kembara** *a.***)**

go jogging (to) **berjoging (joging** *n.***)**

go on foot (to) **jalan kaki**

go out for a stroll (to) **jalan**

go shopping (to) **membeli-belah**

go sightseeing (to) **melancong**

go to school (to) **bersekolah (sekolah** *n.***)**

go up (to) **naik**

go upstairs (to) **naik ke atas**

goat **kambing**

goat meat on skewers in peanut sauce **saté kambing**

good **bagus, baik**

good afternoon **selamat tengah hari**

good evening **selamat petang**

good morning **selamat pagi**

good night **selamat malam**

goodbye **selamat jalan, selamat tinggal**

goodness **kebaikan**

goods **barang**

government **kerajaan (raja** *n.***)**

graduate (to) **tamat pengajian**

graduation ceremony **upacara ijazah**

grandchild **cucu**

granddaughter **cucu**

grandfather **datuk**

grandmother **nénék**

grandson **cucu**

gravy **kuah**

great **bagus sekali**

green **hijau**

grey **kelabu**

grill (to) **bakar**

grilled **bakar**

grind (to) **kisar**

group **kumpulan (kumpul** *v.***)**

guava **jambu**

guess (to) **agak**

guest **tamu, tetamu**

guest room **bilik tamu**

guest singer **penyanyi undangan**

guests' invitation **jemputan (jemput** v.)

guide **pemandu (pandu** n.)

guitar **gitar**

hair **rambut**

half **setengah**

hall **dewan**

hand **tangan**

hand-made **buatan tangan**

hang (to) **sangkut**

hang out (to) **berkumpul (kumpul** v.)

happy **bahagia, gembira, senang**

Happy Birthday! **Selamat hari jadi!**

Happy Eid! **Selamat Hari Raya!**

Happy New Year! **Selamat Tahun Baru!**

hat **topi**

hate (to) **benci**

have (to) **ada**

have a family (to) **berkeluarga (keluarga** n.)

have a wife (to) **beristeri**

have an appetite for (to) **berselera
    (selera** n.) **untuk**

have breakfast (to) **bersarapan
    (sarapan** n.) **pagi**

have children (to) **beranak (anak** n.)

have soy sauce in it (to) **berkicap (kicap** n.)

have the ability to (to) **mampu**

have: I ~ **Saya ada…**

he **dia**

head **kepala**

head teacher **guru besar**

health **kesihatan (sihat** a.)

healthy **sihat**

hear (to) **mendengar (dengar** v.)

heart **jantung**

heavy **berat**

hello **hélo**

help **bantuan (bantu** v.)

help (to) **membantu (bantu** v.)

helper **pembantu (bantu** v.)

here **di sini**

high **tinggi**

high blood pressure **penyakit darah tinggi**

hill **bukit**

historical **bersejarah (sejarah** n.)

history **sejarah**

hobby **hobi**

holiday **cuti**

holiday (to be on) **bercuti (cuti** n.)

holiday resort **tempat peranginan**

Holland **Belanda**

hope (to) **harapkan (harap** v.)

hopefully **harap, mudah, mudahan**

horror **seram**

horror movie **filem seram**

hospital **hospital**

hot **panas**

hot (spicy) **pedas**

hot water/spring **air panas**

hotel **hotél**

house **rumah**

house of worship **rumah beribadat**

How (in what way) are you sick? **Sakit apa?**

How are you? **Apa khabar?**

How do I get there? **Bagaimana nak
    ke sana?**

How is…?/How was…? **Bagaimanakah
    dengan?**

How is the weather? **Bagaimana cuacanya?**

How long (distance)? **Berapa panjang?**

How many…? **Berapakah?**

How many hours? **Berapa jam?**

How many kilos? **Berapa kilo?**

How many nights? **Berapa malam?**

How many times? **Berapa kali?**

How much? **Berapa?, Berapa banyak?**

How much is the cost? **Berapa harganya?**

How old? **Berapakah umur?**

How tall? **Berapa tinggi?**

human being **manusia**

human relationship **hubungan masyarakat**

human resources **sumber manusia**

humanities **kemasyarakatan (masyarakat** n.**)**

humid **lembap**

hungry **lapar**

hurry (to be in a) **terburu-buru, tergesa-gesa**

Hurry up! **Lekas lekas!**

husband **suami**

I **aku, saya**

I am **saya**

I love… **Saya suka sekali…**

ice **ais**

ice cream **ais krim**

identification **pengenalan (kenal** v.**)**

if **jika, kalau**

illness **penyakit (sakit** a.**)**

illuminate (to) **sinar**

impatient to (to be) **tidak sabar**

import (to) **import**

imported from (to be) **diimport dari**

in **dalam**

in another 30 minutes **dalam masa 30 lagi**

include (to) **termasuk (masuk** v.**)**

indeed **memang**

independence **kemerdékaan (merdéka** a.**)**

independent **merdéka**

Indian bread **roti canai**

Indian lentil curry **dhal kari**

Indian pancakes with meat fillings **murtabak**

Indian-style rice with meat **nasi briyani**

indigestion **ketakcernaan**

inform (to) **beritahu (tahu** v.**)**

information **keterangan (terang** a.**), maklumat**

ingredients **bahan**

inject (to) **menyuntik (suntik** v.**)**

inn **penginapan (inap** v.**)**

inspiration **inspirasi**

instead of **sebagai ganti**

Institute of Higher Education **Institusi Pengajian Tinggi**

instructions **cara membuat**

instructor **pengajar (ajar** v.**)**

intelligence **akal**

intelligent (to be) **berakal (akal** n.**)**

interested **tertarik**

interested in (to be) **berminat (minat** n.**), tertarik (tarik** v.**) dengan**

interesting **menarik (tarik** v.**)**

international **antarabangsa**

introduce (to) **perkenalkan (kenal** v.**)**

invariable **tetap**

invent (to) **réka**

inventor **peréka (reka** v.**)**

invitation **jemputan (jemput** v.**), undangan (undang** v.**)**

invite (to) **ajak, jemput, menjamu (jamu** v.**)**

invited: the person ~ **tetamu jemputan**

is, are **adalah**

it **ia**

It is...centimetres long.
   Panjangnya...sentimeter.

Italy **Itali**

itching **gatal**

jacket **jakét**

January **Januari**

Japan **Jepun**

job **pekerjaan (kerja** n.**)**

jogging **joging**

join (to) **gabung**

joint **hubung**

joke **gurau**

joke (to) **bergurau (gurau** n.**)**

joke around (to) **berjenaka
   (jenaka** n.**)**

journalist **wartawan**

journey **perjalanan (jalan** n.**)**

July **Julai**

June **Jun**

just **sahaja, saja**

just now **tadi**

kaffir lime leaf **daun limau purut, daun
   purut**

karate **karaté**

keen **bersemangat (semangat** n.**)**

keep (to) **simpan**

keep an eye on (to) **mengawasi (awas** n.**)**

keep on doing (to) **terus**

keep on walking **jalan terus**

key **kunci**

kilo **kilo**

kilo: one and a half ~s **sekilo setengah**

king **raja**

kitchen **dapur**

know (to) **kenal (dengan), tahu**

know: I don't ~. **Saya tidak tahu.**

knowledge **pengetahuan (tahu** v.**)**

known as **dikenali (kenal** v.**) sebagai,
   terkenal dengan**

lab **makmal**

lack of profit **rugi**

lake **tasik**

lamb **biri**

language **bahasa**

large **luas**

last: the ~ **terakhir (akhir** a.**)**

late **léwat, terlambat (lambat** a.**),
   terléwat (léwat** a.**)**

late at night **malam malam**

later **nanti**

laugh **tawa**

laugh (to) **ketawa (tawa** n.**)**

law **undang-undang**

lawyer **peguam**

leaf **daun**

leather **kulit**

leather shadow puppet **wayang kulit**

leave **cuti**

leave (to) **angkat**

leave (to) **tinggalkan (tinggal** v.**)**

leave for (to) **berangkat (angkat** v.**)**

lecture **syarah**

lecturer **pensyarah (syarah** n.**)**

left: on the ~-hand side **di samping kiri**

leg **kaki**

leisure **lapang**

lemon grass **serai**

lend (to) **pinjamkan (pinjam** *v.***)**

length of stay **tempoh tinggal**

less **kurang**

lesson **pelajaran (ajar** *v.***)**

let **biar**

let go (to) **melepas**

Let me help. **Biar saya bantu., Mari saya bantu.**

Let me introduce… **Perkenalkan, Ini…**

Let's go! **Jomlah!** *(slang)*

letter **surat**

library **perpustakaan (pustaka** *n.***)**

licence **lesen**

life **hidup**

light (of weight) **ringan**

like **macam**

like (similar to) **seperti**

like (to) **suka**

like the most (to) **paling suka**

like: I don't really ~… **Saya kurang suka…**

likewise **pula**

link **penghubung (hubung** *v.***)**

lips **bibir**

list **daftar**

listen to music (to) **mendengar muzik**

live (to) **tinggal**

lively **meriah**

lobster **udang karang**

long **lama, panjang**

long: (For) how ~ (time)? **Berapa lama?**

look, examine (to) **pandang**

look after (to) **mengurus (urus** *v.***), menjaga (jaga** *v.***)**

look for (to) **mencari (cari** *v.***) cari**

look like (to) **kelihatan (lihat** *v.***)**

look out onto (to) **menghadap (hadap** *v.***) ke**

looked for (to be) **dicari (cari** *v.***)**

lose out (to) **rugi**

lose something (to) **keciciran (cicir** *v.***)**

loss **rugi**

lost **sesat**

lost (to be) **tersesat (sesat** *a.***)**

lot: a ~ of **banyak**

loudly **kuat**

love **cinta**

love (to) **mencintai (cinta** *n.***)**

luck **untung**

luck: I wish you ~. **Harap kamu berjaya.**

lucky (to be) **bernasib (nasib** *n.***)**

luggage **bagasi**

lukewarm **suam**

lurid **garang**

made of (to be) **dibuat (buat** *v.***) daripada**

maid **pembantu rumah**

main road **jalan raya**

maize **jagung**

make **buatlah**

make (to) **membuat**

make one's mouth water (to) **menjamu selera**

make plans (to) **merencanakan (rencana** *n.***)**

make yourself at home **buatlah seperti rumah sendiri**

Malay (language) **Bahasa Malaysia**

male **lelaki**

man **lelaki**

manage (to) **urus**

management **pengurusan (urus** v.**)**

manager **pengurus (urus** v.**)**

Mandarin **bahasa Mandarin**

mango pudding **puding mangga**

many: For how ~ people? **Untuk berapa orang?**

many: too ~ **terlalu banyak**

map **peta**

marathon **maraton**

marble **batu marmar**

March **Mac**

marital status **taraf perkahwinan**

market **pasar**

marketing **pemasaran (pasar** n.**)**

maroon **mérah manggis**

marriage **perkahwinan (kahwin** v.**)**

marriage vows **akad nikah**

married **berkahwin (kahwin** v.**), berkeluarga (keluarga** n.**), kahwin**

married: not ~ **belum berkahwin**

marry (to) **kahwin**

massage **urut**

massage parlour **rumah urut**

master's degree **sarjana**

material **kain**

mathematics **matematik**

matter: it doesn't ~ **tak apalah, tidak mengapa**

May **Mei**

May I have...? **Boléh saya dapatkan...?**

May I request....? **Boléh saya minta…?**

maybe **mungkin**

me too **Saya juga begitu**

mean (to) **maksudkan (maksud** v.**)**

measure **ukur**

meat **daging**

mechanic **mekanik**

medicine **perubatan (ubat** n.**)**

meet (to) **bertemu (temu** v.**)**

meet: I am pleased to ~ you too. **Saya juga begitu**.

meeting **mesyuarat**

mention (to) **menyebut (sebut** v.**)**

menu **menu makanan**

Merry Christmas **Selamat Menyambut Hari Krismas**

message **pesanan (pesan** v.**)**

method **cara membuat**

metre **meter**

mind **akal**

minister **menteri**

ministry **kementerian (menteri** n.**)**

miss (a form of transport) (to) **ketinggalan (tinggal** v.**)**

miss (to) **tertinggal (tinggal** v.**)**

mistaken (to be) **tersilap (silap** a.**)**

mistaken: if I'm not ~ **kalau saya tidak silap**

mix **campur**

mix (to) **campur, gaul**

mixed (to be) **dicampur (campur** v.**)**

mixed vegetables **sayur campur**

mobile phone **teléfon mudah alih**

moist **lembap**

moment **sekejap**

Monday **Isnin**

money **wang**

month **bulan**

monument **tugu**

more **lebih**

morning: this ~ **pagi tadi**

mother **ibu**

mother-in-law **ibu mertua**

motivation **semangat**

motorbike **motorsikal**

mountain **gunung**

mountain range **pergunungan (gunung** n.**)**

mouth **mulut**

movement **bergerak (gerak** n.**)**

Mr **Encik**

museum **muzium**

music **muzik**

musician **ahli muzik**

mutton **daging kambing**

mutton curry **kari kambing**

name **nama**

name: My ~ is… **Nama saya…**

namely **iaitu**

nation **bangsa**

national zoo **zoo negara**

nationality **kebangsaan, warganegara, kewarganegaraan**

native **asli**

native: like a ~ **seperti orang asli**

nature **sifat**

nauseous **mual**

near **dekat**

neat **kemas**

neck **léhér**

necklace **kalung, rantai léhér**

need **perlukan (perlu** v.**)**

need (to) **perlu**

need: there's no ~ **tidak usah**

needed for **diperlukan (perlu** v.**) untuk**

neighbour **tetangga, jiran**

nephew **anak saudara lelaki**

net **jala**

net (to) **menjala (jala** n.**)**

never **pernah**

new **baru**

new year **tahun baru**

news **berita**

newspaper **akhbar, surat khabar**

next month **pada bulan hadapan**

next to **di sebelah**

next to it **di sebelahnya**

next week **minggu depan**

niece **anak saudara perempuan**

nine **sembilan**

no **bukan**

no smoking **dilarang merokok**

No, thank you. **Tidak, terima kasih.**

non-stop **terus**

noodles **mi**

noodles in soup **mi kuah**

noodles in spicy gravy **mi rebus**

noodles, black soy sauce, squid and vegetables **mi hailam**

noodles: flat rice ~ **mi kuay teow**

nose **hidung**

not **tak, tiada**

novel **novél**

November **November**

now **sedang, sekarang**

now and again **sebentar-sebentar**

nowadays **kini**

number **nombor**

number: the wrong ~ **salah nombor**

nurse **jururawat**

obliged (to) **terpaksa (paksa** *v.***)**

obtain (to) **oléh**

occasion **masa**

ocean **lautan (laut** *n.***)**

October **Oktober**

odd **pelik**

office **pejabat**

often **sering**

OK **baiklah**

older brother **abang**

older sister **kakak**

once **sekali**

once in a while **sekali-sekala**

one **satu**

one (counter for animals) **seékor**

one by one **satu satu**

one: the ~ in front of that **yang depan itu**

onion **bawang besar**

only **cuma, hanya, saja, tunggal, sahaja**

opened (to be) **dibuka (buka** *v.***)**

opinion **pendapat**

opinion (to be of the) **berpendapat (pendapat** *n.***)**

orang utan **orang hutan**

orange **jingga, orén**

order (to) **pesan**

order some more (to) **tambah lagi**

order: in ~ to **untuk**

ordered (to be) **dipesan (pesan** *v.***)**

original **asli**

other **lain, yang lain**

outside **di luar**

over cooked **terlalu keras**

overcast **mendung**

overeat (to) **kekenyangan**

overtake (to) **memotong (potong** *v.***), mendahului (dahulu)**

own (to) **milik**

owner **pemilik (milik** *v.***)**

oysters **tiram**

package holiday **pakéj percutian**

paddle **dayung**

paddle (to) **mendayung (dayung** *n.***)**

page **muka surat**

pair: (a) ~ of **sepasang**

pale **pucat**

palpitation **debar**

pampered **manja**

papaya **betik**

parcel **bungkusan (bungkus** *v.***)**

park (to) **meletak (letak** *n.***)**

park a car (to) **letak keréta**

part **bahagian**

part time **sambilan**

pass (to) **berlalu (lalu** *v.***)**

pass away **meninggal dunia**

passer-by **pejalan kaki**

passport **pasport**

patient **sabar**

pattern **corak**

pay (for) (to) **bayar**

peaceful **damai**

peanut **kacang**

peanut sauce **sos kacang**

pedal **kayuh**

pedestrian **pejalan (jalan** *n.***) kaki**

Penang **Pulau Pinang**

pencil **pensél**

peninsula **semenanjung**

pepper **lada**

per cent **peratus**

per hour **per jam**

per month **serbulan**

per room **sebilik**

performance **pertunjukan (tunjuk** v.**)**

permission **ijazah**

persistent **terpulang (pulang** v.**)**

person **orang**

personal **peribadi**

personal details **butir peribadi**

phone: by ~ **dengan teléfon**

photo **foto**

photographer **jurufoto, jurugambar**

photography **fotografi**

piano player **pemain piano**

pick up (to) **jemput**

picture **gambar**

piece **keping, kepingan**

piece, slice, to cut **potong**

pink **mérah jambu**

pip **ulas**

pity: It's a ~! **Sayang!**

place **letak**

place of birth **tempat lahir**

place where someone lives **tempat tinggal**

plan **rancangan (rancang** v.**)**

plan (to) **rancang**

plane **kapal terbang**

plastic **plastik**

plate **pinggan**

play **drama**

play (to) **bermain (main** v.**)**

play football (soccer) (to) **bermain bola sépak**

play on the computer (to) **bermain komputer**

play sport (to) **bersukan (sukan** n.**)**

player **pemain (main** v.**)**

pleasant **nyaman**

please come **datanglah**

pleased **senang**

Pleased to meet… **Gembira dapat bertemu dengan…**

pleasing **menyenangkan (senang** a.**)**

plum sauce **sos pelam**

police **polis**

police station **balai polis**

polite **sopan**

poor **miskin**

popular **popular**

population **penduduk (duduk** v.**)**

pork **babi**

porridge **bubur**

porridge: black glutinous rice sweet ~ **bubur pulut hitam**

portray (to) **menggambarkan**

possible: if ~ **jika boléh**

potato **ubi kentang**

prawn **udang**

prawn crackers **keropok**

prefer **lebih suka**

prepare (to) **menyediakan (sedia** a.**), siapkan (siap** a.**)**

present **bungkusan (bungkus** v.**)**

president **presiden**

previous **dahulu**

price **harga**

pricking **perit**

primary school **sekolah rendah**

printed **cap**

private **swasta**

private company **syarikat swasta**

problem **masalah**

problem: (It's) no ~. **Tidak ada masalah.**

problem: no ~ **tidak mengapa**

product **produk**

prohibit (to) **larang**

proud **sombong**

proud (to be) **menyombongkan (sombong** *a.***)**

provided that **asalkan**

psychology **psikologi**

public **umum**

publish (to) **terbit**

publishing house **penerbitan (terbit** *v.***)**

pull (to) **tarik**

pupil (primary school) **murid**

purchases **belian (beli** *v.***)**

purple **ungu**

put (to) **bubuh**

put in **masukkan (masuk** *v.***)**

quality **kualiti**

queen-sized bed, double bed **katil kelamin**

quickly **cepat, dengan pantas**

quite right **betul sekali**

raincoat **baju hujan**

raining **hujan**

rainy season **musim hujan**

rare **setengah matang**

rat: big ~ **tikus besar**

rather **agak**

raw **mentah**

ray **sinaran (sinar** *v.***)**

reach (to) **sampai**

read (to) **membaca**

reading **pembacaan (baca** *v.***)**

ready **sedia, siap**

ready (to be) **bersedia (sedia** *a.***)**

ready to be served up **siap dihidang**

really **sungguh, betul**

Really? **Yakah?**

really: not ~ **tidak begitu, tidak sangat**

rear: the ~ **belakang**

reason for visit **tujuan lawatan**

reason: that's the ~ **patutlah**

receive (to) **terima**

reception **resépsi**

recipe **resipi**

reciprocate (to) **balas**

recommend (to) **cadangkan (cadang** *v.***)**

red **mérah**

red beans with coconut milk and ice **ais kacang**

reduce (to) **kurangkan (kurang), mengurangi**

regards: Give them my ~. **Sampaikan salam saya kepada meréka**.

regulation **peraturan (atur** *v.***)**

relieved **lega**

religious worship **ibadat**

remainder **baki**

remember (to) **ingat**

rent **séwa**

rent (to) **menyéwa (séwa** *n.***)**

renting out **penyéwaan (séwa** *n.***)**

replace (to) **mengganti (ganti** *v.***)**

reply (to) **balas, jawab**

request (to) **meminta (minta** *v.***)**

reservation **tempahan (tempah** v.)

respectful greetings **sembah**

rest (to) **berehat (rehat** v.)

restaurant **restoran**

restriction **peraturan (atur** v.)

retire (to) **bersara**

return **kepulangan (pulang** v.)

return home (to) **pulang**

return ticket **tikét pulang balik**

rhythm **rentak**

rice (cooked) **nasi**

rice field **sawah padi**

rice flour **tepung beras**

rice noodles in coconut gravy **mi laksa**

rice porridge with chicken **bubur ayam**

rice with meat and vegetables **nasi campur**

rice: blue ~ with raw vegetables and salted fish
   nasi kerabu

rice: glutinous ~ **nasi pulut, pulut**

rice: glutinous ~ and coconut pudding **puding
   pulut santan**

rich **kaya**

rich: I'm ~! **Kayalah saya.**

rickshaw **béca**

right: that's ~ **tepat sekali**

river **sungai**

roast **bakar**

roast chicken in spicy sauce **ayam percik**

room **bilik**

room: for one ~, per room **sebilik**

rose **bunga mawar, ros**

roundabout **bulatan (bulat** a.)

rubber **getah**

rubbish (trash) **kotoran (kotor** a.), **sampah**

run (to) **lari**

run out of **kehabisan (habis** v.)

sad **sedih**

safe **aman**

saffron leaf **daun kunyit**

sail **belayar (layar** v.)

salary **gaji**

sales **jualan**

salt **garam**

salt: add ~ to taste **bubuh garam secukup
   rasa**

salty **masin**

same: the ~ as **sama dengan**

sarong **kain sarung**

satiated **kenyang**

satisfied **puas**

satisfy (to) **memuaskan (puas** a.)

Saturday **Sabtu**

sauna **sauna**

say (to) **kata**

scenery **pemandangan (pandang** v.)

school **sekolah**

school hall **dewan sekolah**

scientist **ahli sains, saintis**

scissors **gunting**

scoop **gayung**

sea **laut**

sea level **aras laut**

seafood **makanan laut**

seaside **tepi pantai**

season **musim**

seat **tempat duduk**

seat **duduk**

seat (window) **tempat duduk
   (di sebelah tingkap)**

second **kedua**

secret **rahasia**

secretarial **kesetiausahawan
(setiausaha** n.**)**

secretary **setiausaha**

section **bahagian**

see (to) **melihat (lihat** v.**)**

See you. **Sehingga berjumpa lagi.**

seem (to) **nampak**

seems: it ~ like **nampaknya**

select (to) **pilih**

sell (to) **menjual (jual** v.**)**

seller **penjual (jual** v.**)**

selling **penjualan (jual** v.**)**

send (to) **hantar, kirim,
mengirim (kirim** v.**)**

separately **berasingan (asing** a.**)**

September **September**

serious **serius**

serve (to) **hidang**

served **dihidangkan (hidang** v.**)**

served (to be) **dihidang (hidang** v.**)**

set **set**

settlement **perkampungan (kampung** n.**)**

seven **tujuh**

sex **jantina**

sexy **seksi**

shallot **bawang mérah**

sharp **tajam**

she **dia**

shine (to) **berkilat (kilat** n.**)**

ship **kapal**

shirt **keméja**

shiver (to) **menggigil (gigil** v.**)**

shoe **kasut**

shop **kedai**

shopkeeper **pekedai (kedai** n.**)**

short **péndék**

short trousers **seluar péndék**

should **harus**

shoulder(s) **bahu**

show **persembahan (sembah** n.**)**

show (to) **tunjukkan (tunjuk** v.**)**

shrimp **udang**

shy **malu**

shy person **pemalu (malu** a.**)**

shy: don't be ~ **jangan malu, malu**

shy: If you're too ~ to ask you will get lost in the
street. (proverb) **Malu bertanya nanti
sesat di jalan.**

sick **sakit**

side **sebelah**

sign **tanda**

signal **isyarat**

signature **tanda tangan**

silver **perak**

simmer (to) **merenih (renih** v.**)**

simple **mudah**

since **sejak, semenjak**

sing (to) **menyanyi (nyanyi** v.**)**

Singapore **Singapura**

singer **penyanyi (nyanyi** v.**)**

single **tunggal, bujang**

sister-in-law **ipar**

sit about /down (to) **duduk**

sit: Please ~ down. **Sila duduk.**

six **enam**

size **saiz, ukuran (ukur** n.**)**

ski **ski**

skill **kemahiran (mahir** n.**)**

skilled person **mahir**

skirt **skirt**

sleep (to) **tidur**

slim **langsing**

slow **perlahan**

slowly **perlahan-lahan**

slowly: more ~ **dengan lebih perlahan**

small: too ~ **terlalu kecil**

smell (to) **bau**

smells: it ~ **baunya**

smoke **asap rokok**

smoke (to) **merokok (rokok** n.**)**

snacks **makanan ringan**

snorkel (to) **mensnorkel (snorkel** n.**)**

so **jadi**

so that **supaya**

so that's good **bagus kalau begitu**

so: and ~ on **dan lain**

soap opera **drama lipur lara**

soccer **bola sépak**

socialize (to) **bergaul (gaul** v.**)**

society **masyarakat**

sock **sarung kaki**

soft **lambut**

sold out **dijual**

soldier(s) **askar**

someone **seseorang**

sometimes **adakalanya, kadang**

somewhat **agak**

son **anak lelaki**

songs: types of ~ **rentak lagu**

sorry: I am ~ **maaf!**

sort out (to) **uruskan (urus** v.**)**

source **sumber**

souvenir **cenderamata**

souvenir shop **kedai cenderamata**

soy sauce **kicap**

soybean: fermented ~ cake **tempeh**

Spain **Sepanyol**

speak **bercakap (cakap** v.**)**

special **istiméwa, khas**

specialities (culinary) **hidangan istiméwa**

spectacles **cermin mata**

spend (to) **berbelanja (belanja** v.**), menghabiskan (habis** a.**)**

spend the night (somewhere) (to) **menginap (inap** v.**)**

spent (to be) **dihabiskan (habis** v.**)**

spice **rempah**

spike **duri**

spiky (to be) **berduri (duri** n.**)**

spill (to) **cicir**

spirit **semangat**

spoilt **manja**

spoon **sudu**

sport **sukan**

sports centre **pusat sukan**

spring **musim bunga**

spring onions **daun bawang**

square **persegi**

squid **sotong**

staff room **bilik guru**

stalk **tangkai**

stall **gerai**

stand (to) **diri**

stand up (to) **berdiri (diri** v.**)**

standard room **bilik standard**

star fruit **buah belimbing**

start (to) **mula**

state **negeri**

station **stésen**

statue **patung**

stay (to) **tinggal**

steak **stik**

steam bath **mandi wap**

step (to) **memijak (pijak** n.**)**

still **lagi, masih, pun**

stock **stok, kuah**

stocking **stokin**

stomach **perut**

stone **batu**

stone (to be made of) **berbatu (batu** n.**)**

stop **perhentian (henti** v.**)**

stop (to) **berhenti (henti** v.**)**

storey **floor**

storm **ribut**

stormy (to be) **beribut (ribut** n.**)**

story **cerita**

straight on **terus**

strange **pelik**

street **jalan**

street: On what ~? **Di jalan mana?**

string **tali**

strong **kuat, kental**

strong (of smells) **tajam**

strongly **kuat**

stubborn **keras kepala**

stuck **terjebak**

stuck (to be) **tersangkut (sangkut** v.**)**

student **pelajar (ajar** v.**)**

student (at college or university) **mahasiswa**

study (to) **belajar (ajar** v.**)**

studying **sedang belajar**

stupid **bodoh**

style **gaya**

stylish (to be) **bergaya (gaya** n.**)**

succeed (to) **berjaya (jaya** n.**)**

success **jaya**

suddenly **tiba-tiba**

suffer from (to) **menghidap (hidap** v.**)**

sufficient **secukupnya**

sugar **gula**

suggest (to) **cadang**

suit **jas**

suit (someone) (to) **sesuai**

summer **musim panas**

sunbathe (to) **jemur**

sunbathing **berjemur (jemur** v.**)**

Sunday **Ahad**

sure **pasti, sudah tentu**

Sure (of course). **Ya, betul.**

sure: I'm not ~. **Saya kurang pasti.**

swallow (to) **telan**

swallowed (to be) **ditelan (telan** v.**)**

sweet **manis**

sweet dessert made with ice, syrup and evaporated milk **ais batu campur**

sweet soy sauce **kicap manis**

sweets **manisan (manis** a.**)**

swim (to) **berenang (renang** v.**)**

swimmer **perenang (renang** n.**)**

swimming pool **kolam renang**

swollen **bengkak**

table **meja**

tail **ékor**

tailor **tukang jahit baju**

take **ambillah (ambil** v.**)**

take (to) **membawa (bawa** v.**), ambil, menghantar (hantar** v.**)**

take a bath (to) **mandi**

take a look at (to) **tengok**

take me to... **hantarkan (hantar** v.**) saya ke...**

take medicine (to) **makan ubat**

take off (to) **berlepas**

take part in (to) **ambil bahagian dalam**

take time **memakan masa**

take transport (to) **menaiki (naik** v.**)**

taken (to be) **dititis (titis** n.**)**

talk to (to) **bercakap (cakap** v.**) dengan**

tall **tinggi**

taste (to) **merasakan (rasa** v.**)**

tax **cukai**

tax (to) **mencukai (cukai** n.**)**

taxi **teksi**

taxi driver **pemandu teksi**

tea **téh**

teach (to) **mengajar (ajar** v.**)**

teacher **guru**

teaching **perguruan (guru** n.**)**

telephone **teléfon**

telephone (to) **meneléfon (teléfon** v.**)**

television **televisyen**

tell (to) **ceritakan (cerita** n.**)**

ten **sepuluh**

tender **lembut**

test **ujian (uji** v.**)**

test (to) **uji**

Thai **Thai**

Thai-style rice and beef **nasi patprik**

than (in comparisons) **daripada**

thank you **terima kasih**

Thank you for... **Terima kasih atas...**

Thanks a million. **Terima kasih
  banyak-banyak.**

that **itu**

that's all **sudah cukup**

then **kemudian**

they **meréka**

thick **tebal**

thigh(s) **paha**

think (to) **fikir**

think deeply (to) **rancang**

think: I don't ~ so. **Saya rasa bukan.**

third **ketiga**

thirsty **haus**

thirty **tiga puluh**

this **tu, ini**

this is **ini**

thorn **duri**

thought **fikiran (fikir** v.**)**

three **tiga**

three days **tiga hari**

three of us **bertiga**

three-coloured pudding **kuih lapis
  tiga warna**

throat **kerongkong**

throb (to) **berdebar (debar** n.**)**

throughout **sepanjang**

throw (to) **membuang (buang** v.**)**

thumb **ibu jari**

Thursday **Khamis**

ticket **tikét**

ticket: one way ~ **tikét satu jalan**

tidy **kemas**

tie **tali léhér**

timber **kayu balak**

time **masa**

time: a long ~ ago **suatu masa dahulu**

time: another ~ **lain kali**

time: Have a good ~. **Selamat bersen ang-senang.**

tired **lelah, penat**

tiring **meletihkan (letih** a.**)**

to **ke, kepada**

take **mengambil (ambil** v.**)**

today **hari ini**

toe **jari kaki**

together **bersama**

tomorrow **bésok, ésok**

tonight **malam nanti**

too **juga**

total **jumlah**

tour **lancong**

tourism **pelancongan (lancong** n.**)**

tourist **pelancong**

toy **mainan (main** v.**)**

trade **niaga**

traditional **tradisional**

traditional Malay and Indonesian music **dangdut**

traffic **lalu-lintas**

traffic jam **kesesakan lalu-lintas**

traffic signal **lampu isyarat**

train **keréta api**

train (to) **berlatih (latih** v.**)**

transit: in ~ **dalam transit**

travel **pelancongan (lancong** n.**)**

travel agency **pejabat perlancongan**

travel on/by (to) **menaiki (naik** v.**)**

travelling **bersiar, kembara**

trip: Have a good ~. **Selamat berangkat.**

trouble: don't go to any ~ **tak payah susah, susah**

trousers **seluar panjang**

true **benar**

trumpet **trompet**

try (to) **cuba**

Tuesday **Selasa**

tunnel **terowong**

turmeric **kunyit**

turn (to) **belok**

turn on (to) (an appliance) **menghidupkan (hidup** a.**)**

turn right **belok kanan**

TV film **filem télevisyen**

twenty **dua puluh**

twin **kembar**

twin bed **katil twin**

two **dua**

two by two **dua dua**

two thousand **dua ribu**

two weeks **dua minggu**

type **jenis**

type (to) **menaip (taip** n.**)**

typewriter **mesin taip**

typhoon **taufan**

Typical man! **Inilah sifat lelaki!**

ugly **buruk**

uncle **pakcik**

unclear **tidak jelas**

under the name(s) of **di atas nama**

undercooked **mentah**

underground **bawah tanah**

understand (to) **memahami (faham** v.**)**

understanding **faham**

unfortunately **sayang sekali**

unique **unik**

university **universiti**

unlucky **malang**

unrefundable **tidak boléh kembalikan wang**

until **sehingga**

Until we meet again. **Sehingga kita berjumpa lagi.**

until you reach **hingga sampai**

upstairs **tingkat atas**

urbanized area **perbandaran (bandar** n.**)**

urinate (to) **buang air**

use (to) **mengguna (guna** v.**)**

used (to be) **digunakan (guna** v.**), dipakai (pakai** v.**)**

usual **biasa**

usually **biasanya**

utterance **tutur**

vacancies **bilik kosong, kekosongan**

vacant **kosong**

various **macam macam**

vase **pasu**

vegetable **sayur**

vegetable salad with peanut sauce **gado-gado**

vegetables **sayuran (sayur** n.**), sayur-sayuran**

vendor **jurujual**

very **sekali, sangat**

victory **kejayaan**

video **video**

village **desa, kampung**

violin **biola, violin**

visit (to) **melawat**

visiting relatives **melawat keluarga**

volleyball **bola tampar**

vomit (to) **muntah**

wait (to) **tunggu**

wait: I can hardly ~. **Saya dah tidak sabar lagi.**

waiter **pelayan (layan** v.**)**

waiting: am ~ (for) **sedang menunggu**

walk (to) **berjalan (jalan** n.**)**

wall **dinding**

want (to) **ingin**

want to (to) **nak**

want: if you ~ **kalau suka**

wash (to) **mencuci (cuci** v.**)**

watch **jam tangan**

watch (to) **menonton**

water **air**

way **cara**

way of life **kehidupan (hidup** n.**)**

we **kami, kita**

wear (to) **pakai**

wear a dress (to) **berbaju (baju** n.**)**

wear a silk kebaya (to) **berkebaya (kebaya** n.**) sutera**

weather **cuaca**

wedding **perkahwinan (kahwin** v.**)**

Wednesday **Rabu**

week **seminggu, minggu**

weigh (to) **timbang**

weighed (to be) **ditimbang (timbang** v.**)**

weighs: it ~ **beratnya**

weight **berat**

Welcome to… **Selamat datang ke…**

well **dengan baik**

well (shaft) **perigi**

well: very ~ **dengan baik sekali**

wet **basah**

What about…? **Macam mana dengan…?**

What kind of…? **Bagaimana?** or **Bagaimanakah?**

What luck! **Untung sekali!**

What time? **Pukul berapa?**

What would you like to order? **Mau pesan apa?**

What? **Apa?** or **Apakah?**

What's wrong? **Ada apa?**

What's the fare? **Berapa tambangnya?**

What's your job?/What do you do? **Apa pekerjaan anda?**

What's your opinion of...? **Bagaimana pendapat anda tentang ...?**

when **jika, kalau, apabila**

where **di mana**

where from **dari mana**

Where there's sugar there are ants (proverb). **Ada gula ada semut.**

where to **ke mana**

while **sambil**

whiskey **wiski**

white **putih**

who **siapa**

Who? **Siapakah?**

whole: the ~ (of) **seluruh**

wide **lebar**

widow **janda**

widower **duda**

wife **isteri**

will **akan**

wind **angin**

window **tingkap**

windy (to be) **berangin (angin** *n.***)**

wine **wain**

winter **musim sejuk**

with **bersama, dengan**

without **tanpa**

wok **kuali**

word **kata**

words **perkataan (kata** *n.***)**

work (to) **bekerja (kerja** *v.***)**

work experience **pengalaman kerja**

work out (to) **senam**

workshop **béngkel**

world **dunia**

worried **cemas**

worry **risau, bimbang**

worry: don't ~ **jangan risau, jangan bimbang**

worrying **mencemaskan (cemas** *a.***)**

worship (to) **beribadat (ibadat** *n.***)**

wrap up (to) **membungkus (bungkus** *v.***)**

wrapped up (to be) **dibungkus (bungkus** *v.***)**

write (to) **menulis (tulis** *v.***)**

writer **penulis (tulis** *v.***)**

wrong **salah**

year **tahun**

yellow **kuning**

yes **ya**

yesterday **semalam**

yesterday evening **malam tadi**

yet **pun**

yet: not ~ **belum**

you **anda, kamu, saudari**

you and your family **anda sekeluarga**

young **muda**

younger brother/sister **adik**

youngest **bongsu**